19 78

I0643124

The Federalist Papers
and the
New Institutionalism

This is the second volume of a series on Representation.
Series Editor: Bernard Grofman

Previously published:

Electoral Laws and Their Political Consequences,
edited by Bernard Grofman and Arend Lijphart

The Federalist Papers and the New Institutionalism

Edited by

Bernard Grofman
University of California, Irvine

and

Donald Wittman
University of California, Santa Cruz

AGATHON PRESS
New York

© 1989 Agathon Press
111 Eighth Avenue
New York, NY 10011

Library of Congress Cataloging-in-Publication Data

The Federalist Papers and the new institutionalism / edited by
  Bernard Grofman and Donald Wittman.
     p.   cm.
    Bibliography: p.
    Includes index.
    ISBN 0-87586-084-2 (cloth) ISBN 0-87586-085-0 (pbk.)
    1. Federalist. 2. Representative government and
representation– United States. 3. Social choice. I. Grofman, Bernard.
 II. Wittman, Donald, 1942– .
JK155.F43 1989
328.73'0734—dc19   88-25976
                                      CIP

Printed in the U.S.A.

Contents

Part II.
Optimal Institutions

Part III.
Power: Checks and Balances

Part IV.
The Ratification Debate

List of Tables and Figures

About the Editors

Bernard Grofman, Professor of Political Science, School of Social Sciences, University of California, Irvine, has as his principal area of expertise models of group decision making, with a focus on representation and comparative electoral systems, at the macrolevel, and jury decision making and pooling of expert judgments, at the microlevel. He has published nearly 80 articles in leading journals such as the *American Political Science Review, American Journal of Political Science, Journal of Politics, Sociological Methods and Research, Behavioral Science, Theory and Decision,* and *Public Choice;* and has coedited several books including *Representation and Redistricting Issues* (1982), *Choosing an Electoral System* (1984), and *Electoral Laws and Their Political Consequences* (1986).

Donald Wittman, Professor of Economics, University of California, Santa Cruz, has published extensively in economic analysis of law and politics. Among his more than forty published articles are "Candidate Motivation: A Synthesis," *American Political Science Review* (1983); "Efficient Rules of Thumb in Highway Safety and Sporting Activity," *American Economic Review* (1982); "Optimal Pricing of Sequential Inputs: Last Clear Chance, Mitigation of Damages and Related Doctrines in the Law," *Journal of Legal Studies* (1981); "Optimal Spatial Location Under Pollution: Liability Rules and Zoning" (with M. White), *Journal of Legal Studies* (1981); and "Parties as Utility Maximizers," *American Political Science Review* (1973).

About the Contributors

Steven J. Brams is Professor of Politics, New York University. His most recent books include *Game Theory and National Security* (New York: Basil Blackwell, 1988), coauthored with D. Marc Kilgour; *Superpower Games: Applying Game Theory to Superpower Conflict* (New Haven: Yale University Press, 1985); *Rational Politics: Decisions, Games, and Strategy* (Washington, DC: CQ Press, 1985); *Superior Beings: If They Exist, How Would We Know?* (New York: Springer-Verlag, 1983); and *Approval Voting* (Boston: Birkhäuser, 1983), coauthored with Peter C. Fishburn.

Bruce E. Cain, Professor of Political Science, California Institute of Technology, is author of *The Reapportionment Puzzle* (Berkeley: University of California Press, 1984) and was a Special Consultant to the California General Assembly Elections and Reapportionment Committee in 1981 and a consultant to the Los Angeles City Council in *U. S. v. City of Los Angeles.* His articles on reapportionment include "Simple vs. Complex Criteria for Partisan Gerrymandering: A Comment on Niemi and Grofman," *UCLA Law Review* (October 1985); and (with Janet Campagna), "Predicting Partisan Congressional Redistricting," *Legislative Studies Quarterly* (1986).

John R. Chamberlin is Professor of Political Science and Public Policy, The University of Michigan. His recent articles include "Representative Deliberations and Representative Decisions: Proportional Representation and the Borda Rule" (with Paul Courant), *American Political Science Review* (1983); "Selecting a Voting System" (with Fran Featherston), *The Journal of Politics* (1986); and "An Investigation into the Relative Manipulability of Four Social Choice Functions," *Behavioral Science* (1985).

Henry W. Chappell, Jr., is Associate Professor of Economics, University of South Carolina. His recent articles (coauthored with William Keech) on politics and macroeconomics include "Policy Motivation and Party Differences: A Dynamic Spatial Model of Party Competition," *American Political Science Review* (1986); and "Party Differences in Macroeconomic Policies and Outcomes," *American Economic Review* (1986).

Cheryl L. Eavey, Assistant Professor of Political Science, Florida State University, is currently a Research Associate in Political Economy at the School of Business, Washington University. Her most recent articles include "Choices of Principles of Distributive Justice in Experimental Groups," with N. Frohlich and J. Oppenheimer, *American Journal of Political Science* (1987); and "Bureaucratic Competition and Agenda Control," *Journal of Conflict Resolution* (1987).

Evelyn C. Fink is Assistant Professor of Government at Dartmouth College. Her dissertation, "Political Rhetoric and Strategic Choice in the Ratification of the U. S. Constitution," modelled the effect of political rhetoric, as the manipulation of information, on the campaign for ratification using the spatial choice model of voting. She is currently working on a study of the effects of debate rules in altering the information environment and its influence on concession making in the House and Senate.

Thomas H. Hammond, Associate Professor of Political Science, Michigan State University, was a Postdoctoral Fellow in Political Economy at Washington University in 1987–88. He is coauthor (with Jack Knott) of *A Zero-Based Look at Zero-Base Budgeting* (Transaction Books, 1980). His most recent articles include "Agenda Control, Organizational Structure, and Bureaucratic Politics," *American Journal of Political Science* (May 1986); and (with Gary Miller), "The Core of the Constitution," *American Political Science Review* (December 1987).

Russell Hardin is Mellon Foundation Professor of Political Science, Philosophy, and Public Policy Studies at the University of Chicago. He is the author of *Morality within the Limits of Reason* (Chicago: University of Chicago Press, forthcoming), *Collective Action* (Baltimore: Johns Hopkins University Press for Resources for the Future, 1982), and is the editor of *Ethics: An International Journal of Social, Political and Legal Philosophy.* His articles on rational choice, moral and political philosophy, and nuclear weapons policy have appeared in many journals and books.

W. T. Jones is Emeritus Professor of Philosophy at California Institute of Technology and Emeritus Trustee of Pomona College and of the Wenner-Gren Foundation for Anthropological Research. His books include *Morality and Freedom in the Philosophy of Kant* (1940); *Masters of Political Thought: Machiavelli to Bentham* (1948); *The Romantic Syndrome* (rev. 1975); *History of Western Philosophy* (Second ed., rev., 1975); and *The Sciences and the Humanities* (1966).

William R. Keech is Professor of Political Science at the University of North Carolina at Chapel Hill, where he has taught since 1964. He is author of *The Impact of Negro Voting: The Role of the Vote in the Quest for Equality* (1968, 1981) and coauthor of *The Party's Choice* (1976), a study of the presidential nomination process. A student of public choice, his current work centers around the relationship between the electoral process and macroeconomic policy and outcomes. Examples of this work include "A New View of Political Accountability for Economic Performance," coauthored with Henry Chappell and appearing in the *American Political Science Review* (1985).

Robert A. McGuire is Visiting Associate Professor of Economics, University of California, Davis (1988–89). He is the author of *An Empirical Investigation of Farmers' Behavior Under Uncertainty: Income, Price and Yield Variability for Late-Nineteenth Century American Agriculture* (New York: Garland, 1985). His most recent articles on the formation of the U. S. Constitution include (with Robert L. Ohsfeldt), "An Economic Model of Voting Behavior over Specific Issues at the Constitutional Convention of 1787," *Journal of Economic History* (March 1986); "Constitution-Making: A Rational Choice Model of the Federal Convention of 1787," *American Journal of Political Science* (May 1988); and (again with R. L. Ohsfeldt), "Self-Interest, Agency Theory, and Political Voting Behavior: The Ratification of the U. S. Constitution," *American Economic Review* (1988, forthcoming).

Gary J. Miller is Professor of Political Economy at the School of Business, Washington University in St. Louis. His most recent book is *Reforming Bureaucracy*, with Jack Knott (Prentice-Hall, 1987). He has published articles on committee decision making and bureaucratic politics. These include "Bureaucratic Agenda Control," with Cheryl Eavey, in the *American Political Science Review* (1984); and "Dictatorship, Decentralization, and the Principles of Administration," with Thomas Hammond, in the *American Journal of Political Science* (1985).

Robert L. Ohsfeldt is Assistant Professor at the School of Health Administration and Policy at Arizona State University, Tempe. His recent articles include (with Robert A. McGuire), "Economic Interests and the American Constitution: A Quantitative Rehabilitation of Charles A. Beard" (1984), and "An Economic Model of Voting Behavior over Specific Issues at the Constitutional Convention of 1787" (1986), both in the *Journal of Economic History*. His most recent studies are "The Effect of AMA Membership on Physicians' Earnings," *Industrial and Labor Relations Review*, and (with R. A. McGuire), "Self-Interest, Agency Theory, and Political Voting Behavior: The Ratification of the U. S. Constitution," *American Economic Review* (1988, forthcoming).

Benjamin I. Page is Gordon Scott Fulcher Professor of Decision Making at Northwestern University. His books include *Choices and Echoes in Presidential Elections* (Chicago: University of Chicago Press, 1978); *Who Gets What from Government* (Berkeley: University of California Press, 1983); and *The Rational Public: Fifty Years of Opinion Trends* (with Robert Shapiro, forthcoming.) Among his articles on public opinion, with Shapiro and others, are "Effects of Public Opinion on Policy," *American Political Science Review* (1983), and "What Moves Public Opinion?" *American Political Science Review* (1987).

Mark P. Petracca, Assistant Professor of Political Science, University of California, Irvine, is coauthor (with Benjamin I. Page) of *The American Presidency* (New York: McGraw-Hill, 1983). His research interests range widely over the areas of American political history and national government, political theory, and macropolitical analysis. His recent articles on American national government include: "Prospects for Presidential Leadership and Political Governance," *Polity* (Winter 1986), and "Federal Advisory Committees, Interest Groups, and the Administrative State," *Congress and the Presidency* (Spring 1986).

William H. Riker is Wilson Professor of Political Science at the University of Rochester. His recent books include *The Art of Political Manipulation* (New Haven: Yale University Press, 1986), *Liberalism against Populism: A Confrontation between the Theory of Democracy and the Theory of Social Choice* (New York: Freeman, 1982), and *The Development of American Federalism* (Boston: Kluwer, 1987). All of these partially involve the study of the Constitution, and his first book, *Democracy in the United States* (New York: Macmillan, 1953, 1964), is mainly a study of the origin and operation of the Constitution.

Thomas Schwartz is Professor of Political Science, UCLA. A specialist in the theory of collective choice, he has also done research in American politics, political philosophy, ethics, and logic. His articles have appeared in the *American Political Science Review, American Journal of Political Science, Public Choice, Journal of Economic Theory, Theory and Decision, Journal of Philosophy, American Philosophic Quarterly,* and other journals and anthologies of political science, economics, and philosophy. Two recent articles are "Agendas and the Control of Political Outcomes," *APSR,* Vol. 81 (1987), with P. Ordeshook;

and "Your Vote Counts on Account of the Way It is Counted: An Institutional Solution to the Paradox of Not Voting," *Public Choice*, Vol. 54 (1987). He is the author of *The Art of Logical Reasoning* (Random House, 1980) and *The Logic of Collective Choice* (Columbia U.P., 1986).

Robert Y. Shapiro is Associate Professor of Political Science at Columbia University, and a researcher at the university's Center for the Social Sciences. His articles on public opinion and government policies, in addition to those written with Benjamin Page, include "Public Opinion Toward Social Welfare Policies: The United States in Comparative Perspective" (with J. Young), in S. Long (ed.), *Research in Micropolitics*, Vol. 3 (JAI, 1988), and several articles published in *Public Opinion Quarterly*.

Preface

The idea for the conference which led to this volume came when I taught a course on representation in which the readings included both the *Federalist Papers* and Buchanan and Tullock's *Calculus of Consent*. In teaching that course (and forcing myself to reread the *Federalist* carefully for the first time since my own graduate student days), my admiration for its authors, already high, grew even higher. I also became convinced that theorists of the "public choice" school were the natural heirs to the *Federalist* legacy. I mentioned this idea to Donald Wittman, who confessed his own admiration for the *Federalist Papers* and a willingness to join me in organizing a conference on the "*Federalist Papers* and the New Institutionalism" (originally "The *Federalist Papers* in Public Choice Perspective") in time to celebrate the 200th anniversary of the writing of the *Federalist Papers*. The conference took place March 20–22, 1987, at the University of California, Irvine.

All the contributors to the conference and volume are associated to one extent or another with the "public choice" approach in political science. Remarkably, all, despite their busy schedules, expressed enthusiasm about writing a paper linking public choice ideas to those in the *Federalist Papers*. Most said that they had always wanted an excuse to write about the *Federalist Papers*. Others, like Bill Riker and Bill Keech, who had already done so, were interested in contributing to a volume celebrating the continuing importance of the *Federalist Papers* as a source for what has come to be called positive theory.

I have learned a lot from the contributors to this volume. I still believe that the new institutionalists of the public choice school are the natural heirs to Madisonian political theory, but I am now more sensitive to the features of Madisonian theory that are almost entirely absent from the public choice literature: the role of deliberation and rational persuasion, a concern for justice and the search for the public good, and a respect for civic virtue and civic education. Compare the vision set forth by James Bryce in the opening paragraph of *The American Commonwealth:*

> The institutions of the United States are deemed by inhabitants and admitted by strangers to be a matter of more general interest than those of the not less famous nations of the Old World. They represent an experiment in the rule of the multitude, tried on a scale unprecedentedly vast, and the results of which everyone is concerned to watch. And yet they are something more than an experiment, for they are believed to disclose and display the type of institutions toward which, as by a law of fate, the rest of civilized mankind are forced to move, some with swifter, others with slower, but all with unresting feet.

In that vision, institutions really do matter.

Contemporary theorists of the "new institutionalism" have at their disposal powerful analytic tools which can be used to reformulate and clarify classic issues in political theory. Recently, a leading traditional political theorist wrote that public choice modelers needed to rediscover the Constitution (Mansfield, 1987, p. 41). This volume is intended as a first start in that direction.

Bernard Grofman
University of California, Irvine

Acknowledgments

The conference which led to this volume was funded by the School of Social Sciences, University of California, Irvine. It was the "Third Irvine Conference on Political Economy."[1] We are indebted to William Schonfeld, Dean of the School of Social Sciences, UCI; Kathy Girvin, Management Services Officer; and Lykke Anderson, Secretary of the Department of Politics and Society; for facilitating conference arrangements. We are also indebted to Dorothy Gormick, Wilma Laws, Armik Muradkhanyan, and the staff of the Word Processing Center, School of Social Sciences, UCI, for their invaluable help in manuscript preparation and bibliographic search.

---

1. Proceedings of its predecessor conference were published by JAI Press in 1986 under the title *Information Pooling and Group Decision Making*, B. Grofman and G. Owen, eds.

The *Federalist Papers* and the New Institutionalism: An Overview

Bernard Grofman

By the *new institutionalism*, I mean analyses using tools derived from microeconomics, game theory, and social choice of the effects of decision-making rules and institutional structures on outcomes.[1] Central to the new institutionalism is the idea that preferences can only be understood in the context of the institutionally generated incentives and institutionally available options that structure choice (see, e.g., Schwartz, this volume; Fink and Riker, this volume). In particular, in John Ferejohn's apt phrase, preferences for outcomes condition preferences for institutions.

I see six major foci of work on the new institutionalism, of which five are exemplified by at least one chapter in this volume: efficiency and transaction costs (Wittman); stability (Miller and Hammond); coordination (Hardin); distribution of power or other resources (Brams; Chamberlin; and Schwartz); and representation (Cain and Jones; Chappell and Keech; Page and Shapiro; and, in a one special sense of that term, *agency*, Schwartz).[2]

The sixth focus, procedural fairness, refers to criteria by which rules for preference aggregation and group decision-making might be judged: for example, consistency, and responsiveness to change in voter preferences. In its contemporary form it springs from the seminal work of Arrow (1963). A comprehensive, though rather technical, review is found in Schwartz (1986); a less technical but now somewhat dated review is found in Plott (1976). (See also Sen, 1970.)

As economists use the term *efficiency* (also called *Pareto optimality*) they refer to a distribution of resources from which no further gains can be made by trade. In other words, an outcome is efficient if no one can be made better off without at the same time making at least one person worse off.[3] A great deal of work has been done in law and economics asserting the efficiency of common law practices, especially those in *torts* (see, e.g., Posner, 1981). Another sizable body of literature takes off from the work of Coase (1960), on the one hand, and Buchanan and Tullock (1962), on the other. The former deals with allocations in a fictionless environment; the latter emphasizes the importance of transaction costs. In this volume, Wittman draws on the transaction costs literature and on hypotheses from the *Federalist Papers* to look at inter-actor bargaining among sectors within the government.

As the term *stability* is customarily used in the social choice literature, it refers to an equilibrium outcome which cannot be overturned by any majority coalition of actors. There is a considerable literature—originating with Condorcet (1785) and continuing with Black (1958) and Arrow (1963), down to more recent work by scholars such as Plott (1967), Kramer (1977), McKelvey (1976, 1979), Schofield (1978), Shepsle (1979), and Shepsle and Weingast (1984)—which looks at conditions under which stability can be expected.[4] In this volume, Miller and Hammond reexamine bicameralism from the perspective of its contributions to stability.

The idea of *coordination* refers to the ability of a disparate set of individuals to choose actions which are mutually complementary and which result in net gains for each in the long run. The most familiar example is the agreement to observe the rules of the road. While it is essentially arbitrary whether cars should drive on the right or the left, it is very helpful to everyone, to put it mildly, if everyone picks the same side. Other examples include the coordinating role of customs such as conversational "turn-taking" and agreements such as the Geneva Convention for the treatment of prisoners of war or binding arbitration procedures for labor-management dispute resolution (Wittman, 1982). Research on regulation falls into this area.

The problem of coordination is closely related to the problem of "collective action" (Olson, 1965; Hardin, 1982a), where, as in the prisoner's dilemma game, what is in the interests of each individual to do may lead to outcomes that no individual wants. Agreed-upon rules, and sanctions for their violation, allow for efficient outcomes in situations where the outcomes are determined by the choices of more than one actor. In this volume, Hardin argues that agreement upon a constitution can be thought of as a solution to the coordination problem which does not require an external sanction for its enforcement. The status quo is anchored by the transaction costs involved in creating an alternative regime. Moreover, rather than merely being the solution to a particular prisoner's dilemma game, a constitution specifies rules for the resolution of virtually all collective choice problems both at the time of its adoption and in the future.

The general problem of the effect of decision procedures on resource distribution (or redistribution) is one widely considered in economics. The term *power*, as customarily used in the game theory literature, however, has a quite precise meaning. It refers to the ability of actors to exercise a decisive vote. An actor is decisive if changing his or her vote (or preference) changes the outcome. Most game-theoretic measures of power treat an actor's power as the percentage of situations in which that actor can be expected to be decisive.[5] An important issue from the new institutionalist perspective is the way in which institutional arrangements (such as voting rules) affect the relative power of different actors. In this volume, Brams addresses the relative power of the two chambers of Congress, a question discussed in the *Federalist* nos. 58 and 63. Brams also looks at the relative power of Congress vis-à-vis the President.

Representation has had two closely related usages in the public choice literature. In the law and economics literature, it refers to "principal-agent" relationships, where a key issue is how incentives for the agent may lead to choices that diverge from the desires or interests of the principal. On the other hand, in the political science literature, it usually refers to the concordance between the choices made by a representative and the preferences of his or her constituents. Here, the most important early work is that of Downs (1957). However, in the political science literature, just which voter or voters correspond to the "principal" is not clear. Sometimes the principal is taken to be the "median voter."

There has been a renewed interest in political science in the idea of representation in both senses of that term (see, e.g., Sugden, 1984; McCubbins and Schwartz, 1984; Feld and Grofman, 1986; Greenberg and Shepsle, 1987), but only some of this interest is traceable to a public choice influence (see, e.g., Grofman, 1975; Lengle, 1981; Grofman et al. 1982; Polsby, 1983; Lijphart, 1981; Lijphart and Grofman, 1984; Grofman and Lijphart, 1986).

A number of authors in this volume look at issues of representation both from the perspective of James Madison and from a contemporary public-choice perspective. Cain and Jones, for example, describe in detail the basic elements of a Madisonian theory of representation. They see it as involving a balancing of conflicting desiderata, for example, responsiveness versus deliberation, majority rule versus unanimity, and representation of individuals versus representation of interests; Chappell and Keech pay particular attention to one aspect of the constitutional compromises, the differing term lengths in the two chambers. Page and Shapiro deal with the rootedness of public opinion and its vulnerability to sudden public whims and passions. Schwartz looks at principal-agent relationships between Congress and federal bureaucrats. The themes in these chapters are all to be found in *The Federalist Papers*, even though the terminology in the *Federalist* is usually different from that of contemporary usage.

The Founding Fathers were, I believe, the greatest (if not the first) political engineers—believers in a "new science of politics" (Ranney, 1976). According to Daniel Patrick Moynihan (1987, p. 22), the fundamental question in *The Federalist Papers* was not about the merits or demerits of ratification but about political science: "Could a government be founded on scientific principles?" Scholars in the public choice tradition, too, see themselves as practitioners of a "new science of politics," one rooted in principles of individual rationality.

The chapters in the first section of this volume seek to specify the similarities and differences between the Madisonian approach to institutional design and those of the "new institutionalists." In the next two sections, the authors apply contemporary analytic tools to the issues of institutional design discussed in *The Federalist Papers*, for example, bicameralism, term length, and judicial power. The last section of this volume deals with the dispute over the ratification of the U.S. Constitution and the way in which preferences for outcomes conditioned preferences for institutions. Given the connections we seek to make between the ideas of *The Federalist Papers* and those of contemporary theorists of the new institutionalism, this seems an apt topic with which to conclude our volume.

Notes

1. There are several other usages of the term the *new institutionalism*, including Marxist, historical, and evolutionary (see Langlois, 1986, and Grofman, 1987). Moreover, the "new institutionalism" inspired by public choice theory is not the only source for the current revival of interest in the study of institutions. In the area of representation, there is growing concern about choice of electoral scheme (e.g., at-large versus single-member district, or plurality versus PR). See, for examples Grofman et al. (1982); Lijphart and Grofman (1984); and Grofman and Lijphart (1986).
2. A seventh (rather specialized) focus has been on mechanisms which will provide incentives to individuals to reveal their true preferences (and to avoid shirking). A useful introduction to this literature on "demand revelation" is the special Spring 1977 issue of *Public Choice* edited by Nicholas Tideman.

3. For many economists, Pareto efficiency is the only normative standard that is appropriate for economists to use in reaching policy judgments. This view is controversial among noneconomists (see Rhoads, 1985).
4. For a nontechnical introduction to this literature, see Feld and Grofman (1987). Also see Grofman and Uhlaner (1985) and Schofield, Grofman, and Feld (1988).
5. For a useful and relatively nontechnical introduction, see Brams (1975). See also Barry (1980a,b), and the volume edited by Holler (1981).

Part I

The Madisonian Vision and the Theory of Public Choice: Comparisons and Contrasts

Introduction

In these opening chapters, a number of authors who have done work associated with the "public choice" tradition in political science compare and contrast the views of the public choice school and modern empirical democratic theory with the views expressed in *The Federalist Papers* (especially by Madison) about institutional design.

Schwartz sees an almost perfect identity between public choice ideas and those of Madison. According to Schwartz, the three elements they have in common are (1) the recognition of the importance of institutional detail; (2) an emphasis on the nature of institutionally generated incentives to individual behavior; and (3) an explanation of outcomes in terms of a "balance" or "equilibrium" of "countervailing interests."

Chappell and Keech see *The Federalist Papers* as "in many respects forerunners of modern social choice theory." However, they suggest that the *Federalist* contains a wider vision of representative government than the focus in contemporary social theory on mechanisms for aggregating individual preferences. Chappell and Keech attribute to the authors of the *Federalist* views more consistent with those of Elster (1983, p. 35): "the core of the political process is the public and rational discussion about the common good, not the isolated act of voting according to private preferences." Chappell and Keech suggest that the standard public choice model is limited by its failure to distinguish among types of preferences and its failure to allow for the possibility of rational persuasion.

Cain and Jones, similarly, distinguish the views of *The Federalist Papers* and those of contemporary public-choice theorists on a number of grounds. According to Cain and Jones, "Madison did not think that a representative democracy could succeed in an environment of unbridled self-interest." Moreover, according to Cain and Jones, "Madison's approach to institutional design was experimental, empirical, and circumstantial, not deductive and theoretical."[1] In contrast, Schwartz downplays the significance of these differences.[2] Schwartz also rebuts the claim that the methodological individualism characteristic of the public choice approach and the frequent references to self-interest in that literature imply a narrow view of behavior as exclusively selfishly motivated.

Page, like Keech, emphasizes the importance attached by the authors of the *Federalist* to the need to "refine and enlarge the public views" by deliberation, and to the need to control transient passions and temporary errors and delusions with devices such as six-year senatorial terms. Page's chapter is the most empirical of the four in this section. He presents evidence that "opinion changes are not extremely frequent; when they occur they are not very big; and opinion seldom fluctuates in one direction and then another." Page suggests that, in contemporary society, the Founders' concern about designing representative institutions that would guard against the whims and passions of the public may be less relevant. Page, however, emphasizes that "the public's policy preferences presumably respond to new information from news events, analyses and interpretations, scholarly research, and political rhetoric. . . . This opens up the possibility . . . of demagoguery, manipulation of opinion, systematic biases in information, [and] false consciousness."[3]

Bernard Grofman

Notes

1. Views similar to those of Cain and Jones and Chappell and Keech have been expressed even more assertively by one noted political theorist, a defender of Madison, who finds the public choice approach of limited value in understanding how representative institutions can be expected to function. According to Harvey Mansfield, Jr. (1987, p. 4), "The Constitution . . . relies on what can be expected in human behavior rather than exhorting to deeds that can only be wished for. But what can be expected is not the worst or even the lowest common demoninator: it is a modicum of virtue in the people and outstanding virtue in a few, both of these cooperating with, and under the direction of, an insistence on liberty that can be found in every human being and cultivated in a free people."

2. My own views are far closer to those of Cain and Jones and Chappell and Keech than to those of Schwartz. The Constitution is avowedly an experiment (as we are told on the first page of the *Federalist*; see also Ranney, 1976, p. 141). The authors of the *Federalist* rely heavily on the lessons of history to understand the possibility and limits of institutional reforms; they lack the *a priorist* dogmatism of many economists and political scientists who work in the public choice tradition. While realistic about human behavior, the authors of the *Federalist* recognize the need for civic attachments and "the capacity of mankind for self-government" (no. 39).

3. Keech's chapter makes a similar point.

CHAPTER ONE

Madison's Theory of Representation

Bruce E. Cain and W. T. Jones

Many, if not most, changes in institutional design can hardly be characterized as "designed"; they usually occur as the reactions of shortsighted people to what they perceive as more-or-less short-range needs. This is one reason the Constitutional Convention was a remarkable event. The Founding Fathers set out deliberately to design the form of government that would be most likely to bring about the long-range goals that they envisaged for the Republic. What is most unusual about Madison, in contrast to the other delegates, is the degree to which he thought about the principles behind the institutions he preferred. Not only did he practice the art of what nowadays is called institutional design, but he developed, as well, the outlines of a theory of institutional design.

Thus, it is not surprising that Madison's ideas about representation have profoundly influenced several generations of American political scientists. In the 1950s and 1960s, for instance, the Yale pluralists borrowed heavily and self-consciously from Madison's arguments in *The Federalist Papers* (Dahl, 1956, 1961; Polsby, 1963). At present, although it happens that the new institutionalism in political science has focused most heavily on Congress and on economic regulation, there is no reason that rational-choice, incentive-based approaches could be not also used to analyze and design electoral reforms in a Madisonian spirit. Thus, the revived interest in institutional issues among political scientists gives us reason to reexamine Madison's thought in a contemporary context. As we shall see, there are important similarities between this approach and Madison's. But even more significantly, there are crucial differences. Above all, it is important to remember that Madison did not think that a representative democracy could succeed in an environment of unbridled self-interest. Moreover, Madison's approach to institutional design was experimental, empirical, and circumstantial, not deductive and theoretical.

We will explore Madison's approach to representation by considering two questions: First, what are the similarities and differences between the Madisonian and contemporary incentive-based approaches to institutional design? Second, how did Madison's positions on particular issues of electoral reform fit into the larger Madisonian scheme, which we will sketch in the course of answering our first question? In this connection, what are the Madisonian issues in contemporary American electoral politics?

Madison and Rational-Choice Theory

Madison on the Nature
and the Possibility of Political Science

Madison believed in the possibility of a science of politics—not an exact science modeled on the Newtonian paradigm (which, of course, few people in his day yet thought of as applying to human affairs), but all the same, a good deal more "scientific" than the largely descriptive and classificatory studies that, say, botany, geography, and geology still were in the last quarter of the eighteenth century. Politics, in Madison's view, was—or rather could become—a science capable of formulating, from careful observation of the past, generalizations about political behavior from which predictions about future political behavior are possible. Hence, he believed, as well, in the possibility of an applied science of political design, and he had a well-developed version of such a science, one which underlay his detailed recommendations for the new constitution.

So far, stated in such general terms, Madison's position has much in common with public choice institutionalism, as Professor Schwartz points out in chapter 2. However, Schwartz vastly understates the differences between Madisonian and public choice institutionalism when he says that contemporary institutionalists "are more prone than the Federalist authors to construct deductive models that admittedly simplify the reality they are used to explain." Schwartz maintains that the "Federalist's 'axioms' were offered as laws rather than models or hypotheses," and that modern deductive approaches demonstrate the "shortsightedness of casual inference, hence the value of deductive rigor."

Madison's approach, however, was *explicitly and self-consciously not axiomatic or deductive;* it was strictly empirical, and he did not believe that the generalizations political scientists could formulate, even after the most careful observation, would ever be more than rule-of-thumb guidelines, holding only "for the most," or "usually," or "often." Political generalizations, that is to say, always had to be qualified by a *ceteris paribus* clause, which represented not merely conditions unknown to the present generation of political scientists, and might become known to later generations, but represented complexities which could not be eliminated because they were a part of human nature and so of human institutions.

As Madison himself put it, there are "causes which the foresight of man cannot guard against. Choices always have to be made under conditions of imperfect and incomplete information." He says at one point, "Experience has instructed us that no skill in the science of government has yet been able to discriminate and define, with sufficient certainty, its three great provinces—the legislative, executive and judiciary . . ." (no. 37, pp. 227–8).[1] Another limitation on the would-be constitutional engineer is the imprecision of language because "all new laws, though penned with the greatest technical skill and passed on the fullest and most mature deliberations, are considered as more or less obscure and equivocal, until their meaning be liquidated and ascertained by a series of particular discussions and adjudications." And this is not merely a limitation that can, over time, be removed by the application of improved methods. It is due to an *intrinsic* feature of language: "No language is so copious as to supply words and phrases for every complex idea, or so correct as not to include many equivocally denoting different ideas" (no. 37, p. 229). In a word, the ambiguities of language inevitably obscure the meaning of written constitutions, no matter how carefully they may be crafted.

In the third place, according to Madison, the practice of institutional design is necessarily imperfect because institutional designers are themselves imperfect. Madison was keenly aware of human fallibility. Hence, even the wisest of constitution makers and reformers, those who try to stand apart and give their best judgment as to what is best for society, must "keep in mind that they themselves are but men and ought not to assume an infallibility in rejudging the fallible opinions of others" (no. 37, p. 226).

These are the reasons that, in Madison's view, politics is, and will remain, an inexact science. Given this fact about politics, it was important for the delegates to the convention always to remember "that a faultless plan was not to be expected" (no. 37, p. 225). Mistakes and bad predictions being inevitable, it was best always to take an experimental, incremental approach, because no one could know whether a proposal was good or bad until it had actually been implemented: "is it an unreasonable conjecture," he asked critics, "that the errors which may be contained in the plan of the convention are . . . such as will not be ascertained until an actual trial shall have pointed them out?" (no. 38, p. 233). Since "experience is the oracle of truth" (no. 20, p. 138), Madison was deeply suspicious of abstract theory, which he thought of as being the product of shut-in, "closet" speculation "upon paper," in contrast to the active products of an intelligent observation of the real world. At various points in his writings, he alludes to the prevalent discrepancy between theory and practice: over and over Madison compares theory and practice, to the disadvantage of the former. Thus, whereas some "apparatus of powers" may have seemed "in theory and upon paper . . . amply sufficient for all general purposes. . . . Very different nonetheless, was the experiment from the theory" (no. 18, p. 123). And again he contrasts "that artificial structure and symmetry which an abstract view of the subject might lead an ingenious theorist to bestow on a Constitution planned in his closet or in his imagination" (no. 37, p. 230) with the more complex product which issued from the hands of delegates exposed to the "pressure" of political demands. There is indeed a note in Madison's writings that anticipates what was to come to fruition much later in William James's pragmatism. Practicality and real-life problem-solving, rather than symmetry, elegance, and deductive simplicity, were for him the only appropriate criteria for evaluating theories.

It would also be wrong to characterize Madison's approach as "casual inference," to use Schwartz's phrase. Madison's generalizations were based on a close study of historical cases. And the best historical examples, at least those which chiefly influenced him, were drawn from the experience of classical Greece, especially the problems that excessive factionalism caused the Greek city-states. "I have thought it not superfluous," he explained at one point, "to give the outlines of this important portion of history, both because it teaches more than one lesson and because, as a supplement to the outlines of the Achaean constitution, it emphatically illustrates the tendency of federal bodies rather to anarchy among the members than to tyranny in the head" (no. 18, p. 128). But inductive generalizations from historical experience, far from being universally valid rules, are no more than tentative working hypotheses that must be updated and modified after they are tested. Since perfection is a Utopian dream, reform of faulty institutions should not be postponed in the vain hope that complete solution of political problems will be found.

It follows that any institutional proposal ought to be accepted if it improves the status quo and is the best of various imperfect alternatives: "No man would refuse to quit a shattered and tottering habitation for a firm and commodious building because the latter had not a porch to it" (no. 38, p. 237). This position was, of course, quite compatible with Madison's overall skepticism about the possibility of having complete knowledge and precision.

Madison's advice for would-be institutional designers can thus be summarized in the following three rules of thumb:

1. Accept the fact that knowledge about political organizations and human behavior is imprecise, incomplete and often circumstantial.
2. Rely on induction from past experience to develop working hypotheses about institutional proposals.
3. Observe how institutions are actually operating, and aim to improve them incrementally.

Madison's preference for an experimental, and therefore tentative, approach to political science and his hostility to a deductive, theoretical approach make him closer to Aristotle than to Plato; he would have resonated with Aristotle's remark that an educated man is one who does not seek precision where precision is impossible, and he would have agreed with Aristotle that precision is impossible in this sublunar sphere—closer to Locke than to Descartes, closer to Burke than to Hegel, and more inclined to see the limits of human knowledge than to trust human rationality. Also, like Burke and contemporary limited-rationality, incrementalist theorists, Madison preferred cautious experiments with new institutions to attempts at wholesale renovation.

Madison on Human Nature

Like contemporary theorists, Madison believed that any well-designed representative system had to assume that self-interested motives often prevailed over other-regarding ones. "If the impulse and the opportunity be suffered to coincide," he reminds us, "we well know that neither moral nor religious motives can be relied on as an adequate control" (no. 10, p. 81). So too, the "mild voice of reason, pleading the cause of an enlarged and permanent interest, is but too often drowned, before public bodies as well as individuals, by the clamors of an impatient avidity for immediate and immoderate gains" (no. 42, p. 268). The purpose of government, according to Madison, is to regulate "these various and interfering interests" (no. 10, p. 79).

But Madison did not believe that human beings, or government, lived, or could live, by self-interest alone: "As there is a degree of depravity in mankind which requires a certain degree of circumspection and distrust, so there are other qualities in human nature which justify a certain portion of esteem and confidence. Republican government presupposes the existence of these qualities in a higher degree than any other form" (no. 55, p. 346).

What were these qualities? A capacity to care for others was certainly one. Madison acknowledged that emotional bonds often exacerbated political conflicts, but he also believed that passions could be constructive forces if ruled by reason. Consider patriotism. Americans, Madison observed, were "knit together . . . by so many cords of affection," but especially by "the mingled blood which they have shed for their sacred rights" (no. 14, pp. 103–4). Affection for one's country and for one's fellow citizens, just as much as formal institutional devices and laws, could serve as a check against the destructive forces of factionalism.

Another motive which, as he thought, affects people's behavior is a desire to keep their relations with others in a kind of balance, for instance, to cite an almost trivial case, a desire not to be socially indebted to those who have done one kindnesses. Thus, as a young student in Williamsburg, he was insistent in letters home to his father that he be sent gifts for those who had done him favors; he wanted, as it were, to bring the exchange of gifts into equilibrium. At a deeper level, of course, this can be, and in his case was, a commitment to moderation, to "nothing in excess"; at a still deeper level, it is a passion for equity and justice.

The desire for moderation was not only a powerful motive in Madison's personal life. He was not alone, he believed, in liking moderation and the mean, and in his program of constitution design he took this motive into consideration, both as a good—something that political institutions should be designed to cultivate—and also as a psychological factor on which the framers could to some extent count. Hence, his writings frequently allude to the importance of finding a compromise between opposite positions: "in this, as in most other cases, there is a mean, on both sides of which inconveniences will be found to lie" (no. 10, p. 83). If people always acted moderately, there would be little reason to worry about the dangers of tyranny. The problem, as he saw it, was that "public measures are rarely investigated with that spirit of moderation which is essential to a just estimate of their real tendency to advance or obstruct the public good" (no. 37, pp. 224–225). However, Madison thought that it was possible to design institutions that encouraged moderation, good sense, and compromise.

He certainly recognized that individuals and groups are capable of irrational and immoderate behavior, but he believed that, in a statistical sense (though of course he would not have put it this way), people are more likely to be sensible. For instance, he recognized that the most important check on tyranny in a representative democracy is the power of citizens to vote officials in and out of office. If citizens are incapable of making sensible decisions, then a government run on democratic principles will be vulnerable to instability. Madison believed that, in the aggregate, voters make sensible decisions; though individually they are capable of bad decisions, in large numbers and over a series of many choices their irrationalities tended to cancel out, swamped by a moderate modal tendency: "I am unable to conceive, that the people of America, in their present temper, or under any circumstances which can speedily happen, will choose, and every year repeat the choice of, sixty-five or a hundred men who would be disposed to form and pursue a scheme of tyranny or treachery" (no. 55, p. 344).

We will now summarize our comparison of Madisonian and contemporary rational choice approaches by using a scheme we have developed elsewhere (Cain and Jones, 1986) and now reproduce in Table 1.1. In this framework, it will be seen, theories can differ both in their assumptions about human nature and in the goals they aim at achieving by their proposals. We will first compare Madison with contemporary theorists in terms of five important assumptions about human nature.

1. *Malleability of human nature.* Madison believed that human nature is neither completely malleable nor completely intractable. His strongly marked Aristotelianism disposed him not only to believe that people ought to avoid extremes in their conduct (a moral judgment), but also to believe that human nature itself is a mean between extremes (a factual judgment). Contemporary incentive-based approaches, as one might expect, show few signs, if any, of implicit Aristotelianism, reflecting instead the influence of advances in the

TABLE 1.1. Human Nature Presuppositions Set

	Presuppositions	Range of the Continuum	
Structural presuppositions	HN_1 Malleability of human nature	Intractable (a)	Malleable (b)
	HN_2 Laws governing human nature	Secular (a)	Transcendental (b)
	HN_3 Self-interestedness of preferences	Self-regarding (a)	Other-regarding (b)
Conditions of human knowledge and preference	HN_4 Attitudes toward risk	Risk-averse (a)	Risk-acceptant (b)
	HN_5 Capacity to know real interests	Incapable (a)	Capable (b)

natural sciences during the last two centuries. Thus, they tend to take human nature as given and do not assume that institutions can or should try to alter the ratio of self-regarding to other-regarding behavior. Our view that Madison regarded human nature as partly malleable very much accords with Chappell and Keech's point in chapter 3 that "the authors of the Federalist did not believe that popular preferences were exogenous and fixed." As they point out, this crucial assumption makes possible "constructive deliberation" that "enhances the prospects that public decisions would approximate justice and the common good."

2. *Laws governing human nature.* Like contemporary political scientists, Madison did not regard the laws governing human behavior as having a transcendental origin.

3. *Self-interestedness of preferences.* While Madison acknowledged that self-regarding motives are stronger and more prevalent than other-regarding motives—and thus, his views had much in common with contemporary rational-incentive approaches— he also believed that other-regarding motives play a role in successful societies. By comparison, the role of other-regarding behavior is often overlooked completely in contemporary incentive approaches, although as Schwartz correctly points out in chapter 2, this is not inherent in a rational choice approach.

4. *Attitudes toward risk.* Madison believed that people are typically risk-averse in their political orientation. This explains, he thought, why habit is such an important determinant of human behavior—so much so, indeed, that it sometimes inhibits necessary adaptations to new circumstances. Contemporary theories also acknowledge the strength of risk-aversive attitudes in political life, particularly when

TABLE 1.2. Dispositions Set

	Dispositions	Range of the Continuum	
What is represented	D_1 Time perspective	Short (a)	Long (b)
	D_2 Scope	Parochial (a)	Common (b)
	D_3 Degree of cooperation	Independence (a)	Coordinated (b)
How to represent	D_4 Consistency over time	Changing action (a)	Consistency (b)
	D_5 Reliability of promises	Adaptability (a)	Reliability (b)

critical interests are at stake, but they tend to assume that self-interest is a sufficiently powerful incentive to overcome habit when an agent believes he or she can gain thereby.

5. *Capacity to know real interests.* Madison thought that, on the whole, the human capacity for calculation is severely limited and very short-range: "indirect and remote considerations . . . will rarely prevail over the immediate interest" (no. 10, p. 81). On this dimension, contemporary rational-incentive approaches are divided, some assuming shortsightedness and others imputing considerable rational sophistication to political actors.

Madison and the Goals of Representation

A political theorist's assumptions about human nature obviously influence the means by which he or she proposes to accomplish certain ends, but it is important to see that the ends themselves are not completely determined by those assumptions; rather, they are distinctive components of a particular theory of representation. What does a theorist wish to accomplish by proposing one particular institutional form rather than another? Just as with the set of dimensions that provide a framework for comparing theorists' beliefs about human nature, we can define a set of dimensions which schematically represent some of the principal goals that political theorists have discussed (see Table 1.2).

One frequent concern of many theorists is which of many diverse interests in a policy should be represented. Their differing positions on this issue can be specified in terms of two dimensions, with Madison's position on these issues being specified as follows.

1 *Time perspective of representatives.* Madison sought a system that

reflected a balance between short- and long-range policymaking perspectives. It was important that representatives be familiar with the electorate's preferences, however parochial and whimsical they might be. But at the same time, he felt that they should resist temporary public whims in favor of long-term interests.

2. *Scope of representation.* Similarly, Madison wanted a compromise between faithful representation of the many different concerns of the various regions and localities and representation of the common concerns of the nation as a whole.

The other sorts of goals that political theorists frequently discuss concern how representatives should act, for example, the desired degree of independence and adaptability. For specifying how goals can vary, two other dimensions are relevant.

3. *Degree of cooperation between representatives.* Madison recognized that representatives would form factions with one another and that any idea of totally independent legislators (liberal formalism) was unrealistic. Characteristically, he favored the mean between these extremes. He feared stable divisions of political conflict and saw enormous benefits in fluid, diverse coalitions. At the same time, his observations of history indicated that republics more frequently succumbed to the former than to the latter.

4. *Consistency and reliability of representatives.* Madison was very much inclined toward compromise and adaptability. He understood that a society that made too many changes undermined its own legitimacy, but he was equally fearful of people who were inflexibly wedded to a particular viewpoint.

In short, Madison's positions on many of the key dimensions of representation were predictably at the mean. The challenge for Madison was to design institutions that encouraged mean values when the natural tendencies in politics pulled societies toward the extremes. A strong assumption in Madison's thinking was that, in large societies, there would inevitably be a wide distribution of opinion and behavior, and that the best that one could do was a moderate consensus. The mean is a compromise that denies large numbers of people their ideal points. Hence, we would take issue with Chappell and Keech (chapter 2) when they say that the concept of Pareto improvement is "one that may help define the common good for *The Federalist* as well." In the large, diverse, factionalized society Madison was thinking about, representatives could not hope to get unanimity or make no one worse off. Rather, they could, if they were good representatives, serve as a moderating force, but in order for that to happen, many constituents would have to compromise their interests, and those at the extreme of the distribution would have to sacrifice more than those in the middle.

Madison's Proposals for Electoral Reform Examined in a Contemporary Context

The best way to illustrate how Madison's overall goals and his assumptions about human nature combined to generate the specific positions he took on various constitutional proposals is to examine a few institutional examples closely. We will discuss three problems about which Madison worried and which are still of concern—indeed of increased concern—today.

Terms of Office for Elected Officials

Madison understood the importance of the "electoral connection" to the success or failure of representative democracy: "It is essential to liberty that the government in general should have a common interest with the people, so it is particularly essential that the branch of it under consideration should have an immediate dependence on, and an intimate sympathy with, the people. Frequent elections are unquestionably the only policy by which this dependence and sympathy can be effectively secured" (no. 52, p. 327). Assuming, then, that frequent elections are the key to the people's ability to control representative behavior, the next question for Madison was: How frequent should House elections be?

His discussion of this issue focused almost exclusively on whether two-year terms, as opposed to one-year terms, would be too long to maintain "the requisite dependence of the House of Representatives on their constituents" (no. 52, p. 328). After considering the experience in Great Britain and various state governments, Madison concluded that "the liberties of the people can be in no danger from biennial elections" (no. 52, p. 329). The worry that elections every two years might make representatives too independent of the electorate seems almost fantastic from today's perspective. The research of Mayhew, Fenno, Fiorina, and others has convincingly shown that the electoral connection has become an obsession for many members of Congress, and that many aspects of congressional behavior can be traced to electoral motivations (Mayhew, 1974a; Fenno, 1978; Fiorina, 1977a). Indeed, had Madison been aware of the future role that reelection fears would play in American political life, it is likely that he, too, would have been concerned, since he was instinctively suspicious of extreme and imbalanced behavior of any sort.

Even without the benefit of knowing about the problems that two-year terms have created for contemporary members of Congress, Madison worried about a legislature's being too closely tied to public opinion. Indeed, his arguments for bicameralism and for an indirectly elected Senate clearly indicated that he wanted to strike a balance between the likely ephemeral perspective of the House and the more deliberative judgment of the Senate. Madison thought that because the Senators would be appointed by the state legislatures for six-year terms, the Senate could check any intemperate decision by the lower house and offset the inexperience caused by the high turnover that he expected to result from frequent direct elections.

Implicit in Madison's discussion is a behavioral model linking the likely actions of legislators to the method by which they are elected to office and to the length of the terms they serve in such a way that (1) legislators who are directly elected are more sensitive to public opinion than those indirectly elected, and (2) those who have to run for office more frequently are more responsive to the popular will than those who serve longer terms. Clearly, the underlying assumption is that, at least in the situation described, legislators will be at least partly influenced by the self-interested motive of reelection. A legislator exclusively motivated by other-regarding interests (e.g., what the legislator thought was the best policy for the country) would disregard the incentives of the electoral system, and Madison knew this did not happen. Electoral arrangements mattered to him precisely because he saw that different rules provide different incentives to actors with self-regarding motives.

Just as Madison worried about the proper length of office terms, it is also a much discussed contemporary question. Two-year electoral cycles, some argue, are not consistent with, and still less conducive to, long-range planning. Granted that the problem has become more acute in recent years, even had Madison foreseen it, as Hamilton did—at least in connection with his discussion of the presidential term[2]—we suspect that Madison would not have argued for longer terms of office in the House. He believed that *public whims, however ephemeral, should be represented,* but that they should also be balanced by other perspectives in the government. If the time horizons of modern governments are too short, as many contemporary critics claim, it is possible that Madison would have held that the abandonment of an indirectly elected Senate and the growing tendency to select presidential candidates by directly elected primaries, rather than the parochial nature of the House, are responsible for the failure. Thus, a solution more attuned to Madisonian themes would attempt to remedy any perceived imbalance in the perspective of representatives by giving other parts of the system a longer time horizon, rather than changing the time horizon of the House of Representatives per se. Madison did not want all representatives to have the same viewpoints. Rather, he wanted to balance various contending viewpoints.

The Qualifications of Voters and the Represented

Because Madison believed that the "definition of the right of suffrage is very justly regarded as a fundamental article of republican government" (no. 52, p. 326), he argued that the qualifications for voters in House elections should be the same as "those of the most numerous branch of the state legislatures." What was his reasoning here? On the one hand, it would be improper to pass over silently such a fundamental right as that of voting; on the other hand, it was important to respect the different customs of the various states. To "have reduced the different qualifications in the different states to one uniform rule" would doubtless have satisfied the desires of closet philosophers for symmetry, but it was not in the realm of practical politics. It "would probably have been as dissatisfactory to some of the States as it would have been difficult to the convention" (no. 52, p. 326). Hence, Madison concludes, the Convention was right to adopt the compromise that the qualifications to vote in federal House elections would be the same as those specified in the state constitutions.

This is a characteristically Madisonian solution. Pegging the federal standard to that of the existing state constitutions avoided controversy among the various views at the Convention of who was and was not qualified to vote, and it was a neat compromise between allowing the states the freedom to conduct elections as they saw fit and putting federal limits on suffrage qualifications. Here again, we see how compromise, moderation, and adaptability affect every aspect of the Madisonian scheme.

Implicit in the position of the framers of the Constitution was the notion that it was legitimate to exclude some individuals in the electorate, but not others—the only question for them being who was to be included and who excluded. Age, property rights, sex, and race were some of the most common qualifications applied by the states in the determination of voting rights. Madison himself gives no hint of which qualifications he thought most important, this presumably being a matter which he held should be determined by local circumstances and tastes.

Once the decision had been made to exclude some people from voting, the next question that had to be faced was whether all people or only some (and if only some, which) should be counted in the apportionment of representatives. Madison believed that all people, including those who were ineligible to vote, should be counted when allocating shares to the states. This proposal was highly controversial because, if it were adopted, slaves would be counted, to the advantage of the southern states, which would thereby gain representation in the national legislature. Today, the notion that representation be apportioned by population rather than by the electorate is once again controversial. Because the number of House seats allocated to a state depends on the most recent census figures, and because these figures include noncitizens and age-ineligible groups, this method of apportionment has significant political consequences, especially in the southwestern states with large noncitizen populations. These states obviously benefit from an allocation of seats by a population-based formula, whereas many midwestern and eastern states would have greater representation if registered voters, eligible voters, or even citizens were used instead.

Apportionment by population also differentially affects the political power of various ethnic groups in the United States. For instance, the Latinos, with young populations and numerous noncitizens, get more representation under the current, population-based rule than groups like the Irish- or Japanese-Americans, with a higher proportion of native-born and older members (Cain and Kiewiet, 1987). Population-based apportionment even has partisan consequences. Since the Republican party tends to draw from a more upscale electorate, Republican areas usually have a higher ratio of voters to population than do Democratic areas. In California, for instance, it is not uncommon for Republican seats to have two or more times the number of voters as Democratic seats. Republicans would benefit greatly if they could persuade the courts to allow apportionment on some other basis than population.

There was no way, of course, that Madison could have foreseen all of this, but it is useful, in thinking about the problem in its current form, to understand the logic behind his view that all people, including slaves, should be counted in the apportionment process. First and foremost, Madison's position reflected a pragmatic compromise between the position that slaves were property and therefore should count for taxation purposes only and the opposing view that slaves were people and should be counted for apportionment purposes only. Slaves, he pointed out, were considered, by the law at that time, "in some respects . . . persons, and in other respects . . . property" (no. 54, p. 337). A slave was property in the sense that he or she was compelled to work for another, could be bought and sold, and was restrained in his or her liberty. At the same time, a slave was "protected . . . in his life and in his limbs, against the violence of all others." In this sense, a slave was "no less evidently regarded by the law as member of the society, not as a part of the irrational creation; as a moral person, not as a mere article of property" (no. 54, p. 337). Given the mixed status of slaves, it would not have been "impartial or consistent" to have included slaves in apportionment but not in taxation, or vice versa. Even more important, it was unreasonable to expect that "the southern states would concur in a system which considered their slaves in some degree as men when burdens were to be imposed, but refused to consider them in the same light when advantages were to be conferred" (no. 54, p. 338).

Though slavery has long since been abolished and the issue in the form that agitated the delegates at the Convention and led to so much debate in the discussions that followed is moot, the question of rights remains all too alive and well. For instance, does a person who enters the United States illegally forfeit some basic human rights, for instance, the constitutional rights of free speech and association? What other basic services (e.g., health care, schooling, fire, and police) is this person entitled to? And, most important from the perspective of this chapter, does this person have a right to representation?

A consequence of the compromise on slavery is that the U.S. Supreme Court currently holds that, because the right to representation is a fundamental one connected to the protection of life and property, all people should therefore be represented and population, not voters, should be the basis for allocating representatives to the states. The Court, in other instances, however, has moved away from Madison's position. For instance, while Madison gave the states total freedom to determine the voting franchise, the Court has greatly restricted the rights of the states to exclude certain classes of people *from electing public officials* by the widespread application of the Fourteenth Amendment and the Voting Rights Act, which we will discuss shortly.

Before leaving the subject of electoral qualifications, we shall note one more issue on which contemporary opinion is at odds with Madison's views. A prevalent contemporary view is that people and not property are the sole legitimate basis of representation. The opinions of the Supreme Court in *Baker* v. *Carr* and *Reynolds* v. *Sims* gave strong weight to the doctrine of one person, one vote. Geographic, wealth, and occupational interests are secondary, and representation schemes that diminish the one person, one vote principle are potentially unconstitutional. Thus, a second house in a legislature that assigns extra seats to rural areas can be ruled illegal by the courts.

Madison, in contrast, held that "Government is instituted no less for the protection of property than of the persons of individuals." He pointed out, with approval, that in New York, "one branch of the government is intended more especially to be the guardian of property and is accordingly elected by that part of the society which is most interested in this object of government," and he observed that since in the federal constitution, "the rights of property are committed into the same hands with the personal rights . . . some attention ought . . . to be paid to property in the choice of those hands" (no. 54, p. 339).

Such a position would today be viewed as elitist and extremely antiegalitarian. The evolution of law on this subject has been toward giving each vote the same weight as far as possible. In redistricting, this has been interpreted to mean achieving as near arithmetical equality in district size as possible. In campaign finance law, it has meant limiting the amount of money that individuals contribute so that some voters do not have more influence over the system than others. Would Madison agree? Would he move with the times? Perhaps. But his views on the representation of groups, to which we next turn, would cause him to see virtue in the distribution of power unequally among individuals within the system. He believed that even if people of wealth and property did not have especially valued personal qualities, they at least had perspectives that contributed to the quality of lawmaking. And the current doctrine that voters should be treated as formally equal, whatever their differences in attributes and endowments may be, would not, it is likely, have impressed Madison in view of the difficulty of implementing it, as well as the unfortunate side effects which follow its implementation.

We will conclude this section by turning from speculation about his approach to this or that specific right in circumstances very different from any he knew, to the question of his approach to rights in general. As we have already said, Madison took the matter of justice and equity seriously, but he was not interested in them as abstract ideals. (He would, we suspect, have written off Rawls's original position as typical of the speculation of "closet" thinkers.) Rather, he aimed at achieving a balance of competing claims—a balance, as it were, of dissatisfactions. The point of balance would obviously change across time as the competing claims changed, old claims disappearing and new claims emerging. But the balance achieved at any particular time (say, 1787, or 1987) is "just" at that time and defines—provisionally, of course—what people's rights, whether the right to vote or the right to be represented, are. Madison, we think, would have focused on the procedures—on "due process"—by which a balance is achieved, not on getting the result which he (or any one else) had decided in advance was "right."

The Representation of Groups

Madison's thoughts on factionalism are well known. As we observed earlier, he assumed that conflicts of interests are inherent in human nature, and he recognized that, as a consequence, people fall into various groups. He wanted to avoid a situation in which any one group—with one bundle, as it were, of interests—controlled the decisions of a society. Free elections and the majority principle protected the country from dictatorship, that is, the tyranny of a minority. However, he was equally concerned about the danger that he thought was more likely in a democracy, that is, the tyranny of the majority. A central institutional issue for him was how to minimize this risk.

Madison's solution characteristically relied not only on formal institutions, which could be designed, but also on the particular sociological structure of American society, which he took as a fortunate starting point for the framers of the new constitution. The institutional component in his solution was checks and balances, so that there were multiple entry points into the government and multiple ways to offset the power that any one branch of the government might otherwise acquire over another. In this system, "the constant aim is to divide and arrange the several offices in such a manner as that each may be a check on the other" (no. 51, p. 322).

These institutional arrangements were reinforced by the sociological fact that the Republic contained a multiplicity of interests that could, and did, offset one another: "Whilst all authority in it will be derived from and dependent on the society, the society itself will be broken into so many parts, interests and classes of citizens that the rights of individuals, or of the minority, will be in little danger from interested combinations of the majority" (no. 51, p. 324). This line of argument was further developed by pluralist thinkers such as Dahl, who maintained that the tyranny of a minority is best prevented by fluid coalitions of interests. It is good that there are many group interests; that they be numerous is less important than that they be impermanent and shifting alliances whose components vary with the specific policy issue.

From the standpoint of representation theory, this leads to several important problems in institutional design. Assuming that American society is not at the mercy of sociological forces outside lawmakers' powers—and that is indeed an unproven assumption—how can electoral law be designed to help result in there being fluid coalitions? And how far should group identity be deliberately supported in American society? Obviously, these two questions are especially salient in race relations problems.

In the 1960s, the problems of civil rights and racial tensions were uppermost on the political agenda. The Vietnam war and the economic troubles of the mid-1970s temporarily displaced race relations, but the changing demographic composition of the United States and the growing concerns about immigration policy have brought racial politics to the foreground once again. When the problem of race relations is reinterpreted in Madisonian terms, the relevant questions are: To what extent should racial or ethnic groups be acknowledged in law and policy? What implications do the various programs that are intended to help minorities (e.g., the Voting Rights Act and affirmative action policies) have for factionalism in America?

These questions are best illustrated by exploring one example in some detail. The Voting Rights Act is an important contemporary attempt at institutional design. Initially passed in 1965 and then amended in 1982, the Voting Rights Act has caused many states and municipalities to reexamine their electoral institutions. As amended, section 2 of the Voting Rights Act prohibits any voting procedure that results "in a denial or abridgment of the rights of any citizen of the U.S. to vote on account of race or color." The tests and criteria of when such an abridgment or denial has occurred have evolved out of the Senate Report in 1982 and subsequent case law. For the present discussion, these details are unimportant. The crucial point is that the kind of ballot procedure, redistricting plan, or electoral arrangement that a community uses (e.g., at-large election, single-member simple plurality, or multimember districts) may not now have the effect of systematically denying representation to a racial or ethnic minority.

The assumptions of the Voting Rights Act are that voters and candidates can be classified by racial and ethnic groups (i.e., factions), that the systematic exclusion of a particular group from representation is undesirable, that certain institutional arrangements systematically contribute to the effect of excluding groups, and that these arrangements can be redesigned so as to assist the excluded group. If these conditions hold, then the Voting Rights Act can be construed as an attempt to protect minorities against the tyranny of the majority when the type of electoral institutions employed by a community, combined with the prevailing voting patterns, has the effect of excluding minorities from fair and effective representation. At the same time, opponents of the Voting Rights Act often raise questions that also derive from Madisonian and pluralist interests. If district lines are drawn by racial and ethnic criteria, will excessive factionalism be encouraged? Does the provision of bilingual ballots to Latino and Asian-American voters tend to destroy the assimilationist forces that create social unity? What about the institutional arrangements that make it possible for minority candidates to get elected by the votes of a single minority without depending on the votes of other minority groups or of the Anglo majority? Does this not undermine the pluralist ideal of fluid coalitions on specific issues—do institutional arrangements designed to assist groups have the incentive effect of strengthening group identity, and so of hardening factional divisions rather than promoting fluid coalitions?

Clearly, therefore, there are Madisonian concerns on both sides of this issue. On the one hand, a Madisonian pluralist acknowledges that factions (including racial and ethnic groups) are inevitable because the extreme individualism of liberal formalism is impossible, and that because the goal is to achieve an extended Republic with a large number of groups to offset one another, not a government dominated by one or just a few groups, it was necessary to form a stable government through the joint product of formal institutions and informal sociology and to recognize that what was created at the formal level could affect the informal arena, and vice versa. Modern Madisonian thinkers cannot be oblivious to biases in the informal sociological sector.

On the other hand, a Madisonian pluralist must also be concerned about any evidence that the incentive effects of minority districts harden coalitional positions or that Voting Rights Act interventions increase racial polarization. What would the outlines of a "reasonable" compromise of these concerns look like? It would involve, perhaps, the introduction of institutional devices that would encourage coalitional behavior at the constituent level or a highly circumstantial application of the Voting Rights Act that avoids transforming its remedies into permanent rights.

Conclusion

We conclude this discussion of Madison's theory of institutional design by asking how contemporary political scientists will evaluate it and its relevance to late twentieth-century America. We think it safe to predict that they will not be unanimous, and we believe that the deepest division of opinion will turn out to reflect differing attitudes toward Madison's implicit presuppositions (his underlying metaphysical and epistemological orientations, especially his preference for an empirical, experiential approach, his readiness to accept tentative, provisional results, and his admiration for balance and moderation). Those whose orientations are different—who regard moderation as a sign of weakness of will, preferring "thorough" and "root and branch" policies, or who prefer a deductive approach because it approximates to the natural science model—will be inclined to write Madison off as a poor sort of political scientist, no more than a politician.

There is no doubt that the trend among political scientists and lawyers in recent years has been in the direction of rational-choice theory and liberal formalism, that is, the assumption that voting mechanisms can be adequately accounted for from the standpoint of anonymous, formally equal individuals. The one person, one vote doctrine, which follows from this assumption, epitomizes this point of view. When we enter a caveat, as we do here, we recognize that our own Madisonian orientations are showing. But we think it worth pointing out that many minorities believe liberal formalism to have unspoken biases that favor better-educated, better-to-do, and more highly assimilated individuals. And though we agree that liberal formalism avoids the incentive effects of giving legal recognition to groups, we also believe that such recognition is a legitimate concern. Faced with such a dilemma, which is not exceptional but typical of the kind of problem with which political science must deal, provisional moderating and circumstantial remedies—Madisonian remedies, indeed—may well be the best answer.

Notes

1. Quotations are taken from the New American Library edition of *The Federalist Papers*, 1961, Clinton Rossiter, ed.
2. Hamilton felt it essential that the President have a broad time horizon and the capacity to resist public opinion when "the interests of the people are at variance with their inclinations" (no. 71, p. 432).

CHAPTER TWO

Publius and Public Choice

Thomas Schwartz

L ike an object seen from different angles in different lights by observers with different interests, a text can bear any number of very different but equally correct interpretations. An interpreter might examine *The Federalist Papers* for literary style or debate strategy; for evidence of its authors' educational, religious, or regional backgrounds; for its practicality or idealism; for its reflection of prevailing intellectual currents; or for any number of other things. I examine the *Federalist* for its original and enduring contribution to political theory.

That contribution is not, of course, the system of government it expounds, which was the work of the Federal Convention. It is not the set of problems that would be solved or avoided, according to the *Federalist*, by the new system, for these were mostly the problems that had occasioned the Federal Convention or had exercised the antifederalists. It is not the broad structural features that the *Federalist* attributes to the Constitution (republicanism, federalism, separation of powers, and the like), nor the general normative principles to which the *Federalist* appeals (justice, property rights, personal liberty, the public good), for these were mostly current coin, and Hamilton's plan provided little room for elaborate philosophical elucidation.

The original and enduring contribution to political theory made by Hamilton, Jay, and especially Madison lies less in the positions they espoused than in the way they argued. It consists in the *Federalist*'s principles of political analysis, the general principles by which Publius reasoned about the consequences of alternative political arrangements. No less original than the individual arguments that they underlie, these principles are more likely to endure change in time and place. Evinced more than stated, the *Federalist* principles of political analysis are strikingly similar to those of the contemporary public-choice school. Both constitute institutionalist theories of politics.

After locating the *Federalist* on the map of political theory, I outline its principles of political analysis, then compare them with those of the public choice school.

Cartography

In speaking of political theory, I cast my net widely. Political theory can be positive or normative—concerned with explanation and prediction or with evaluation and prescription. The distinction is easily exaggerated. A normative theorist who specifies the grounds of political authority has at least implicitly described a motive that people might have for adopting certain institutions and, hence, a possible explanation of their adoption; Hobbes does both at once. A positive theorist who works out the consequences for public policy or for the character and behavior of citizens of instituting one form of government rather than another has provided possible grounds for choosing the one form in preference to the other.

My net holds styles of political argument and approaches to political analysis as well as single, highly articulated systems of propositions. That distinction, too, is easily exaggerated. A systematic theory presented in a single book may prove more valuable for the general form of analysis that it introduces and exemplifies than for its particular assumptions and findings; a good example is Anthony Downs's *An Economic Theory of Democracy*.

Politics are the possessions of polities, each comprising people (citizens or subjects) who act or interact within a set of institutions (a political constitution and a basic legal system). Some outcomes of action or interaction are public-policy decisions, broadly conceived; others would conventionally fall in the private sphere. Even the latter owe their character to institutions as well as individual decisions—to contract law, the criminal code, religious establishment, and whatnot. Public-policy decisions can, in turn, alter institutions as well as the opportunities and even the tastes and beliefs that give rise to individual choices. So all three elements of politics—people (or their behavior), institutions, and policy decisions—are interdependent.

Yet, many theories of politics treat one element as primary, either saying little about the other two or grounding a more comprehensive theory in a single-element theory. To do so is not necessarily to deny interdependence. It is hard to explain or prescribe the relationships of all things to all things all at once. A theorist might emphasize a single element because of personal taste, past neglect, or a belief that more can be explained in one direction than in another. Not every theorist has treated a single element as primary, of course. Aristotle was as eclectic and antireductionist in his politics as in his metaphysics, and continental philosophers of the nineteenth and twentieth centuries have tried to explain all three elements of politics in terms of fourth factors, such as history and technology. Still it is interesting to compare political theories according to the elements of politics that they emphasize.

A single-element theory that focuses on persons (or their actions) is a political psychology. It is concerned with what is fixed and what is malleable in human nature, with the determinants of political behavior, and with the virtues associated with citizenship and other political roles. Plato was the quintessential political psychologist. For him, good policy, which he did not define, would be produced by just insti- tutions, which he did define but in psychological terms: just institutions are those that divide labor according to people's innate capacities and propensities. Behavioralism, too, is a political psychology.

Theories that emphasize policy decisions and other outcomes are concerned with moral constraints on actions (such as the absence of certain biases) and with the consequences of alternative policies—chiefly, magnitude and incidence of costs and benefits—apart from the procedures and motivations that led to their adoption. The utilitarians are outcome theorists. So are contemporary theorists of distributive justice, casuistical moralists who examine the rights and wrongs of particular policies, and policy analysts who study the effects (the "impact") of adopting one policy rather than another.

Institutional theories are concerned with the justification or explanation of the existence of coercive institutions and with the ways in which specific institutions or types of institutions constrain behavior, affect policy, allocate power, and secure or impair procedural or representational fairness. The Roman Lawyers and St. Thomas Aquinas were institutionalists. So were the medieval partisans of *imperium* and *sacerdotum*. So, to a great extent, were the classical contractarians—Hobbes, Locke, and, in a significant part of his work, Rousseau. So, certainly, was Montesquieu. And so were the authors of *The Federalist Papers*.

Although concerned with policy problems—notably problems of peace and security, of trade and diplomacy, of monetary stability and the protection of property—the *Federalist* authors saw policy decisions chiefly as outcomes of interaction among persons within an institution. Rather than prescribe policy, they recommended an institutional instrument for arriving at policy decisions, arguing that it combined energy enough to solve policy problems with safeguards sufficient to prevent tyranny.

Although the *Federalist* authors were very much concerned with behavior, their political psychology, if it could be said to exist at all, was vanishingly thin and commonsensical: avarice and ambition existed alongside virtuous sentiments, people varied in their capacities and propensities, and sectional and other factional interests were likely to clash and to provide a motivation for the aggrandizement of power. To admire Publius's portrait of his countrymen, with its nice balance of cynicism and generosity, is not to find an elaborate psychological theory.

For the most part, the *Federalist* theory of behavior is institutional rather than psychological. It is a theory of *institutionally induced* behavior: institutional roles *select for* certain capacities and propensities and influence strategies by imposing constraints and providing opportunities. Elections would select the capacity and inclination to serve constituents' interests (Madison, *Federalist*, no. 35). Different bases of representation and different terms of office in the two chambers of Congress would select different motivations (Madison, no. 10). The small size of Congress compared to the electorate and the need to secure votes would give an individual congressman the incentive to become well informed. By contrast, the role of voter is nonselective, and an individual voter has far less an incentive than a congressman to become well informed. So voters would be less likely than elected representatives to make sound policy decisions and more likely to respond to demagogic appeals (Hamilton, no. 35; Madison, no. 48). True, the *Federalist* authors were concerned with certain untoward motivations, chiefly greed, ambition, and factionalism. But they did not explain these motivations or say much about their incidence. The assumption that such motivations exist—that men are not angels—was used to argue for some government rather than none, for national as well as state government, and for care in matters of constitutional design. Beyond that, this assumption served not as a premise of any argument but as a worst-case hypothesis—an "even if" assumption—in an argument for the robustness of the constitutional order (Madison, no. 52).

Themes of the Federalist

What distinguishes the theory of *The Federalist Papers* from earlier institutional theories is a combination of three themes.

Importance of institutional detail. More than the classical contractarians, more even than Montesquieu, the *Federalist* authors emphasized the fine details of institutional structure. Of course, this was because they had a specific constitution to expound. But whatever the reason, they argued that small, subtle details—the specific terms of office of representatives and senators, the Electoral College, the specific form of the executive veto, the time limit on appropriations—were consequentially important.

Incentives. The *Federalist* authors based prediction and prescription on institutional incentives. To ensure that officeholders have the right motivations, offices must be designed so that the right motivations are selected: "The interests of the man must be connected with the constitutional rights of the place" (Madison, *Federalist*, no. 51). Looked at the other way around, to predict or explain the way an institution works or to evaluate its design, we must examine the incentives it creates and therewith the motivations it selects.

Equilibrium. Undesirable behavior by one official or branch of government, and particularly the aggrandizement of power, is best prevented neither by "parchment barriers" to untoward action (Madison, no. 48) nor by attempting to form a "nation of philosophers" (Madison, no. 49) nor again by entrusting government to "angels" (Madison, no. 51) but by designing institutions so that untoward interests are held in check by countervailing interests: "ambition must be made to counteract ambition" (Madison, no. 51). Outcomes are then explained as the creatures of an "equilibrium" (Madison, no. 49) or "balance" (Madison, no. 51) of such interests—a state of affairs whence any ambition to deviate is checked by a counteracting ambition. Stated another way, a constitution is an allocation of power to positions, a written constitution an allocation of initial endowments of power, and a durable constitution an equilibrium allocation. A written constitution will endure, therefore, only if it is an equilibrium allocation, and to predict the system established through a written constitution is to predict equilibria from initial endowments.

Public Choice

The public choice school, too, is an institutional approach to political analysis, drawing on three older institutional theories. One is social choice theory, the mathematical study of voting rules and other institutions that transform individual preferences into a collective choice (Arrow, 1963; Sen, 1970; Schwartz, 1986, 1987). Another is game theory, which investigates the ways in which rules governing interactive decisions shape strategies and give rise to equilibria (Luce and Raiffa, 1957; Ordeshook, 1986). The third is neoclassical economics, from which the public choice school draws a style of reasoning (Downs, 1957; Buchanan and Tullock, 1962; Olson, 1965; Tullock, 1967; Mueller, 1979) more than specific findings. It, too, is about institutions, specifically market economies—or, if you prefer, the legal and political rules that make economic exchange possible. One might contend that economics is about behavior more than institutions. Producers, for example, are assumed to maximize profits. But that assumption is institutional rather than psychological. People may or may not be avaricious by nature, but those who do not act avariciously do not long survive in the role of producer: the role selects for avarice.

The public choice approach to political analysis shares the three themes of the *Federalist*. Much work by public choice scholars argues that political outcomes are highly sensitive to the fine details of institutional structure—that legislative decisions are highly sensitive to the precise form of agendas, that budgets chosen by majority voting are highly sensitive to prescribed points of reversion, that subtly different electoral systems can yield surprisingly different choices, that the achievement of common goals by an interest group depends critically on the exact nature of certain institutional rewards and penalties, that the stability of voting outcomes depends on the precise size that majorities are required to have and the precise number of issues they are required to decide, and so on.

Like the *Federalist* authors, public choice scholars either make minimal assumptions about individual behavior or analyze individual behavior as the product of institutional incentives: roles select for motivations. Officeholders are assumed to try to please constituents, for example, because that is a good strategy for achieving reelection, and they are assumed to seek reelection not because political ambition is part of human nature but because those who do not are not well represented among officeholders. The role of citizen, on the other hand, affords such a small incentive to participate in politics that it is a wonder anyone bothers to vote.

And, of course, public choice scholars view political outcomes as equilibria of interests in an institutional setting—as solutions to games defined by institutional rules. Sometimes equilibria of specified sorts are shown not to exist. But the goal of analysis is still to explain political outcomes as equilibria in some sense—as possible outcomes, or members of sets of possible outcomes, to which institutional interaction predictably converges and from which deviations are punished.

Although policy figures prominently in public choice research, policies are mostly studied as creatures of interaction within institutional settings or as institutional changes that alter the incentives of actors and therewith the subsequent outcomes of institutional interaction.

Public choice research is also concerned with behavior. In most cases, however, either nothing is assumed about individual motivations or they are assumed to be institutionally induced. Sometimes strong assumptions are made about people's tastes or the information available to them, but they are presented as special-case assumptions, not general principles.

The frequent reference in the public choice literature to self-interest, methodological individualism, and rationality may convey the opposite impression, that the public choice school assumes a particular political psychology. More often than not, however, the term *self-interest* is just poor diction: it refers to whatever interests, selfish or altruistic, the self happens to pursue. And methodological individualism is no more than the doctrine that all political and economic outcomes are ultimately the results of individual choices constrained by institutions and available resources: it denies any explanatory role to irreducible collective consciousness or to historical forces. Finally, "rationality" is a formal constraint on individual choices, requiring (roughly) that people act as though maximizing something—something or other, that is, not anything in particular. It is true that the classical rationality assumptions have been criticized for excessive substantive import. But the criticisms (along with proposed revisions) have come chiefly from within the public choice community.

There are differences, of course, between Publius and public choice, some too obvious to merit much comment. Our experiences and concerns are not those of the *Federalist* authors, who worked for the sole and immediate goal of ratification, and we enjoy advantages in information and technical tools.

More important, their enterprise was normative, and ours is often positive. But to repeat, that difference is easily exaggerated: an argument to the effect that institution X would induce behavior Y leading to outcome Z can be put to the service of explanation and prediction as well as evaluation and prescription.

More important still, we are more prone than the *Federalist* authors to construct abstract deductive models that admittedly simplify the reality they are used to explain; the *Federalist*'s "axioms" (Hamilton, no. 61, 31; Madison, nos. 45 and 59) were offered as laws rather than models or hypotheses. If we have learned anything from public choice research, it is that apparently clear and weak assumptions, once made precise, often have surprising and anomalous deductive consequences (Brams, 1976; Schwartz, 1987), consequences that conflict with our casual inferences, demonstrating the shortsightedness and unreliability of casual inference, hence the value of deductive rigor. But for deductive rigor we need precise, mathematically tractable assumptions. The problem is that such assumptions often simplify reality and that their mathematical meaning sometimes is clearer than their substantive import. We trade good fit of assumptions to reality for good fit of inferences to assumptions. Yet this difference, too, is easily exaggerated. It is less a difference in trade-offs than a difference in awareness of the need to make a trade-off. And as contributions to a continuing scientific inquiry rather than a one-time exercise in political advocacy, deductive findings in public choice carry standing invitations to weaken or eliminate questionable assumptions and to identify inferences as mere artifacts of such assumptions.

Conclusion

The *Federalist* authors were institutionalists not because they ignored policy and behavior but because they saw these elements of politics chiefly as the creatures of institutional structure. Their patrimony is public choice research, committed to the study of institutions, to the view that fine institutional details are important, to the explanation of political behavior in terms of institutionally induced incentives, and to the analysis of policy decisions as equilibria of contending interests within institutional settings.

Acknowledgments. This research was supported by NSF grant SES 8612120.

CHAPTER THREE

Electoral Institutions in
The Federalist Papers:
A Contemporary Perspective

Henry W. Chappell, Jr., and William R. Keech

In many respects, *The Federalist Papers* may be considered forerunners of modern social-choice theory. And social choice theory can be considered a modern reflection of Madisonian thinking. Such arguments are to be found in Riker (1982, pp. 8–11, and Ch. 10) and in Schwartz (chapter 2). Other observers, such as Cain and Jones (chapter 1), call attention to differences between the views of Madison and those of contemporary analytical theorists.

This chapter relates the insights of *The Federalist Papers* to theory and insights from social-choice and other modern sources with respect to electoral institutions. We find a fundamental compatibility between the *Federalist* and modern theory, but we will argue that there are important points of divergence between them. We do not find the points of divergence to be irreparably damaging to either. We will show how modern theory can help to clarify some issues in the *Federalist*, and we will show how modern theory would profit by attention to the views of Madison, Hamilton, and Jay.

By focusing on electoral institutions, we concentrate on a pervasive and essential aspect of the political system defined in the *Federalist*. Perhaps the central feature of the republican form of government defended there is that government is ultimately dependent on the people. Hamilton contends that "the consent of the people" is the "pure original fountain of all legitimate authority" (*Federalist*, no. 22, p. 152), and Madison argues that "the ultimate authority resides in the people alone" (no. 46, p. 294).[1] More specifically, "a republic [is] a government which derives all its powers directly or indirectly from the great body of the people, and is administered by persons holding their offices during pleasure for a limited period, or during good behavior" (no. 39, p. 241).

What does this mean? How active and controlling a role are the people expected to play in the political system defended in the *Federalist*? How are they to exercise their authority? The answers to these questions as reflected in actual constitutional rules have, of course, changed over time in the direction of enhanced popular participation and more direct accountability of public officials to a broad electorate.

Yet, in the original constitutional arrangements, only one body, the House of Representatives, was to be chosen by direct popular election. The people were to have only an indirect role in the selection of other public officials. Moreover, this system has been associated with the idea of further limits on popular influence because of its features of separated powers and of checks and balances. Since elections played such a limited role in the *Federalist* system, and since they receive so little discussion in *The Federalist Papers*, it might seem that these papers are not a very promising place to look for theory about electoral institutions. We will show that this is not so.

On the other hand, modern social-choice theory has perhaps the most explicit and elaborate theory about elections in existence. But even so, the most sustained effort to relate the theory of social choice to the theory of democracy returns to the *Federalist* as capturing the fundamental insights of this modern theory. William Riker (1982), a leading contemporary social-choice theorist, argues that the view of democracy that is most compatible with modern theory is a "liberal" interpretation of voting that he calls "Madisonian" (pp. 8–11, chap. 10). We will argue that there are more ways than Riker has identified in which social choice theory might profit by building on the insights of the *Federalist*.

The general framework of this chapter is guided by modern social-choice theory's effort to distinguish and relate (1) popular preferences; (2) decision rules and electoral institutions; and (3) collective decisions or policy outcomes. As we will show, each of these elements is discussed in the *Federalist*, but there is something to be gained by separating them more consciously than is done there.

Modern social-choice theory usually models popular preferences as given and stable, if not fixed. It models collective decision rules and procedures and describes the properties of the outcomes that result. These properties may be defined in terms of their relationship to the individual preferences, or in terms of "real valued" social-welfare functions. (See Mueller, 1979, chaps. 9 and 10, for an elaboration of the difference.)

The *Federalist* has a more fluid view, though the papers do reflect a concern with each of the three components of the framework discussed above. The concern with the nature of human preferences (1) is one of the best known features of *The Federalist Papers*, as is indicated by the attention given the discussion of passions and interests in the famous Number 10. The observations on the institutional framework of the three branches of government (2) are also widely acknowledged. Since the observations on the nature of the desired outcomes (3) are less developed, less original, and less well known, we discuss them first.

A Concern with Outcomes: Justice and the Common Good

William Riker (1982) intimates that the essential feature of "Madisonian liberalism" is a set of institutions and procedures that ensure that it will always be possible to reject and replace public officials. He criticizes the Rousseauian populism that suggests that proper electoral procedures will identify a "general will" based on common interests. Riker implies that Madisonian liberalism and (by extension) the *Federalist* are not concerned with defining desirable outcomes or showing how they can be achieved.

In fact, the *Federalist* makes repeated references to the public good, and to justice, which is described in virtually Rawlsian language as "the end of government" (no. 51, p. 324). The *Federalist* does not contain anything we might call a theory of justice or of the common good, but justice seems to be used in a way that refers to individual rights (see Epstein, 1984, pp. 60, 83, 98–99, 163). The common or public good refers to "the permanent and aggregate interests of the community" (no. 10, p. 78). In some respects, Madison's view of the common good may be as utilitarian an idea as aggregate interests imply. "But the whole is more than the sum of its parts because the whole has or is intended to have a permanence which the parts . . . lack" (Epstein, 1984, pp. 65–66).

Justice and the common good are what William Connolly calls "essentially contested concepts." These are concepts that describe things that are valued, complex, and "open," in that different parties will interpret rules of application differently as new situations arise. Following W. B. Gallie, Connolly (1983) argues that such concepts "essentially involve endless disputes about their proper uses on the part of their users" (p. 10).

To refer to an essentially contested concept such as the common good without much more specificity is understandable in terms of the strategic setting of the *Federalist*. It is a way to appeal for broad support for the proposed constitution without touching on the applications that might be divisive. However, another reason may be that Hamilton, Madison, and Jay did not have much choice in the sense that there was then no clear way to define the common good any more specifically than to name it.

Modern social-choice theory makes it possible for us to do somewhat better. Runciman and Sen (1965) have modernized Rousseau's theory of the general will in a way that may be relevant to the task of the *Federalist*. They have suggested that the widely discussed prisoner's dilemma game is a way to make precise and concrete Rousseau's distinction between the will of all and the general will. The will of all is the product of the aggregation of selfish individual interests. The Pareto inferior Nash equilibrium that results when individuals jointly defect in a prisoner's dilemma game represents well Rousseau's idea that individual selfishness can produce collectively undesirable outcomes.

Similarly, the Pareto improvement that is possible when individuals jointly cooperate captures in very concrete terms the possibility that everyone can be better off if everyone acts in consideration of common interests. This insight from modern theory is one that may help to define the common good for the *Federalist*.

Such a view of the common good has the realistic feature that it is not always defined; on some issues or for some purposes, it may not exist. Some situations may involve a pure conflict of interest in which there is no *common* good. These situations may lend themselves to some theory of justice that is not grounded in Pareto or unanimity criteria in the way that the prisoner's dilemma game is. Or they may involve conflicts of interest for which there is no rationale for public resolution.

While the conception of *permanent* as well as aggregate interests suggests a concern on the part of the *Federalist* with considerations above and beyond those of the prisoner's dilemma, it does seem clear that the authors did not have something much more radical or redistributive in mind than the kinds of collective action and collective goods problems that are implied by that game-theoretic metaphor. The *Federalist* does not have an elaborate theory of outcomes, and our interpretation of their references to the common good unquestionably reads something into the essays that was not explicitly there originally.

Still, there are enough references in the *Federalist* to the desirability of outcomes so that we might call it an *instrumentalist* or *consequentialist approach* to the justification of collective decision rules, as contrasted with a *proceduralist* or *contractarian approach*. That is to say, the justification of decision procedures is defended more in terms of promoting the often-undefined goals of the collective enterprise than in terms of procedural ideals (as in Arrow's criteria for collective decision rules), or an *ex ante* agreement to act contrary to one's preferences under certain circumstances (as in Rawls's original condition). (See Coleman and Ferejohn, 1986, pp. 6–8, for an elaboration of these alternatives, and Epstein, 1984, pp. 7, 162–166, for a suggestion that the *Federalist* was instrumentalist in design.)

Another modern concept for the relationship between procedures and outcomes implicit in the *Federalist* is Rawls's (1972) concept of "imperfect procedural justice" (pp. 83–90). The metaphor is a criminal trial in which the desired outcome is clear: correct determination of the true guilt or innocence of the defendant. The adversary proceeding of trial by jury is designed to achieve the desired outcome, but it does not do so without fail. By the same token, the *Federalist* system is designed to achieve justice and the common good, but it does not do so without fail or by definition (in contrast to pure and perfect procedural justice).

The procedures laid out in this system were not flawless, as was recognized by the early and repeated amendments to the Constitution. In fact, many of the amendments can be seen as a continuing series of efforts to improve the procedures in order to better achieve the goals of justice and the common good. At the same time, there is room for adaptation to changes in the understanding of what justice and the common good mean. Most of the amendments that were not oriented to procedures were redefining rights or establishing new ones. This is in keeping with the experimental and incremental approach that Cain and Jones (chapter 1) find in Madisonian thought.

Modern social-choice theory is impatient with concepts that are as difficult to define and operationalize as the *Federalist's* considerations of justice and the common good. Madison and his colleagues might be just as impatient with efforts at mathematical precision in identifying them. We find the efforts at precision to be enlightening and clarifying. However, sympathetic as we are, we do not expect them to override individual and collective human deliberations about justice and the common good. In this respect, the style of thinking reflected in the *Federalist* may be informed by social choice theory but may still have the last word.

Human Nature and the Nature of Preferences

While the *Federalist*'s view of the common good *may* be compatible with at least one interpretation of that of Rousseau, its view of human nature and preferences is certainly more pessimistic. The *Federalist* holds out no Rousseauian hope that a small-scale society might induce individuals to rise above their selfishness and consider instead the interests they have in common. Madison writes that "a pure democracy, by which I mean a society consisting of a small number of citizens, who assemble and administer the government in person, can admit of no cure for the mischiefs of faction" (no. 10, p. 81).

Federalist no. 10 is a ringing statement of the irreducible diversity of political views that can be expected to exist in a society that does not suppress liberty. These views are not necessarily desirable, because "As long as the connection exists between [man's] reason and his self-love, his opinions and his passions will have a reciprocal influence on each other, and the former will be objects to which the latter will attach themselves" (no. 10, p. 78).

The main danger is not the diversity or subjectivity of views, but the violence of faction, which is "a number of citizens, . . . who are united and actuated by some common impulse of passion, or of interest, adverse to the rights of other citizens, or to the permanent and aggregate interests of the community" (no. 10, p. 78). In distinguishing passion and interest, rather than using them as synonyms, Madison reflects a historic distinction that has since become obscured. As Albert Hirschman (1977) points out, interests in material things were once seen as a relatively harmless outlet for human energies that might otherwise be directed toward more dangerous passions for glory and power.

In fact, Hirschman suggests that the famous prescription that "Ambition must be made to counteract ambition" between branches of government (*Federalist*, no. 51, p. 322) was, in fact, an application of a principle then better understood as involving counteracting passions within a single soul: "The comparatively novel thought of checks and balances gained in persuasiveness by being presented as an application of the widely accepted and thoroughly familiar principle of countervailing passion" (1977, p. 30).

In emphasizing the diversity of preferences, the *Federalist* is only to a degree congruent with modern social-choice theory, which typically models diverse preferences either as an ordering of preferences over a definable set of alternatives, or as a variety of ideal points in n-dimensional issue space. Most social-choice theory sees these preferences as capable of being misrepresented for strategic purposes, but as otherwise in principle knowable, fixed, and exogenous.

Clearly, the *Federalist* view of preferences is that they are less fixed and more fluid than that implied by social choice theory. Hamilton speaks of *momentary* passions and *immediate* interests. Even popular assemblies are subject to the *impulses* of rage, resentment, jealousy, avarice, and of other *irregular* and violent propensities (no. 6, p. 56; italics added). These views of evanescent and fluid preferences suggest that, if they are correct, the modeling of individual preferences as fixed and totally exogenous is a quite limited and limiting assumption, though an understandable one for purposes of analyzing the effects of alternative decision rules.

There are modern conceptualizations of preferences (not too far afield from social choice), which may capture the nature of the *Federalist* view of preferences better than fixed ideal points in a utility space. Perhaps the closest of these is Schelling's view of multiple selves. Schelling (1984, pp. 57–82) conceives of the self as having competing manifestations, some of which are less disciplined, reasonable, and farsighted than others. Jon Elster (1983) maps ways in which preferences may be endogenous. He distinguishes drives and desires and shows how the "broad rationality" of desires may be distorted by drives, which are nonconscious psychic forces. He identifies several ways in which this can happen, including adaptive preference formation (the adjustment of wants to possibilities) and preference change by framing (the attractiveness of options changes when the choice situation is reframed; 1983, pp. 25–26).

Benjamin Page and Robert Shapiro in chapter 4 show that public opinion on a variety of issues is remarkably stable. They suggest that the *Federalist*'s concerns about sudden and violent passions and temporary errors and delusions "simply do not correspond to the realities of twentieth century America." Yet modern research has also shown that in some ways publics can be shortsighted.

For example, most studies of retrospective evaluation of economic performance suggest that the public looks back over only a very short period of time and is potentially vulnerable to manipulation. Kiewiet and Rivers (1985) have shown that the overall economic performances of the Carter and the first Reagan administrations were quite similar, but the timing of the most satisfactory portions was such that shortsighted voters may have given Reagan an undeserved advantage. Furthermore, the issues that Page and Shapiro report on are, by definition, issues that have been around a long time. Others, like bomb shelters, "the social issue," and the tax revolt may come and go in a way that is more reminiscent of the *Federalist*'s concern.

Modern social-choice theory has a clarity and precision about the nature of preferences that must be considered an advantage for purposes of theory building. Yet, in many respects, the *Federalist* has a richer notion of the nature of preferences. The standard social-choice model of preferences is being enlarged and enhanced by scholars operating largely within the tradition, such as Schelling and Elster. Its limitations are being directly addressed and mitigated by these scholars, whose work makes it clear that social choice theory is potentially even richer than its characteristic current manifestation. Our return to *The Federalist Papers* makes it clear to us that they are a rich source of insight that we in social choice theory can use to suggest ways to enhance our models of preferences.

Collective Decision Procedures:
The Design of Institutions

Representative government is essential to the *Federalist* system of rising above the "mischiefs of faction." The delegation of the government to a small number of citizens elected by the rest would have as an effect "to refine and enlarge the public views by passing them through a chosen body of citizens whose wisdom may best discern the true interest of their country and whose patriotism and love of justice will be least likely to sacrifice it to temporary or partial considerations" (*Federalist*, no. 10, p. 82). Clearly, the *Federalist* expected representation to involve something more than the delegate model that underlies much modern empirical research on the relationship between representatives and their constituencies. Its writers did not hope for maximum governmental responsiveness to the immediate preferences of the electorate. However, as the *Federalist* (no. 57) makes clear, they did expect that representatives would pay close attention to these preferences.

But this delegation of the government should not be to a single body: "The accumulation of all powers, legislative, executive and judiciary, in the same hands, whether of one, a few, or many, and whether hereditary, self-appointed, or elective, may justly be pronounced the very definition of tyranny" (no. 47, p. 301). Yet, the separation of powers must be more than a "mere demarcation on parchment of the constitutional limits of the several departments" (no. 49, p. 313). Ideally, "each department should have a will of its own," and each department should have "the necessary constitutional means and personal motives to resist encroachments of the others. . . . Ambition must be made to counteract ambition. . . . the constant aim is to divide and arrange the several offices in such a manner as that each may be a check on the other—that the private interest of every individual may be a sentinel over the public rights" (no. 51, pp. 321–322).

How are these bodies to be selected? We may now come closer to the aspirations of the framers than the original Constitution. Ideally, each department was meant to

> be so constituted that the members of each should have as little agency as possible in the appointment of the members of the others. Were this principle rigorously adhered to, it would require that all the appointments for the supreme executive, legislative, and judiciary magistracies should be drawn from the same fountain of authority, the people, through channels having no communication whatever with another. (no. 51, p. 321)

The main exception noted at the time was the rationale for an appointive judiciary.

Since the Electoral College has been given an unambiguous popular basis, and since the Senate has been directly elected, now three national institutions are chosen in a way that approximates the ideal arrangement noted above. State legislatures no longer play the role they once did in choosing U.S. Senators or in defining how presidential electors are chosen. The fountain of authority for the executive and for both legislative branches is more directly than ever the people. Of course, the *Federalist* sidestepped the question of suffrage, but subsequent constitutional amendments have narrowed considerably the grounds on which states can define the right to vote.

The observations in the *Federalist* on related issues of term length and renewability are still of interest. The rationales for the selection and tenure of the two houses of Congress and of the President seem designed to ensure a diversity of perspectives, with the apparent presumption that agreements coming out of such diversity must be healthy and desirable. We discuss the grounds and arguments for such a presumption in the next section.

Madison defends two-year terms for members of the House on the grounds that "frequent elections are unquestionably the only policy" by which it can be ensured that government will have "a common interest with, . . . an immediate dependence on, and an intimate sympathy with, the people" (no. 52, p. 327). The expectation that the popularly elected House would be the dominant agency of the national government was also a ground for short terms, since "the greater the power is, the shorter ought to be its duration" (no. 52, p. 330). The inference that the House would be dominant has not been confirmed in all contexts, but it is sustained by Brams in chapter 8.

The Senate was to be selected in an entirely different way: for longer terms, by state legislatures, and on a basis that represents states equally rather than people. This body was meant to be "a salutary check on the government" (no. 62, p. 378). The Senate would not only be a check on "the propensity of all single and numerous assemblies to yield to the impulse of sudden and violent passions, and to be seduced by factious leaders into intemperate and pernicious resolutions" (no. 62, p. 379); it would also be well situated to be responsible for programs that take time to bear fruit. Some kinds of policies have immediately noticeable effects. Others, however, depend "on a succession of well-chosen and well-connected measures, which have a gradual and perhaps unobserved operation" (no. 63, p. 383). The Senate was meant to have sufficient permanency to attend to such a train of measures as require continued attention (no. 63, p. 384).

One wonders how the *Federalist* would view the contemporary issue of federal budget deficits. In the eyes of many, these deficits involve borrowing to support current consumption at the expense of the future, and thus as a violation of the "permanent," as opposed to the aggregate, interests of the community (no. 10, p. 78). Could longer terms such as those for the Senate be expected to prevent such present orientation? According to one estimate (Gramlich, 1984), it will take twenty or more years for the consequences of the deficits to be reflected in current consumption. Thus, for some kinds of problems, a six-year term may not perhaps ensure a long enough time horizon. On the other hand, Madison would surely have hoped that well-chosen legislators could take a long view that extended far beyond their own term of office and would evince a concern for the "permanent interests" of the community.

Hamilton's defense of the term length and renewability for the President sounds more like the argument for the Senate than for the

House. Energy in the presidency is to be enhanced by longer duration in office. Longer terms are also a means for the president to avoid "feebleness and irresolution" and to resist the transient impulses that "the people may receive from the arts of men, who flatter their prejudices to betray their interests" (no. 71, pp. 432–433). There are some empirical questions implicit here. According to one modern model, the most desirable length of the President's term depends on the length of the voters' memories of an administration's performance (Chappell and Keech, 1983). Most empirical estimates suggest that these memories are not very long.

Hamilton's argument for reeligibility may be one of the earliest developments of the rationale for retrospective voting. The possibility of reelection "is necessary to enable the people, when they see reason to approve of his conduct, to continue him in his station in order to prolong the utility of his talents and virtues, and to secure to the government the advantage of permanency in a wise system of administration" (no. 72, p. 437). Excluding the possibility of reelection would diminish "the inducements to good behavior" as well as have a series of other effects that are, in effect, arguments against the two-term limit set out in the Twenty-second Amendment (no. 72, pp. 437–440).

The tone of this argument is very compatible with public choice modeling of behavior in terms of motivations and incentives. Hamilton's President may not be a vote maximizer or a single-minded seeker of reelection, but his behavior is clearly expected to be motivated in constructive ways by the desire to be returned to office. In much the same spirit, Chappell and Keech (1983) have shown that politicians who maximize reelection prospects over a long time horizon may behave much more constructively than those who maximize votes for the next election.

Perhaps the congruence of the *Federalist* with modern social-choice theory is greater with respect to institutional design than we showed it to be regarding preferences or outcomes. The concern with the use of rules and procedures to structure human motivations in collectively constructive ways is a theme they clearly share. Still, the social choice view of the world may be somewhat limited to the content of its models. The *Federalist*, on the other hand, reflects both a recognition that base motives may, from time to time, defeat the lofty purposes that defined the institutions and a hope that wisdom and enlightenment will prevail more often than might be guaranteed by the institutional arrangements.

The Nature of the *Federalist* System

In the view of William Riker (1982), the "Madisonian" theory in the *Federalist* is almost entirely negative. Specifically, Riker sees the electoral process as arbitrary and without substantive meaning. Nonetheless, he endorses the Madisonian system and the associated constitutional restraints. He sees them as realistic, as compatible with the maintenance of liberty, and as the most that can be hoped for, given the limits that modern social-choice theory identifies on the possibilities that elections can be meaningful.

Riker's defense of a "Madisonian" system that has so little of a positive nature to recommend it becomes more plausible in view of his criticism of the alternative, a populist view he associates with Rousseau. This latter view is said to claim that elections can "discover the general will, which is the objectively correct common interest of the incorporated citizens," and which will be accurately identified if citizens make their choices on the basis of common and not private interests (Riker, 1982, p. 11). Riker finds this view to be unrealistic and incompatible with modern social-choice theory.

In fact, we have shown that the tone and argument of the *Federalist* is not nearly so negative as Riker's. Surely it is possible that a system of checks and balances could have an entirely negative effect. It could be that the framers simply thought that the risks of bad legislation outweighed the gains of good legislation and therefore set up a system deliberately designed to block change. This seems not to have been the case, though Madison and Hamilton may disagree on the point.

Madison acknowledges that for the Senate to act as a check on the House "may in some instances be injurious as well as beneficial." But he suggests further that the two houses are less likely to agree on perfidious schemes than on proper measures and genuine principles of republican government: "The improbability of sinister combinations will be in proportion to the dissimilarity in the genius of the two bodies" (no. 62, pp. 378–379). Moreover, the prospect that the interests of the people will be betrayed is less "where the concurrence of separate and dissimilar bodies is required in every public act" than it is where the "whole legislative trust is lodged in the hands of one body" (no. 63, p. 386). Unfortunately, Madison gives no supporting argument, but he clearly expresses the belief that something constructive rather than something obstructionist will emerge from the need of two legislative bodies to agree.

Hamilton seems prepared to acknowledge a more fundamentally

conservative character of the Constitution. He grants that "the power of preventing bad laws includes that of preventing good ones; and may be used to the one purpose as well as to the other" without explicitly claiming that the latter is more likely than the former. His defense is different:

> But this objection will have little weight with those who can properly estimate the mischiefs of that inconstancy and mutability in the laws, which form the greatest blemish in the character and genius of our governments. They will consider every institution calculated to restrain the excess of lawmaking, and to keep things in the same state in which they happen to be at any given period as much more likely to do good than harm; because it is favorable to greater stability in the system of legislation. The injury which may possibly be done by defeating a few good laws will be amply compensated by the advantage of preventing a number of bad ones. (no. 73, pp. 443–444)

Hamilton is not denying that as many good laws as bad will be prevented, but he is arguing that stability is a virtue in and of itself. He does not explicitly defend the status quo; he defends stability, and he does so without implying that the relative prospects of rejecting good and bad proposals are different. Miller and Hammond (chapter 6) show that the bicameral legislature does, in fact, induce stability. Their modern social-choice analysis can be seen as verifying rigorously the insights of the *Federalist*s.

We have shown that the *Federalist* deals with preferences, institutions, and outcomes, just as modern social-choice theory does. Yet, unlike modern social-choice theory, the links between these elements are not clearly modeled or spelled out. Rather, they are left rather vague. To the modern theorist, this vagueness may reflect a weakness, or the necessities of political rhetoric, given the very practical purposes of the *Federalist*.

But there is another way to look at the lack of explicit links between preferences, institutions, and outcomes. The authors of the *Federalist* would not look favorably on the idea of simply aggregating the preferences of citizens. They make very clear that they do not consider the passions and interests of individuals or factions to be the bedrock of public policy formation. They would consider the following view of Jon Elster (1983) to be much more acceptable: "the core of the political process is the public and rational discussion about the common good, not the isolated act of voting according to private preferences" (p. 35). As Steven Rhoads (1985, ch. 11) points out, such discussion can occur through the process of deliberation that takes place in representative government, wherein delegation can "refine and enlarge public views" (*Federalist*, no. 10, p. 82). The result may be the transformation of preferences rather than their aggregation (Elster, 1983, p. 35).

The Federalist Papers are, in many respects, forerunners of modern social-choice theory. In our view, the most important respect is in their attention to realistic views of preferences, institutions, and outcomes. Yet, the absence of anything that looks like a formal model of the links between these elements reflects more than the absence of modern theory and techniques. The authors of the *Federalist* did not believe that popular preferences were exogenous and fixed. They believed in a process of representative rather than direct democracy, in part because representation would introduce an element of constructive deliberation. This deliberation would enhance the prospects that public decisions would approximate justice and the common good, terms which the *Federalist* uses without a shadow of embarrassment. Modern social-choice theory has enormously enhanced our understanding of the nature of democratic institutions and processes. It has enabled us to add to the precision of our conceptual and analytical tools. But while these very constructive achievements sharpen the insights of *The Federalist Papers*, they do not replace them or even substitute for them.

Acknowledgments. We would like to acknowledge the helpful comments of Michael Gillespie, Harvey Mansfield, Jr., Timothy McKeown, and Mark Petracca.

Notes

1. Page references are to the New American Library edition of *The Federalist Papers*, 1961, Clinton Rossiter, ed.

CHAPTER FOUR

Restraining the Whims
and Passions of the Public

Benjamin I. Page and Robert Y. Shapiro

A t first glance, public choice theory would seem to conflict with
the views of the Founders of the U.S. government concerning
public opinion. Alexander Hamilton, James Madison, and other
Founders, while advocating what they called a "wholly popular"
system of republican government, did not hold the policy preferences
of ordinary citizens in very high regard. At the outset, their politically
relevant "public" was narrowly defined to exclude women, slaves,
native Americans, and (often) the propertyless. Beyond that, the
government institutions the Founders designed were explicitly intended to restrain the "irregular passions," "transient impulses," and
"temporary delusions" of the public.

The Federalist Papers argue for some of the principal features of the
Constitution in precisely such terms. In *Federalist* no. 10, for example,
Madison defined the evil of faction in terms of a "common impulse of
passion, or of interest" adverse to the rights of other citizens or to the
permanent and aggregate interests of the community (p. 78) and
argued (p. 81) that, if a majority of citizens shared such a passion or
interest, the majority must be rendered unable to carry it into effect.[1]
The cure: a large and diverse republic, where a "rage" for "improper
or wicked projects" like paper money or an equal division of property
would be less apt to pervade the union, and where delegation of
government to a small number of elected officials would "refine and
enlarge the public views" (pp. 82–84).

In *Federalist* no. 49, Madison criticized Jefferson's old plan for popular conventions to alter the Constitution or correct breaches in it, maintaining that "the *passions*, therefore, not the *reason*, of the public would sit in judgment" (p. 317). In no. 63, he defended the selectly appointed Senate, with long terms of office, as necessary in order to defend the people against "their own temporary errors and delusions" (p. 384) or "violent passions" or "popular fluctuations" (p. 385). In no. 68 (p. 412), Hamilton upheld the indirect selection of the President, by electors in the separate states, as avoiding the "tumult and disorder," "violent movements," or "heats and ferments" of a direct election or even of electors meeting in one place. In *Federalist* no. 71, Hamilton argued for the four-year presidential term as allowing the President to avoid complaisance to "every sudden breeze of passion" or to "every transient impulse" or "temporary delusion" of the people (p. 432). And in no. 78, he favored permanent tenure for judges, giving them independence to guard the Constitution and the rights of individuals against "ill humors" among the people that occasion "dangerous innovations" or "serious oppressions." A "momentary inclination" of a majority of citizens would not justify violation of the Constitution (p. 469).

To many contemporary thinkers, including public choice theorists, these concerns have an odd ring. Are not citizens' preferences the bedrock upon which political decision-making is supposed to be built? At least since the publication of Kenneth Arrow's classic work (1951/1963) many have viewed politics as consisting of the aggregation of individuals' preferences into collective choices. They have celebrated the way in which two-party electoral competition may lead to democratic outcomes, with parties and candidates and officials choosing the policies most preferred by the public (e.g., Downs, 1957, ch. 4; Davis and Hinich, 1966, pp. 182, 185, 187; Davis, Hinich, and Ordeshook, 1970, pp. 441–442; Enelow and Hinich, 1984, pp. 221–222; McKelvey and Ordeshook, 1986). Under some circumstances, at least, the invisible hand of competition in political markets is said to ensure responsiveness to ordinary citizens. If it cannot be relied upon to do so, because of lack of equilibrium or for other reasons, that is considered a cause for concern. To a substantial extent, then, modern public choice theorists have embraced the values of what Dahl (1956) called "populistic democracy."

Not only does the Founders' wariness about citizens' policy preferences seem peculiar from a public choice perspective, but public choice theory seems even to lack a vocabulary with which to talk about some of the Founders' concerns. If a citizen is viewed primarily as the possessor of a utility function defined over a set of government policies, or as the occupant of a most preferred point in an issue space, what on earth is a political "passion," as opposed to any other sort of preference? If (as is sometimes assumed) information is both complete and perfect, or if rational expectations rule, what is a "temporary delusion"? Can public choice theorists make any sense of the worries that so influenced the Founders in their design of the U. S. Constitution?

In this essay, we shall try to show that the conflict is more apparent than real. Some simple ideas about rational decision-making, consistent with the Founders' views, can illuminate both normative and empirical aspects of the role of collective public opinion in policymaking. But we will also argue that some of the Founders' concerns do not apply to public opinion in the twentieth-century United States. Some of the institutional arrangements they advocated would impose unnecessary or harmful restraints on the public.

What the Founders Meant

The first step is to consider the Founders' conception of the problem of public opinion as expressed in their own terms. The best discussions are found in three relatively little-known *Federalist* papers that we have already mentioned, nos. 49, 63, and 71, as well as in the familiar no. 10.

It is evident from passages in those papers that the Founders had in mind at least two distinct kinds of policy preferences that they considered illegitimate or undesirable and did not wish to count in making collective decisions. We can refer to them as *intrusive preferences* (for policies that would infringe on others' "rights") and *narrow preferences* (for policies that would harm the "public good"). The Founders also offered a brief account of the origins of such preferences, in self-interest, in "passions" (sometimes inflamed by demagogues) and in *error*.

Our distinction between intrusive and narrow preferences corresponds to Madison's important distinction between two fundamental aims of government: protection of the "rights" of citizens (i.e., "justice") and furtherance of the "permanent and aggregate interests of the community" (i.e., the "public good"). (See *Federalist*, no. 10, p. 78, and Epstein, 1984, ch. 3.) The rights that Madison had in mind involved, especially, protection of "the faculties of men, from which the rights of property originate"—hence his opposition to paper money or equal distribution of property. But these rights presumably also included civil liberties of other sorts. Madison's conception of the public good particularly involved "safety" from foreign invasion or domestic disorder, as well as prosperity of commerce.

As *Federalist* no. 10's definition of faction indicates, one source of intrusive or narrow preferences could be simple self-interest. A majority faction, for example, might be tempted to confiscate the property of a wealthy few. The Founders were respectful of the strength and pervasiveness of self-interest in human affairs, designing institutions to set "ambition . . . to counteract ambition" among officials and to resist certain kinds of selfishness among the people.

Another source of (intrusive or narrow) factions, according to Madison, is an impulse of "passion," a topic pursued in several other papers. In *Federalist* no. 49, for example, where Madison opposed popular conventions to remedy breaches of the Constitution, he followed his assertion that passion rather than reason would sit in judgment by declaring that "it is the reason, alone, of the public, that ought to control and regulate the government. The passions ought to be controlled and regulated by the government" (p. 317). In *Federalist* no. 50 (p. 319) he again alluded to the distinction between passion and reason. Concern with passions also appears—among other places—in no. 62 (p. 379), no. 63 (p. 384), and no. 71 (p. 432).

Passion, as used in the *Federalist,* suggests strong emotion attached either to an opinion (e.g., a religious belief) or to a person (e.g., a political leader). Madison offered only a hint of a psychological theory (No. 10, p. 78): "self-love" and reason interact, so that fallible opinions are sometimes pursued with passionate zeal (see Epstein, 1984, pp. 69–71).

Still another source of undesirable policy preferences is *error.* In *Federalist* no. 63, for example, Madison spoke of "temporary errors and delusions," as opposed to "the cool and deliberate sense of the community" (p. 384). The Founders felt that citizens' preferences ought to be ignored or resisted if they rested upon erroneous beliefs about what effects policies would have. People should be saved from the fatal consequences of their own mistakes; they would be grateful afterward (no. 71, p. 432). The Founders therefore put much emphasis upon the need for careful *deliberation* about policy by a "temperate and respectable body of citizens" like the Senate (p. 384; see Bessette, 1980). They stressed the importance of substantive knowledge and experience (e.g., no. 53, p. 332) and the need for "cool and sedate reflection" (no. 71, p. 432). Hamilton wrote that "the people commonly *intend* the PUBLIC GOOD," but they sometimes err about "the *means* of promoting it" (p. 432).

The framers often blurred the distinctions among different kinds and sources of illegitimate or undesirable policy preferences, sometimes suggesting that the only real problem is temporary error. This may have resulted from unwillingness to offend the public—since the aim of the *Federalist*, after all, was to win ratification of the Constitution—or it may reflect a certain wishful thinking. In no. 63 (p. 384), Madison implied that the people would later "lament and condemn" policies resulting from their own passion or advantage, as well as those resulting from being misled, although we would consider delay and deliberation a more certain cure for the latter than for the former. It is not at all obvious that time or correct information tends to eradicate self-interest. Hamilton distinguished the "interests" of the people from their "inclinations" (e.g., no. 71, p. 432) and argued that a four-year presidential term would provide time enough to make the community "sensible of the propriety" of measures it might originally have opposed (p. 434). In no. 78, he flatteringly noted that the people's "ill humors" might "speedily give place to better information, and more deliberate reflection" (p. 469).

Thus, the Founders implied that, if narrow and intrusive passions and interests were temporarily restrained, the exercise of reason would eventually lead people to see that their true interests coincided with private rights and the public good. Perhaps so; this is consistent also with the argument (e.g., in no. 63, pp. 383–384, and no. 71, pp. 432, 434) that people are better at judging results than policies and (in effect) are better entrusted with the electoral reward and punishment of responsible officials than with referendum-style democracy. But such a cheerful view of enlightened self-interest takes a lot for granted and lumps together some concerns that are better kept analytically distinct.

The Founders also linked together different concerns by means of the concept of demagoguery: the notion that ordinary citizens could be "misled by the artful misrepresentations of interested men" (no. 63, p. 384), or by "the wiles of parasites and sycophants, by the snares of the ambitious, the avaricious, the desperate" (no. 71, p. 432). Here, too, the precise ways in which citizens may come to have illegitimate or unworthy policy preferences are somewhat mixed together. Ceasar (1979) points out the important difference, for example, between "soft" demagoguery that flatters and insinuates and "hard" demagoguery that arouses fears and exacerbates class or other divisions in society. We would distinguish also between demagoguery that simply arouses or mobilizes self-interest (to the detriment of others' rights or the common good) and that which misleads people as to their own or others' interests. The Founders' notion of demagoguery as the swaying of popular passions by an excess of passionate appeals (see Tulis, 1987) lumps together these diverse phenomena. Perhaps the central point here, however, is simply that the Founders attributed to certain leaders the power to influence citizens' policy preferences in undesirable ways that could render those preferences illicit or unworthy of response by policymakers.

Whims, Passions, and Rational Decision-Making

Once we have distinguished among the types of defects that the Founders attributed to public opinion, we are in a position to see some connections with public choice or economics-style thinking. It is clear, for example, that the Founders simply ruled out certain policy alternatives, no matter how popular, as illicit on the ground that they violated individuals' rights. Intrusive preferences for such policies were not supposed to count.

It is possible, though a bit awkward, for public choice reasoning to deal with rights. The source and the precise nature of rights is problematic, given a modern reluctance to treat them as natural, self-evident, or God-given. An absolutist stand for rights conflicts with the economist's usual conviction that everything should be subject to trade-offs (Barry, 1973). And the idea of resisting intrusive preferences violates some widely accepted normative principles of social choice theory, such as the "neutrality" axiom of Arrow (1963) and May (1952)—that preferences should be aggregated without discrimination among policies. Indeed, the protection of rights (even "minimal liberalism") is generally inconsistent with the Pareto principle (Sen, 1970, ch. 6; see Fishkin, 1979; Schwartz, 1986, pp. 269–273). Still, with some stretching, the protection of rights can be incorporated—normatively and empirically—in public choice work. (To what extent the institutions that the Founders designed actually tend to restrain intrusive preferences, and thus to prevent tyranny, is, of course, another question. For a skeptical view, see Dahl, 1956.)

Much the same thing is true of narrow preferences that neglect the common good. The Founders' examples of the public good are mostly compatible with modern economists' concepts of "public goods" or "social goods" that private markets fail to provide optimally; it is a short (though not unavoidable) step to conclude that government should provide them. What is more problematic from a public choice perspective is why a majority of voters would fail to demand them. What need is there for any special provision other than the aggregation of citizens' preferences? And why, exactly, should we expect the common good to emerge from the Founders' institutional arrangements better than it would from populistic voting? A skeptical analyst might argue, for example, that any advantages of superior judgment and experience among elite Senators might be outweighed by the disadvantages of unrepresentative values and preferences associated with their exalted economic and social positions. Still, such issues can be discussed, and a particular conception of the common good can be dealt with, in public choice terms.

The Founders' concerns about erroneous preferences, too, are amenable to public-choice-style reasoning. They are of particular interest to us—and are worth more extensive treatment—because they raise central questions about the nature of public opinion and the way it changes.

Obviously, the concepts of *error* or *delusion* in opinion (unlike the notions of *narrow* or *intrusive preferences*) necessarily imply that information is not perfect and that preferences are not fixed. So does the idea of *demagoguery*. In order to deal with them, we need a theory of public opinion that goes beyond the assumption of a fixed set of preferences or utility functions defined over policy alternatives, one that incorporates informational considerations in a different way from the usual treatments of uncertainty.

McCubbins and Page (1984) have attempted to sketch the beginnings of such a theory, based on assumptions of individual rationality under uncertainty and incomplete (costly) information. Here, we will note a few of its main features relevant to the issues at hand.

The main point is that people are not at all well informed about public policy. Their information is very incomplete, and they face a high degree of uncertainty about the consequences—for themselves and for those they care about—of different policy alternatives. In evaluating a policy alternative, therefore, citizens are concerned with its expected utility, which depends upon the probability that various different states of nature are true, as well as the utility of the policy alternative contingent upon each possible state of nature. The expected utility of an alternative is the sum of many terms, each consisting of the probability of a particular state of nature's being true times the alternative's conditional utility given that state of nature.

That is to say, (according to this theory) an individual evaluates a policy alternative in terms of how desirable it would be under each of various possible circumstances, weighted by the individual's beliefs about how likely it is that each of those possible circumstances holds in the real world. We do not imagine that this is usually done by precise calculation; more often, people just make casual (even unconscious) estimates.

Thus, people do not have utility functions or preferences defined directly over policy alternatives; their preferences are *conditional* upon a variety of *beliefs:* beliefs about real-world facts and conditions and causal connections, beliefs that can be summarized by subjective probability distributions concerning the truth or falsehood of various states of nature. What a citizen wants to do about nuclear power, for example, may be conditional upon beliefs about the likelihood of serious accidents and about the cost and feasibility of disposing of radioactive waste. How a citizen judges foreign aid or counterinsurgency policies may be contingent upon beliefs about the living conditions of peasants in Third World countries and about the costs and benefits of alternative roads to economic and political development.

Once we have acknowledged the central role of beliefs, it becomes possible to talk about "errors" or "delusions" in policy preferences. People's beliefs can be wrong, that is, factually incorrect. People may misunderstand the consequences—the likely costs and benefits—of policy alternatives, so that they support policies that would harm their own (or their loved ones') interests and oppose policies that would help. Moreover, false or misleading information that distorts policy preferences can be deliberately conveyed to citizens by (among others) those we may choose to label *demagogues.*

What is true of individual citizens might well be true of the public collectively. Especially in an age of mass media, when much the same information finds its way into nearly every household, the same misconceptions or falsehoods might reach a large segment of the public and deflect their policy preferences in the same direction, creating an error in collective public opinion. For that matter, a single demagogue (say, hypothetically, a President intent upon deceiving the people about foreign policy) might convey false information to large audiences and thereby mislead public opinion. Unless we believe some peculiar things about markets for information, there is no particular reason to expect that the publicly available political information at any moment is unbiased. (On some matters like foreign affairs, information monopolies arguably exist. At best, the production and dissemination of true and false information presumably responds to those able and willing to pay for it, not to equally weighted citizens. In any case, the movement toward truthful equilibrium in a "free marketplace of ideas" might well be very slow.)

Starting from assumptions of individual rationality, therefore, we emerge with a theoretical picture of public opinion rather different from the fixed preferences found in much public-choice work. Now, the public's policy preferences presumably respond to new information from news events, analyses and interpretations, scholarly research, and political rhetoric. The information conveyed to the public may be true or false, helpful or misleading; if it is false or misleading, public opinion may fall into error. This opens up the possibility (though, of course, not a certainty) of demagoguery, manipulation of opinion, systematic biases in information, and false consciousness.

Thus, the Founders' concerns are not inconsistent with a public choice approach to public opinion. In fact, they fit quite well with a theory of public opinion based on rational decision-making under uncertainty. But the question remains; How well do the Founders' concerns reflect empirical reality? Are the policy preferences of the public, in fact, subject to whims and passions, errors, delusions, fluctuations, and manipulation by demagogues? If so, to what extent and under what conditions? We will now turn to some evidence that bears on these points.

The Stability of Public Opinion

Over the course of several years, we have assembled a large body of survey data on the collective policy preferences of Americans, in order to study the causes and consequences—and the extent—of changes in public opinion. We have gathered the marginal frequencies of responses to more than six thousand policy questions asked of national samples since 1935. In fact, we have attempted, with considerable success, to obtain data from *every* publicly available survey of the American public that inquired about policy preferences. Most important, we have found more than one thousand questions that were repeated with identical wording at two or more times (sometimes months apart, sometimes years), so that we can say something about opinion change.

In an early paper (Page and Shapiro, 1982), we drew upon some preliminary data to report on the nature and extent of changes in Americans' policy preferences. We can now use a considerably expanded data set—about twice the size of the early one—from a variety of survey organizations (NORC, AIPO, SRC/CPS Michigan, Harris, and OPOR), to investigate some matters relevant to the question of whims and passions in public opinion (for a more full discussion of the data, see Page and Shapiro, 1987b).

We have data on 1,128 policy questions that were repeated at least

TABLE 4.1. Significant Changes in Repeated Policy Questions[a]

	No Change	Change	Total Questions
Foreign and defense policy	51% (215)	49% (210)	38% (425)
Domestic policy	63% (440)	37% (263)	62% (703)
Total items	58% (655)	42% (473)	100% (1,128)

[a]Gamma = Yule's $Q = -.24$

once between 1935 and the present. These questions cover a wide range of topics, from foreign aid, defense spending, and military action abroad, to economic regulation, social issues, and social welfare policy. They deal with action by the U.S. Congress, the President, administrative agencies, the U.S. Supreme Court, and state and local government. They should not be thought of as a random sample of policies or of possible survey questions (though they constitute a large part of the universe of actual repeated survey questions); they are very diverse and, in that sense, representative.

The most striking finding from these data is the great stability of public opinion. For each of the 1,128 repeated survey questions, we examined whether or not opinion changed significantly, using the standard of a six-percentage-point shift in responses (excluding "don't know" and "no opinion" replies) to constitute a significant change. (In our surveys, a 6% change is statistically significant at better than the .05 confidence level; see Page and Shapiro, 1982, p. 26 and footnote 4.) Table 4.1 shows that, even by this rather generous measure, well over half (58%) of the repeated survey questions showed no significant opinion change at all.

Stability was somewhat greater on domestic than on foreign issues, where dramatic events and new information are more common, but even in foreign and defense policy, there was no significant change on about half (51%) of the questions. In many cases, these questions were repeated a number of times, over the course of several years, so that there was abundant opportunity for change. Still, stability was the rule.

Not only was there general stability, but most of the 556 changes that did occur (in responses to the 473 questions that showed one or more significant opinion changes) were relatively small. Nearly half of them (242, or 44%) were less than 10 percentage points. Most of those involved preference changes of only 6–8 percentage points, hardly startling movements. Contrary to what one might expect, foreign and defense items did not differ much overall from domestic

TABLE 4.2. The Magnitudes of Significant Changes in Policy Preferences[a]

	6–7%	8–9%	10–14%	15–19%	20–29%	30% +	Total
Foreign/def. policy	21% (54)	22% (55)	28% (71)	15% (38)	12% (30)	3% (7)	46% (255)
Domestic policy	24% (71)	21% (62)	30% (91)	14% (41)	8% (23)	4% (13)	54% (301)
Total	22% (125)	21% (117)	29% (162)	14% (79)	10% (53)	4% (20)	100% (556)

[a]Gamma $= -.05$ (n.s.).

items in the magnitudes of significant changes, although opinion changes on foreign policy tended to be more abrupt. (See Table 4.2)

Since the time intervals between repeated survey questions varied a great deal, it is useful to divide the magnitudes of change by the length of time over which they occurred in order to measure the *rates* of opinion change. By this measure, too, public opinion is not very volatile. The mean rate of change for all our foreign-policy instances of change was 31 percentage points per year—a rate that may seem very high but that, in fact, just reflects small changes (often of less than 10 percentage points, as we saw in Table 4.2) that occurred quite rapidly, usually after major international events. On domestic policy, where opinion change tends to be more gradual, the average rate of change was only 12 percentage points per year. To make the same point a different way, of the 255 instances of significant opinion change on foreign and defense policy, 58% proceeded at a rate of 10 percentage points or more per year, whereas only 27% of the 301 domestic opinion changes did so.

Another important aspect of stability in public opinion is the infrequency of fluctuations, that is, of significant reversals in the direction of opinion change within a moderate interval of time. We took two or more significant changes in opposite directions within two years, or three or more within three years (a fairly generous criterion), as constituting a fluctuation. By this measure, fluctuations occurred seldom, on only 18% of the 173 survey questions that were asked frequently enough to allow detection of fluctuations. There was no significant difference between foreign and domestic issues in this respect. Indeed, most of the fluctuations were explicable in terms of changing policy realities (compared to which changing proportions of Americans wanted "more" or "less" than the policy of the moment), rather than actual alterations in preferences. This would not seem to support the notion that the public has fickle and vacillating moods toward either foreign or domestic affairs.

In short, according to our evidence, opinion changes are not extremely frequent; when they occur they are not very big; and opinion seldom fluctuates in one direction and then another. As is apparent from our larger study, the stability in survey responses does not merely reflect poor measurement or unchanging "nonopinions." Stability is a real feature of collective public opinion about policies.

What does this tell us about the Founders' concerns? Of course, our data say nothing about the nature of public opinion in 1789, which is likely to remain a mystery. But our findings do suggest that now— with high levels of formal education, widespread communication of political information, and close connections between government activity and peoples' lives—public opinion concerning policy does not much suffer from some of the infirmities that worried the Founders. *Fluctuations,* as we understand that notion, are not common. Insofar as phrases like "sudden and violent passions" or "temporary errors and delusions" or "transient impulse(s)" or "sudden breeze(s) of passion" imply that public opinion changes capriciously, by large amounts, they simply do not correspond to the realities of twentieth-century America.

As Joseph Bessette and Jeffrey Tulis (among others) have pointed out to us, the stability of contemporary public opinion, far from refuting the views of the Founders, may actually confirm them: the extensive commercial republic that the framers designed, with its diverse interests, obstacles to coordinating factions, and increasing prosperity, may well have contributed to the result.

Causes of Change in Public Opinion

Others of the Founders' concerns (errors and demagoguery, for example) refer to the nature and the causes, rather than the extent, of opinion change. Our research has cast some light on these matters as well.

Examining the historical contexts in which our hundreds of opinion changes occurred, we have found that the changes can very seldom be characterized as capricious or whimsical. Policy preferences generally change in response to new events or new information that a rational citizen would find relevant to evaluating policies. That is, changes in opinion generally correspond to changes in reality (or interpretations of reality) that bring about widespread changes in the beliefs that underlie policy preferences.

We have alluded to the role of international events. In our data, the most important single cause of opinion change has been *war.* The outbreak of war, or the tide of battlefield events (especially with World War II), has quite understandably changed Americans' opinions about preparedness, military spending, alliances, aid, peace terms, and a variety of foreign policy matters, as well as about working conditions, strikes, domestic spending, taxes, and various domestic policies. Similarly, the business cycle, with rises and declines in unemployment, inflation, and per capita income, has greatly affected Americans' opinions about social welfare programs, government taxes and spending, and many other matters.

Our assessment is that in these and other situations the public has generally reacted in a sensible fashion to events, based on the information and interpretations made available to it. This is not something that is easily demonstrated through quantitative evidence; it requires scrutiny of the particular cases (see Page and Shapiro 1982, 1987b). We judge that the public has tended to respond in an instrumentally rational fashion, changing policy choices so as to take account of changing conditions. Therefore, we speak of a *rational public*. Our data provide little evidence of a capricious or unreasonable public.

We have been able to use some of our survey questions—those repeated at sufficiently short intervals so that the causes of opinion change can be narrowly bracketed in time—in order to study more precisely what affects aggregate public opinion. We have found that the contents of network TV news, coded according to the directional thrust of information from various news sources, can account for a very large proportion of opinion change: about half the variance in it. Specifically, news reports of the findings and testimony of experts, as well as editorial remarks by newspersons and commentators, have strong positive effects on policy preferences. Reports about popular Presidents, but not unpopular ones, also tend to have positive effects; other sources, such as interest groups, tend to have no effect or even a negative impact (Page, Shapiro and Dempsey, 1987; see also Page and Shapiro, 1984). Here, too, the public does not seem to be at all whimsical; it responds most positively to the sources of information it deems most credible. We see nothing to suggest flighty or capricious opinion change.

Demagogues and Manipulation of Opinion

The most important of the Founders' concerns, however, are also the hardest to assess. Is the public prone to serious errors or delusions, brought about by the artifices of demagogues? Is opinion manipulated? Is it distorted by biased or misleading information?

To grapple with these questions, we must go beyond asking what sorts of actors or events bring about opinion change and must consider the *quality* of information involved in influencing opinion. We have to ask whether particular assertions are true or false, helpful or misleading. If we wish to distinguish between the deliberate and the accidental provision of misinformation, we must also discern the knowledge and motivations of the providers. Such inquiries involve many pitfalls. States of mind are seldom knowable with certainty. Often, the nature of truth and falsehood is subject to dispute. Basic facts, to say nothing of causal relationships, may be controversial. Answers to these questions are therefore likely to be much less certain than answers to others, but they are so important as to justify making an effort.

At this point, we can offer only some tentative observations. First, outright manipulation of public opinion by individual demagogues seems to have been only a limited danger in the 1935–1985 period we have studied. To be sure, Senator Joseph McCarthy's reckless Communist-hunting at the height of the Cold War coincided with low public support for civil liberties, but McCarthy himself appears to have had rather little impact on policy preferences; rather, the events of the Cold War and the reactions of American leaders generally (as exemplified, for example, by President Truman's "loyalty-security" program) eroded tolerance of dissent. Polling began just too late to tell much about the effects of the Depression-era oratory of Father Coughlin or others. Few other clear, nationally important cases of demagoguery (successful or unsuccessful) can be identified.

Public opinion is quite resistant to change. Extreme circumstances of war, depression, or civil unrest might, of course, alter the picture, and the nearly universal ownership of television sets means that the technology for mass appeals is now readily available, but for the most part, the United States, in recent decades, has not seen the sort of successful inflammatory rhetoric by individual politicians that the Founders feared.

The nearest thing to effective demagoguery in contemporary American politics is deceptive or misleading rhetoric from Presidents— especially popular Presidents—who are in a strong position to dominate political communications. Presidents have sometimes deceived the public, as Lyndon Johnson did about the Tonkin Gulf incident off Vietnam (Wise, 1973) and Ronald Reagan did about Nicaragua and arms sales to Iran. More often, Presidents have misled the public by oversimplifying problems and overselling solutions, as Johnson did with his War on Poverty and Jimmy Carter did with the "energy crisis" (see Tulis, 1987).

Still, even popular Presidents, with all the communications resources they command, must ordinarily work intensively for months to win a 5- or 10-percentage-point increase in support for their favorite policies (Page and Shapiro, 1984). We have not identified many cases in which a misleading persuader—presidential or other— has been able to create a large swing in public opinion. The "sudden breeze(s) of passion" or "transient impulse(s)" that the Founders feared demagogues might provoke do not seem to have occurred very often in recent times.

There are, however, indications of a problem that is perhaps more fundamental: systematic biases in the totality of the political information conveyed to the public. It may be the case that false or misleading or biased information of certain sorts, coming from many sources— not just from individual demagogues—tends to give the American public a distorted picture of the political world and, systematically, to deflect policy preferences away from what a well-informed citizenry would want.

We will not attempt any substantial discussion here (see Page and Shapiro, 1987a,b) but will merely note our impression that important biases in the twentieth-century American information system include a strong *nationalistic* or ethnocentric bias, a tendency to see the world in American terms and to think the worst of nations or movements defined as "enemies"; a *procapitalist* slant that proclaims (or assumes) the virtues of free enterprise, downplays its deficiencies, and ignores or criticizes alternative economic and social arrangements (see Parenti, 1986); a strong *anticommunist* bias, particularly in information about foreign affairs, that draws upon both nationalism and procapitalism; a *minimalist government* view that exaggerates the deficiencies of government action; a *proincumbent and pro-status-quo* bias friendly to power holders; and a *partisan* bias (resulting from deference to power holders) that follows the cycles of party control of government.

Biases are difficult to measure. It is not sufficient simply to count favorable and unfavorable messages; the thrust of the available information must be compared to some baseline model of what "unbiased" information would look like. Such a model is difficult to conceptualize, let alone to make operational. (Would unbiased information mirror reality? Reality as perceived by average people, or by average experts, or as it objectively is? Who gets to define *objective reality?*) Observers seem to use a wide variety of implicit baseline models—models that vary, naturally enough, according to the observers' own values and what they believe to be true.

Thus, we should be cautious about our analysis. But biases of the sort we have listed, in the contents of the mass media and other sources of information, could result from the normal operation of market forces. Nationalism follows from the mass audience's preoccupation with matters close to home, as well as from the power-wielding interests of officials (who have a near-monopoly on much foreign-policy information) and the economic interests of multinational corporations and other producers and influencers of news. Procapitalism reflects the average American's reasonably satisfactory experience with the U.S. economic system, but also the influence of the owners of corporations (including those who own the highly concentrated mass media and those who dominate foundations) upon the conduct and publicizing of research (e.g., what sorts of people, with what views, emerge as "experts"), the production and dissemination of news and commentary, and the stands of political parties and officials. Minimalist government is embraced for much the same reasons. The proincumbent and partisan biases in information follow from the dependence of the news media upon official sources, as well as from the flow of money to scholars and think tanks and commentators who represent the politically dominant ideas of a particular historical period.

If these or other significant biases exist, they clearly have important consequences for democratic politics. To the extent that policy is made by aggregating individuals' preferences into collective choices, the democratic quality of that process is seriously undermined when preferences themselves are systematically manipulated or distorted by misleading information.

How Well Did the Founders Cope with Public Opinion?

It is worth inquiring how well the Founders' institutional designs deal with the actualities of public opinion.

We have argued that some of the Founders' concerns were exaggerated or, at least, are not very pressing today. Public opinion is not capricious. It does not change rapidly by large amounts or for whimsical reasons; it responds reasonably to new information and to events, as they are interpreted. Simple demagoguery is uncommon. Thus, some of the restraints that the Founders put upon the policy-making influence of public opinion are not now necessary. The movement in American history toward a broader electorate and toward greater popular control of the presidency (with voters now participating in primary elections and choosing pledged electors in November) and of the Senate (with direct elections) could be viewed as consistent with this point. Again, this could represent success rather than failure of the Founders' scheme.

We are not in a good position to judge whether or not the Founders' institutional arrangements have helped control the kinds of intrusive or narrow preferences that would trample on others' rights or work against the common good. We consider it possible, but by no means certain, that they have done so (depending partly, of course, upon one's definition of rights and the common good), especially through the creation of an extensive commercial republic rather than by means of particular institutions like the Senate or the Supreme Court.

The institutional arrangements have probably helped prevent some errors due to temporarily misinformed public opinion. Delay and multiple veto points and insulation from frequent elections undoubtedly do help to foster deliberation. Having two chambers in Congress rather than one, long terms in office for Senators, and a presidential veto, no doubt does prevent some foolish legislation from being passed (though it is not clear how often foolish proposals originate with the public as opposed to elites) and does permit some adoption of unpopular measures that the public later accepts when the results turn out to be good. The Founders' arrangements are particularly well suited to retrospective voting and electoral reward and punishment.

The danger, obviously, is that good as well as bad legislation is hindered; that the effect is to retard change and favor the status quo, rather than to prevent error; and that popular control is reduced without enough corresponding gain. The Founders were impressive political theorists, but not purely disinterested ones. They also had economic class (and individual) interests not shared by the average citizen: they were lawyers and landowners and merchants, creditors and speculators, not debtors or workers or small farmers (Beard, 1913), and their avid protection of private property may have reflected their own interests as well as perceptions of the common good. By the same token, the leeway (in foreign policy, for example) that the framers provided for officials to strike off on their own, contrary to the public's will, may lead as often to disaster as to success and popular ratification.

For one important kind of problem—namely, systematic biases in the political information provided to the public—the Founders did not offer much in the way of remedies. If the citizenry is regularly misled about public policy, so that it consistently favors alternatives contrary to its values and interests, no amount of delay or official autonomy is likely to help. The biased information and the distorted preferences will presumably persist; elites may be equally deceived and, in any case, cannot resist forever. (If they could, they might do nothing better than pursue interests of their own contrary to those of the public.)

Perhaps the Founders did not worry much about systematic biases because of the existence, in their day, of lively and diverse sources of information. They relied on a free press to carry many viewpoints, and on distance and isolation to limit the effects of any particular information. But the highly centralized mass media of today, reaching nearly every home, create a new situation. The very similar fare that appears in the *New York Times*, on the Associated Press wire, and on TV network news is bound to have pervasive effects. Even if outright demagoguery is rare, any biases in media content are bound to reach and affect the public. An extensive republic, with diverse interests, turns out not to guarantee diverse (or unbiased) information.

The kind of deliberation by which Americans could reliably discover and correct errors presupposes an information system that, at minimum, makes available correct information about crucial matters and does not systematically mislead. What such an information system might look like, how closely it would resemble our current arrangements, and how it might be implemented are questions of great importance that the Founders did not address.

Acknowledgments. Support for the data analysis reported here came from the National Science Foundation grant SES 83-08767; the responsibility for analysis and interpretation is our own. We are grateful for comments and suggestions from Joseph Bessette, Tom Ferguson, Bernard Grofman, Peter Ordeshook, Mark Petracca, David Prindle, Tom Schwartz, Jeffrey Tulis, Donald Wittman, and the participants in the Irvine conference on "*The Federalist Papers* and the New Institutionalism."

Notes

1. Page references are to the New American Library edition of *The Federalist Papers*, 1961, Clinton Rossiter, ed.

Part II

Optimal Institutions

Introduction

One can analyze the U. S. Constitution in terms of the standard economic dichotomy: distribution and efficiency. Economic efficiency means that there is no other feasible alternative that makes one person better off without making another person worse off. Distribution is concerned with the allocation of political and economic wealth (there may be many different distributions which are economically efficient). In this section, we show that the Constitution has many characteristics that promote efficiency; in the sections on ratification and checks and balances, we will concentrate on the distributive issues.

The Federalist Papers demonstrated that the U.S. Constitution was the optimal (efficient) social contract for the people of the thirteen colonies. Miller and Hammond and Wittman show that various constitutional arrangements promote efficiency. This should be expected: the months of deliberation and debate at the constitutional convention meant that if there were any mutual gains from trade (on policies and institutional arrangements), they would have been made.

Miller and Hammond show that bicameralism is efficient and more stable (i.e., less likely to be subject to intransitivity) than unicameralism. The potential for majority rule intransitivity had been discussed by Condorcet (1785) in a book reviewed by Madison. While the review is lost and there is no specific mention of the voter's paradox by Madison at the convention or in *The Federalist Papers*, there is considerable discussion of the problem of instability in general by Madison (examples are provided in Miller and Hammond's chapter). In turn, the instability problem can be viewed as a problem of inefficiency. If laws are unstable, then property rights are unstable, and therefore, individuals will underinvest (since they may not obtain the fruits of their investment under a different property-rights regime) and instead will devote their resources to changing the rules and obtaining the quick benefits from these changes (this paraphrase of Madison's arguments could be put under the general rubric of *rent-seeking*). While bicameralism is more stable than unicameralism, Miller and Hammond show that it is not so stable that it prevents efficient rules from displacing the status quo. Hence, when there is a bill that all of the Senators and Representatives prefer or are indifferent to over the status quo, then it will be passed.

Wittman shows that constitutional provisions regarding due process and the commerce clauses promote economic efficiency. He also analyzes the ability of the government to transact around the separation-of-powers concept. The Federalists were aware of the possibility of groups' implicitly exchanging their constitutional rights and thereby transacting around the institutional arrangements. However, Wittman argues that the Federalists underestimated the ease of creating a national coalition of factions: the political party. The political party coalition has enabled the party to overcome the separation of power between the various branches of government. Wittman also shows how the high transaction costs between the judiciary and the other branches have made this branch more independent of the other branches.

A number of authors (including Hobbes, Brennan, and Buchannan) have used the concept of a *social contract*. Hardin argues that their concept implicitly used the analogy of a short-term bilateral contract, although long-term multilateral contracts are more appropriate metaphors for constitution theory. He shows how these latter contracts have dramatically different characteristics from short-term bilateral contracts and, therefore, dramatically different implications for constitutional theory. For example, long-term contracts may not involve unanimous agreement (as in union contracts), and therefore, contractarian theory should not be based on unanimous consent. Furthermore, the glue holding the agreement together need not be some external authority, but the transaction costs involved in creating another regime.

Donald Wittman

The Constitution as an Optimal Social Contract: A Transaction Cost Analysis of *The Federalist Papers*

Donald Wittman

The Federalist Papers is the premier document in applied political philosophy. By arguing that the provisions of the proposed U.S. Constitution were superior to other alternatives, the authors of *The Federalist Papers* implicitly demonstrated that the Constitution was the optimal social contract for the people of the thirteen former English colonies. Here we provide an economic analysis of *The Federalist Papers*, the U.S. Constitution, and constitutional theory in general.

The concept of transaction cost is shown to play an important role in our understanding. We demonstrate that when there are low transaction costs, there is a blurring of the separation of powers and, at times, the separation of power; conversely, we demonstrate how high transaction costs make certain institutional differences not merely apparent, but real. We also show that the authors of the Constitution were intimately aware of the role of transaction costs in constitutional design.

There are both historical and substantive reasons that economics might provide an especially cogent explanation of the constitutional provisions. On the historical side, the same intellectual currents that altered political philosophy and led to the American Revolution also led to the writing of *The Wealth of Nations* in 1776. The nontemporal explanation derives from the subject matter of economic investigation. Economists have been extremely interested in the design of efficient institutions and contracts.[1] The U.S. Constitution can be viewed as our social contract and the foundation for our political institutions.

Economic science can provide a strong theoretical framework for understanding the Constitution and a methodological basis for the scientific testing of hypotheses. Just as Newton was able to combine the obvious (objects at rest tend to remain at rest) with the nonobvious (for every reaction, there is an equal and opposite reaction) in creating a general theory of physical behavior, economic theory often makes use of commonsense insights into the Constitution in developing a general theory of political behavior. Furthermore, unlike much of the legal scholarship on constitutional interpretation, economics can provide hypotheses which are capable of being tested.[2]

In contrast to the practicing lawyer who searches for exceptions and critical distinctions, I will be searching for tendencies and similarities. The methodology used can best be understood by taking an archetypal economic example: the demand for apples. In almost any society, when the price of apples increases, the demand goes down. There may be individual exceptions, as some people may buy even more apples when the price goes up; however, the tendency is for the demand to go down. In the same way, I will be interested in, for example, the general tendency of procedural rights to be more extensive when the potential punishment is higher (and I will ignore the particular exception).[3]

Transaction Costs

Before considering the constitutional issues, I will first introduce the concept of transaction costs. Transaction costs are the social costs involved in making a transaction or agreement. In perfectly competitive economic markets, these costs are often very low. For example, my purchase of a loaf of bread involves the time costs of my counting out the money and the seller's time expenditure waiting at the cash register. Bilateral monopoly involves higher transaction costs because of the social cost of bargaining and of carrying out threats such as strikes and, in international politics, war. Another case of high transaction costs arises when many people are involved in a *single* transaction. The bargaining necessary to make a majority agreement among 200 million people involves very high costs. The costs involved in making the agreement unanimous among so many people is practically infinite.

When transaction costs are low, people may "transact around" the law. This is especially true when the people involved have some ongoing contractual arrangement. For example, a sales tax to be paid by the seller of groceries has the same effect as a sales tax to be paid by the buyer. In the former case, the seller will collect the tax (t) and therefore charge t more than when the tax is on the buyer. In either case, the total cost to the buyer is the same. When there is no ongoing contractual relationship and transaction costs are low, there may only be an effect on wealth distribution. For example, Coase (1960) showed that whether a rancher is liable or not for his or her cows damaging a neighbor's corn crop, the effect on the number of cows or the amount of corn grown is the same. Thus again, the law can be partially transacted around, since the assignment of liability will have no allocative effect (although it will have a distributive one in this example). Of course, the intent of the law may have been to be transacted around.

We now show that this simple concept of transaction costs provides numerous insights into constitutional issues.

Separation of Powers

> He [Montesquieu] did not mean that these departments [legislative, judicial and executive] ought to have no *partial agency* in, or no *control* over, the acts of each other. (Madison, *Federalist*, no. 11, p. 482).

In the United States, both the federal and the state constitutions have well-defined separation of powers. The President is to be the chief executive, Congress is to legislate, and the courts are to judge. Other countries (even those without written constitutions) have similar, although not identical, separation of powers. In this section, I show (1) that some separations of powers have no practical effect and (2) that the Constitution promotes a separation of power more than separation of powers.

Separation of Power Having No Effect

The U.S. Constitution (Article I, section 7) requires that the House of Representatives initiate all revenue bills. However, all bills must also be passed by the Senate in order to become law. It makes no difference who initiates the bill, the result will be the same, as the House and the Senate must agree. The Senate can indicate its preferences to the House before any revenue bill is formulated. But even if it cannot, the Senate can always reject a bill if it is not acceptable. This is just an example of the law's being completely transacted around when there is an ongoing contractual relationship. One would have to create a farfetched theory of information in order to create any affect of singling out the House as an initiator of revenue bills.

Madison was aware of this, as can be seen from the excerpts from his Constitutional Convention notes: "Experience proved that it [the exclusive privilege of originating money bills] had no effect."[4] "If both branches were to say yes or no, it was of little consequence which should say yes or no first, which last."[5]

The Federalist Papers were very concerned with creating separation of power. They hoped to foster competition among the several branches of power.[6] Madison was quite aware that if a coalition formed, it might overcome the separation of power built into the Constitution; however, he felt that the possibility of a coalition in a republic was quite unlikely: "If a majority be united by a common interest, the rights of the minority will be insecure. There are but two methods of providing against this evil. . . . The other [second method], by comprehending in the society so many separate descriptions of citizens as will render an unjust combination of the majority of the whole very improbable" (Madison, no. 51, p. 323).

Madison overestimated the transaction costs involved in creating an extensive political coalition. In fact, *The Federalist Papers* does not explicitly consider the possibility of a political party (a grand coalition glued together with implicit contracts). But there have been many periods when one political party has dominated more than one branch of government, enabling itself to greatly transact around the branches-of-government concept. Is it really the Senate and the House and the Presidency in competition with each other, or the Democratic Party in competition with the Republican Party, or the liberals versus the conservatives? The Constitution creates power positions for individual players. Individual Senators and Representatives will promote their own (possibly their constituents') interests (ideological or otherwise) by entering into coalition (transacting) with people in the other house of Congress and with the presidency.

Separation of Powers or of Power?

In the previous section, I suggested that it was less appropriate to view the House as being in competition with the Senate and both as being in competition with the presidency than to view the political process as a coalition acting across constitutional lines. In this section,

I show that even if we view the Congress as a coalition against the presidency, we still do not have separation of powers.

Because of the relatively few people involved, we can expect lots of implicit trading around the intent of the law. Logrolling within either branch of Congress is well documented. This kind of *quid pro quo* can exist across branches even when one branch ostensibly has no control over a particular activity. For example, if the President does not enforce a certain law that Congress desires to be enforced, Congress can use the threat of not passing a revenue bill that the President desires. In this way, Congress can affect enforcement even though the Constitution delegates enforcement only to the President. Similarly, the executive may extract legislation in order to enforce the law. An example of this was presented by Franklin at the Constitutional Convention: "When the Indians were scalping the western people, and notice of it arrived, the concurrence of the Governor [of Pennsylvania] in the means of self defense could not be got, till it was agreed that his Estate should be exempted from taxation."[7]

How does the Supreme Court fit into the picture? It appears that exchanges between the other branches and the Supreme Court involve higher transaction costs than exchanges among the other branches (say, between the Senate and the House), but these costs are not so high that transacting around the constitutional creation of an independent judiciary via some (implicit) *quid pro quo* bargaining is impossible.

Although there are only nine people on the Supreme Court, it is quite difficult for the Supreme Court to bargain with the President. For example, it is unlikely for the Court (or a majority of the Court) to agree that the President's bill is constitutional in return for the President's promoting legislation that the Court desires. On the other hand, the Court can influence the President's enforcement behavior by finding certain enforcement (or nonenforcement) nonconstitutional. On the other side, the Court is influenced by the President's behavior. The Court cannot find too many of the laws or the President's enforcement of the laws unconstitutional. This caution by the courts implies that the court decision concerning constitutionality is influenced by the President's behavior (of course, the President's influence may be even more direct, in the making of new appointments). Influence means that the President indirectly decides what laws are found constitutional and the Supreme Court indirectly decides what laws are passed and enforced. To that extent, the constitutional separation of powers is transacted around. What the Constitution does is to delegate a certain set of rights to various branches. The branches, to a greater or lesser degree, exchange these rights. Thus, we no longer have a separation of powers as much as a separation of power. That is, the initial type of rights delegated by the Constitution determines the wealth (power) of each branch more than the final use of these rights, just as the initial delegation to the rancher of a property right to damage (or to the farmer of a property right to nondamage) has an effect only on wealth, and none on where the property right will end up.

The question still remains why exchanges between the Supreme Court and the other branches, while not insignificant, are not more widespread. In the first place, the Court is much more limited by precedent and the logic of its argument than the other branches of government. While the Court can bend precedent and stretch logic, it is still constrained in its activities. Therefore, its ability to bargain is limited. In the second place, its control of the lower courts is much more constrained than the President's control over the bureaucracy, and the transaction costs of engaging in exchanges with these lower courts is much higher. In turn, these lower courts are constrained by their precedents. The Supreme Court may not decide the case at all, and the transaction costs of the President and the Congress in dealing with the diffuse lower court system are very high. Thus, we would expect the courts to exchange their rights with the rights of the other branches at a much lower level than the other branches exchange rights among themselves.

In the United States, one role of the Supreme Court is to allocate the initial distribution of property rights to the various branches of government. Because of relatively low transaction costs, it is easy for one branch of the federal government to delegate some of its functions to another branch in the federal government. Thus, Congress often delegates some of its legislative powers to the executive branch (e.g., when an administrative agency is to set up rules for protecting the environment). The Constitution also explicitly states that the Congress may delegate its appointment powers to the other branches of government for lower level offices.

Transaction between the federal government and the states around the Constitution are also possible, although they involve higher transaction costs than exchanges among the branches of the federal government. States are represented in the federal legislature via the members of Congress, who are, to greater or lesser degrees, in coalitions with local politicians. Federal legislation can transact around the constitutional delegation of powers to states by bribing the states to undertake certain behavior. The terms of trade for highway construction are ninety cents on the dollar.

The delegation of powers by the Constitution makes sense in that certain activities naturally group together. The Constitution presumably reduces transaction costs by creating branches of powers. If the Constitution has chosen an ineffective branch for a certain power, low transaction costs will allow this particular power to be delegated to a more appropriate branch. In a low-transaction-cost situation, more important than the type of power delegated to individuals is the amount of power embodied in that type. To the extent that there are low transaction costs, the Constitution is more important for its separation of power among individuals than for its separation of powers among branches.

Judicial Interpretation

In this section, I concentrate on developing testable propositions regarding interpretation by the courts. I will use economic theory to explain the difference in court behavior between statute and constitutional interpretation. First, from the *Federalist* (Hamilton):

> where the will of the legislature, declared in its statutes, stands in opposition to the people, declared in the constitution, the judges ought to be governed by the latter. (No. 78, p. 468)

Hamilton contrasts this with the case where the Constitution is not involved:

> In such a case [where there is a conflict between statute laws and no constitutional questions are at issue], it is the providence of the court to liquidate and fix their meaning and operation. . . . (Ibid.)

When a court interprets a legislative statute, it is relatively easy (especially if the statute is a recent one) for Congress to pass new legislation if the majority of both houses are dissatisfied with the court's interpretation. That is, if the court's interpretation is incorrect, the "transaction costs" are low enough for the Congress to transact around the court's rulings (as in the possibility of Congress's rewriting the Endangered Species Act so as not to include minor fish species). The role of the courts in statute interpretation is to provide reasonably consistent rules of interpretation so that those who are affected by the legislation can predict the court's interpretation and Congress can write legislation in the future in light of the court's previous interpretations. Thus, if the court interprets a list of prohibited behavior as "express mention, implied exclusion," so that behavior not specifically prohibited in the legislation is not implicitly prohibited, legislatures have two options in the future if they prefer a broader interpretation: (1) listing every possible kind of behavior which they intend to prohibit (clearly, this involves enormous costs if the law is to have a long life) or (2) stating in the statute specifically that similar but not identical behavior is also to be prohibited. In this way, the statute directs the courts to interpret more broadly. On the other hand, if the courts tend to interpret too broadly, legislatures can always add at the end that the law applies only to the actual list of prohibited activities.

Because legislative transaction costs are relatively low compared to constitutional amending procedures, one would expect the courts to make use of background material in order to discover intent more for constitutional interpretation than for statute interpretation. After all, with regard to statute making, it is easier for the legislature to expressly indicate its intent than for the courts to sift through background material. If the courts do not sift through background material, then in the future Congress will be more likely to put in the express intent when writing a statute. They know their intent better than the courts.[8] The same cannot be argued for constitutional interpretation.

Due Process

> Bills of attainder, *ex post facto* laws, and laws impairing the obligation of contracts are contrary to the first principles of the social compact and to every principle of sound legislation. (Madison, *Federalist*, no. 44, p. 282).

Due process is readily justified on grounds of economic efficiency. Due process (e.g., formal charges and the right to be heard) reduces error. Needless error involves unnecessary economic costs. Jailing innocent people involves the costs of guards and lowered productivity. Furthermore, optimal behavior may be deterred if innocent activity is punished. Due process, being a type of transaction cost, involves economic costs. For example, trials involve the time of the judge, the jury, the lawyers, and so on. Therefore, due process is also rationed. The more serious the cost of error, the more economically justified it is to expend resources on avoiding error, and the more due process is guaranteed. Putting someone in jail requires more due-process safeguards than denying the person food stamps.

The U. S. Constitution as well as most state constitutions does not allow *ex post facto* laws by the legislature. Yet, courts are allowed to determine the law *ex post facto*. Why is this so? As argued earlier, legislatures are not bound by any previous legislative action. As the majority changes, so can the statutes. Thus, there is little predictability of legislative statutes, compared to court decisions, which are restrained somewhat by precedent. An *ex post facto* law cannot be said to be expected. In contrast, court behavior is much more predictable. When a court enunciates a new precedent, the court is only taking out of "fine print" what existed in the law. Therefore, the court is rewarding good predictors, that is, people who can know the rules before they are explicitly stated. This activity should be encouraged; therefore, court decisions are almost always retroactive. Thus, it is efficient for the courts, but not for the legislature, to be retroactive.

Bills of attainder, where the government passes legislation singling out an individual for subsequent condemnation or imprisonment, are also not allowed, for the same reasons that *ex post facto* laws are not allowed. The specified person is punished for past behavior that he or she cannot alter and could not have reasonably predicted would become illegal.

Due process is like an insurance policy. It reduces risk to the individual. To a certain degree, the courts are asked to estimate how much insurance (due process) the individual would have purchased. If the courts are good predictors, they will emulate private markets for due process. For example, in the private market, unions often bargain for strong procedural safeguards to prevent the firing of people who are now employed. The employer must show good cause. In contrast, the decision by the employer not to hire someone in the first place is much more arbitrary. There are a number of reasons. Unions represent their current members, not their potential members. More important (as the same holds true for long-term contracts between businesses), in a long-term contract an employee may undertake certain investments (e.g., investment in training specific to the firm or the purchase of a nearby house) which are not fully fungible. In a contract, the employee is willing to undertake lower wages in exchange for a reduced likelihood of being fired. Efficient contracts are made in the private sector, and to a remarkable degree, the court's ruling of what is implied in public sector contracts coincides. Thus, more due process is required for denying disability payments once they have been initiated than before initially applying for them. A hearing is required before stopping these payments; but a person is not automatically given disability payments and then submitted to a hearing as to whether they should have been initiated. Expectations work in the same way. If people have long-term expectations concerning a job, then more due process is forthcoming when these expectations are unanticipatedly not met. Thus, when a junior college teacher was fired from an institution which almost always granted tenure, the U.S. Supreme Court held that the college must grant a hearing *(Perry* v. *Sindermann,* 4408 U.S. 593, 1972) before deciding not to renew a contract. In contrast, in *Board of Regents* v. *Roth* (408 U.S. 564, 1972) the Court held that the state university had no past custom of semiautomatically granting tenure, and that therefore, there was no requirement of a hearing for the nonrenewal of a contract.

The courts have often thrown out laws because they are too vague. Vagueness creates unnecessary costs. Some people will avoid doing something which is not meant to be illegal because they are not sure what the law implies. This is costly behavior that could have been prevented by a less vague statute. The legislature or some executive body is better at promulgating the specifics than the average citizen. By declaring the statute unconstitutionally vague, the court is shifting the onus of interpretation from the average citizen to the legislature (or other body), which can interpret at lower cost.

Commerce Clause

> The interfering and unneighborly regulations of some States, contrary to the true spirit of the Union, have, in different instances, given just cause of umbrage and complaint to others, and it is to be feared that examples of this nature, if not restrained by national control, would be multiplied and extended till they became not less serious sources of animosity and discord than injurious impediments to the intercourse between the different parts of the Confederacy. (Hamilton, *Federalist,* no. 22, p. 144).

Article II, section 10, of the Constitution disallows states from imposing export or import duties without the consent of Congress unless absolutely necessary for executing inspection laws, and the U.S. Supreme Court has maintained that there are constitutional limitations upon state interference with interstate commerce. States and other jurisdictions may enact legislation which affects interstate commerce when these regulations serve valid goals, such as safety. However, the courts are not likely to find constitutional "state efforts to protect local economic interests by limiting access to local markets by out of state suppliers" (34 U.S. 349, 1951). Thus, the court struck down a municipal ordinance forbidding the local sale of milk that had not been pasteurized and bottled at an approved plant within five miles of the center of the city. This ordinance was clearly economically inefficient. For the system as a whole, such an ordinance is a net loss.

While the Court does not always swing with the economic argument because sometimes local interests reduce competition from other states under the guise of safety, the rulings are predominantly toward economic efficiency. Thus, the Court has consistently struck down those state taxes which it concludes unjustifiably benefit local commerce at the expense of out-of-state commerce. For example, in *Hale* v. *Bimico Trading Inc.* (300 U.S. 375, 1939), the Court held unconstitutional a Florida statute which imposed an inspection fee sixty times the actual cost of inspection upon cement imported into the state for sale or use, because that statute excluded locally produced cement from all inspection and inspection fee requirements. This Florida statute was meant to reduce competition from out-of-state suppliers.

One might ask why the Court doesn't allow the states to decide, since presumably the states would be interested in promulgating optimal contracts. In the absence of such a proscription by the Court, there would be some tendency for states to engage in efficient contracting with each other. Unfortunately, there are relatively high transaction costs between the states and among the citizens. Thus, there might be numerous attempts to gain a bargaining advantage by threatening to pass tariffs and other restraints of trade to increase the rents accruing to the citizens. Hence, it is more efficient just to outlaw inefficient transactions in the first place. Because the economic implications of the Commerce Clause are so transparent, I will not spend any further time demonstrating its economic content.

Concluding Remarks

The Federalist Papers argue in favor of particular institutional arrangements. We have demonstrated that in some areas, the design of the institution has little effect (e.g., whether the Senate or the House of Representatives can initiate a revenue bill is irrelevant), while in other areas, the organizational structure is critical (e.g., the fact that Congress cannot determine the constitutionality of a law greatly reduces the influence of Congress). In turn, the importance of the institutional design has been shown to depend upon whether the transaction costs are high.

In this chapter, we have suggested an economic approach to understanding constitutional provisions. Many questions remain unanswered. For example, under what circumstances is bicameralism more (or less) efficient than unicameralism? Or when is a confederation more (or less) efficient than a more centralized federation? Dealing with these other questions is beyond the scope of this chapter and, of necessity, requires research efforts by a great number of people.

Notes

1. It is useful to contrast this approach with that of Beard's "economic" analysis of the Constitution (1913/1935). His explanation for certain constitutional provisions is that they distributed wealth to particular groups. Our analysis argues that, with the exception of voting rules (for example, each state has two Senators), constitutional provisions were made because they were efficient.
2. Although our focus is on *The Federalist Papers*, the theory of constitutions (or basic rules of the game) developed here is meant to apply to all modern-day large-scale nations. Some nations have no actual written document known as a constitution, while others have *de facto* constitutions which are not consistent with their written constitution. It is the claim of this paper that all these *de facto* constitutions possess certain similarities to each other and that each is partially determined by the "universal laws" of economics.
3. Just as economics often ignores why at sixty cents a pound Person X will buy less than Person Y (and instead concentrates on the fact that each will tend to buy less at eighty cents), in this study I will also ignore the cross-national differences in level (of due process, for example) and instead concentrate on the similar relative relationships that hold within the nation.
4. From Madison's notes on Madison (1:527; Madison, 5 July). See Philip Kurland and Ralph Lerner, *The Founders' Constitution* (1987), Vol. 2, 376.
5. From Madison's notes on Wilson (1:543; Madison, 6 July). Kurland and Lerner, supra at note 3, page 377.
6. "Ambition must be made to counter ambition," Madison, no. 51, *The Federalist Papers*, Clinton Rossiter, ed., New American Library (1961), p. 322. "The different governments will control each other, at the same time that each will be controlled by itself" (ibid., p. 323). Further quotations are from this edition of *The Federalist Papers*.
7. Madison's notes from Franklin's speech (1:97; Madison, June 4). Kurland and Lerner (1987), supra at note 3, vol. 1, 320. The speech was mainly concerned with the power of the veto.
8. This may be the underlying explanation for Justice Scalia's antagonism toward the use of background material in determining legislative intent.

CHAPTER SIX

Stability and Efficiency in a Separation-of-Powers Constitutional System

Gary J. Miller and Thomas H. Hammond

In constructing the legislative and executive branches of the federal government, the delegates to the Constitutional Convention had in mind three principles of design. One principle was that the constitutional system should be responsive to the views and concerns of the public. This presented no great difficulties: the popular election and the two-year terms of House members were thought to be sufficient. But a constitutional system could be too responsive: responsiveness had to be tempered by a second principle, that of stability in the laws. Ensuring this stability was a more difficult problem. The solution which emerged involved the creation of a bicameral Congress and an independently elected President with a veto power over legislation. A third principle was that policies adopted by the Congress and the President had to be good for the society as a whole. Stability and responsiveness would be of little consequence if clearly undesirable policies were routinely produced.

An abundant literature in political science and history has explored the extent to which the Constitution has met these three principles. However, these explorations have usually been conducted in an informal style, and one is hard-pressed to determine, even in the abstract, whether or not the constitutional system actually has the desired properties. The purpose of this chapter is to show how the workings of the constitutional rules can be studied in a somewhat more formal fashion. We will focus primarily on the second and third goals, involving stability in the laws and the desirability of the laws that are adopted. We will show, first, that both bicameralism and the executive veto do contribute to stability in the laws. Second, we will demonstrate that the legislative veto override undermines this stability, at least to some extent. Third, we will show that any stable public policies which are produced by Congress and the President are, in general, desirable, in the sense that there will be no policies which are unanimously preferred to those policies which are actually adopted. Our observations about stability are based on the more formal treatment in Hammond and Miller (1987).

The Federalist Papers on Efficiency and Stability

There can be little doubt that the designers of the Constitution saw good public policy and stability in the laws as paramount concerns. In *Federalist* no. 62, for example, Madison defended the Senate in the proposed bicameral Congress on the grounds, in part, that the Senate could block passage of undesirable policies which a unicameral legislature might approve:

> Another advantage accruing from this ingredient in the constitution of the Senate is the additional impediment it must prove against improper acts of legislation. No law or resolution can now be passed without the concurrence, first, of a majority of the people, and then of a majority of the States. (p. 378)[1]

Similarly,

> a senate, as a second branch of the legislative assembly distinct from and dividing the power with a first, must be in all cases a salutary check on the government. It doubles the security to the people by requiring the concurrence of two distinct bodies in schemes of usurpation or perfidy, where the ambition or corruption of one would otherwise be sufficient. (p. 378)

One reason that House members could not always be trusted stemmed from their short terms of office. To Madison, this meant that these legislators would be unable to develop the necessary wisdom about public policy. As he remarked about the virtues of a Senate whose members have longer terms,

Another defect to be supplied by a senate lies in a want of due acquaintance with the objects and principles of legislation. It is not possible that an assembly of men called for the most part from pursuits of a private nature continued in appointment for a short time and led by no permanent motive to devote the intervals of public occupation to a study of the laws, the affairs, and the comprehensive interests of their country, should, if left wholly to themselves, escape a variety of important errors in the exercise of their legislative trust. (p. 379)

It was thought that a Senate with a slow turnover and whose members had long terms of office would be able to avoid the unwise policies that a unicameral legislature might be expected to produce.

A bicameral legislature could also be expected to help prevent instability in the laws. There was no doubt in Madison's mind that instability in the laws had great costs: "To trace the mischievous effects of a mutable government would fill a volume" (p. 380). These effects were both external and internal. Externally, instability causes the nation to forfeit

the respect and confidence of other nations. . . . An individual who is observed to be inconstant to his plans, or perhaps to carry on his affairs without any plan at all, is marked at once by all prudent people as a speedy victim to his own unsteadiness and folly. His more friendly neighbors may pity him, but all will decline to connect their fortunes with his; and not a few will seize the opportunity of making their fortunes out of his. . . . Every nation, consequently, whose affairs betray a want of wisdom and stability, may calculate on every loss which can be sustained from the more systematic policy of its wiser neighbors. (pp. 380–381)

Internally, the consequences of instability were even worse:

The internal effects of a mutable policy are still more calamitous. It poisons the blessings of liberty itself. It will be of little avail to the people that the laws are made by men of their own choice if the laws be so voluminous that they cannot be read, or so incoherent that they cannot be understood; if they be repealed or revised before they are promulgated, or undergo such incessant changes that no man, who knows what the law is today, can guess what it will be tomorrow. (p. 381)

This instability had distributional consequences:

Another effect of public instability is the unreasonable advantage it gives to the sagacious, the enterprising, and the moneyed few over the industrious and uninformed mass of the people. Every new regulation concerning commerce or revenue, or in any manner affecting the value of the different species of property, presents a new harvest to those who watch the change, and can trace its consequences; a harvest, reared not by them-selves, but by the toils and cares of the great body of their fellow-citizens. (p. 381)

Commerce could also expect to suffer from an unstable government:

> The want of confidence in the public councils damps every useful under-taking, the success and profit of which may depend on a continuance of existing arrangements. What prudent merchant will hazard his fortunes in any new branch of commerce when he knows not but that his plans may be rendered unlawful before they can be executed. What farmer or manufacturer will lay himself out for the encouragement given to any particular cultivation or establishment, when he can have no assurance that his preparatory labors and advances will not render him a victim to an inconstant government? In a word, no great improvement or laudable enterprise can go forward which requires the auspices of a steady system of national policy. (pp. 381–382)

It is possible to distinguish three different causes of instability. One cause of instability stems from the frequent turnover of the member-ship of the legislature. Madison defended the proposed Senate, with its slower turnover of members, in the following terms:

> The mutability in the public councils arising from a rapid succession of new members, however qualified they may be, points out, in the strongest manner, the necessity of some stable institution in the government. Every new election in the States is found to change one half of the representa-tives. From this change of men must proceed a change of opinions; and from a change of opinions, a change of measures. But a continual change even of good measures is inconsistent with every rule of prudence and every prospect of success. (p. 380)

A second cause of instability involves quickly occurring changes in the views of the legislators. In *Federalist* no. 62, for example, Madison defended bicameralism in the following terms:

> The necessity of a senate is not less indicated by the propensity of all single and numerous assemblies to yield to the impulse of sudden and violent passions, and to be seduced by factious leaders into intemperate and pernicious resolutions. Examples on this subject might be cited without number. (p. 379)

A third cause of instability stems from the very nature of majority rule. The problem here is that, in a single legislative assembly, for any policy that might be proposed there is virtually always another policy that a majority prefers to the first policy. Simple majority rule, in other words, could not be counted on to produce stable public policies. In 1785, the Marquis de Condorcet published his *Essai*, in which he explicitly noted and discussed this particular problem of majority rule instability. While *The Federalist Papers* do not specifically discuss the problems of majority rule instability, McGrath (1983, chap. 3) points out that Madison had read Condorcet's essay and is known to have written a review of it, a review which is now, unfortunately, lost. In this chapter, we will evaluate constitutional provisions for the extent to which they reduce this particular kind of instability. This work provides the foundation necessary for understanding the impacts of membership turnover and preference change on the stability of public policies.

The Instability of Simple Majority Rule

When there are three or more legislators in a unicameral legislature, simple majority rule will generally produce unstable policies, in the sense that for each possible legislative choice, there will almost always exist other alternatives which are majority-preferred (McKelvey, 1976, 1979; Schofield, 1978; Cohen, 1979).

This is illustrated in Figure 6.1. In this case, there are six legislators voting over four alternatives. If they vote by majority rule, four legislators (H_2, H_3, S_2, and S_3) prefer alternative x to alternative z. A different four (H_1, H_2, H_3, and S_1) prefer alternative z to alternative y. All six prefer alternative y to w. Yet a different majority (H_1, S_1, S_2, and S_3) prefer alternative w to x. Thus, x is majority-preferred to z, z is preferred to y, y is preferred to w, but w is preferred to x. Every outcome can be beaten by a majority coalition preferring something else, in a potentially endless cycle of majority rule voting. While the institutional features of the unicameral legislature may provide a "stopping rule," the stopping rule is necessarily arbitrary as regards the majority preferences. Any alternative which is chosen will be chosen not because of the preferences of some majority but because of the arbitrary stopping rule. The question is: Can bicameralism end this kind of cycling? The answer is that it can.

Let us introduce some terminology which will be useful in our discussion. One alternative will be said to *dominate* another alternative when there is a set of individuals whose members all prefer the first alternative to the second and who can, given the rules of the game (such as majority rule), enforce the first alternative over the second. The *core* of this institution is the *set of undominated alternatives*. If there is a core to a simple majority-rule game in a unicameral legislature, that means there is some alternative which can defeat any other alternative in a paired comparison. If an institution has a core, its policies will (at least, in principle) be stable, since no alternative in the core can be upset by some other alternative.

Let us call a particular preference pattern of a group of individuals

FIG. 6.1. Example of simple majority rule and bicameral majority rule.

Legislative preference profile

H_1	H_2	H_3	S_1	S_2	S_3
z	x	x	z	y	y
y	z	z	y	w	w
w	y	y	w	x	x
x	w	w	x	z	z

Votes each option gets in paired comparisons

x: H_2,H_3,S_2,S_3 w: H_1,S_1,S_2,S_3
z: H_1,S_1 x: H_2,H_3

z: H_1,H_2,H_3,S_1 z: H_1,H_2,H_3,S_1
y: S_2,S_3 w: S_2,S_3

y: H_1,H_2,H_3,S_1,S_2,S_3 y: H_1,S_1,S_2,S_3
w: — x: H_2,H_3

Dominance relationships among options
under simple majority rule

"———▶" means ". . . dominates . . ."

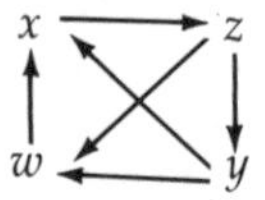

Dominance relationships among options
under bicameral majority rule

"———▶" means ". . . dominates . . ."

$$x \longrightarrow z$$

$$w \longleftarrow y$$

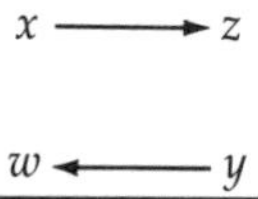

(as in Figure 6.1) a *preference profile*. The problem with simple majority rule in a single chamber is that there are very few preference profiles which result in a core. Instead, for most preference profiles (as in Figure 6.1), there is no core, and majority rule is unstable: every possible alternative can be upset by some majority which prefers a different outcome and has the votes to enforce it.

We will say that voting rule A *is more stable than* voting rule B if two conditions are met: (1) if a given preference profile has a core under B, then it must be the case that it has a core under A; and (2) there is some preference profile that has a core under A, but the same preference profile will not have a core under B. In other words, if A is more stable than B, then it is strictly an improvement on B in terms of undominated outcomes.

The claim we make for bicameralism is that it is more stable than simple majority rule. That is, a preference profile which is unstable under unicameral majority rule may nonetheless be stable under bicameral majority rule; moreover, a preference profile which is stable with unicameral majority rule will always be stable with bicameral majority rule. Thus, bicameralism at least partly solves the problem of majority rule instability.

Stable and Efficient Outcomes from Bicameralism

If we divide any group of legislators into two mutually exclusive and collectively exhaustive subgroups and require that a majority of each subgroup approve any new legislation, then some of the simple majorities which previously were able to upset some options are now powerless under bicameral majority rule.

Refer again to the preference profile in Figure 6.1. Suppose H_1, H_2, and H_3 constitute one chamber called the "House," and S_1, S_2, and S_3 constitute another chamber called the "Senate." For a bill to pass, it requires not just a majority of the six votes but a majority of each chamber, called a *joint majority*. Thus, not all majority coalitions are decisive—only joint majority coalitions. This is a limitation on simple majority rule, in that the majority coalition of H_1, H_2, H_3, and S_1 cannot now enforce its preference for z over y. Likewise, the coalition of H_1, H_2, H_3, and S_1 cannot enforce its preference for z over w, and the coalition of H_1, S_1, S_2, and S_3 cannot enforce its preference for w over x.

Under simple majority rule, each option in Figure 6.1 is dominated by some other option or options. Under bicameral majority rule, x beats z and y beats w, but no other dominance relations hold (see the description of the dominance relationships in Figure 6.1). Since z no longer beats y, y is undominated and must be in the core; since y and w no longer beat x, x must also be in the core. By disempowering some majorities, then, bicameralism can break up majority rule cycles, thereby creating stability.

The fact that a public policy is stable—that it is undominated—does not necessarily mean that it is, in some sense, "good" public policy. There is a simple test which we can apply to the legislature's choice to determine if it is good public policy. The principle upon which this test is based is the *Pareto principle*. To say that a policy is *Pareto-efficient* simply means that there is no other policy that is *unanimously* preferred to it. If a policy is *Pareto-inefficient*, that means there is some other policy that is *unanimously* preferred to it. Thus, one way of defining a "good" public policy is to say that it is a policy which is Pareto-efficient: there is no other policy which is unanimously preferred.

Bicameral cores are always Pareto-efficient. If there is a bicameral core, this means that for every alternative in the core, there is no other policy which is preferred by a joint majority. And since there is no other policy which is preferred by a mere joint majority, it obviously follows that there is no other policy which is preferred unanimously, by all the members of both chambers. Hence, we can conclude that bicameral cores are Pareto-efficient and thus meet this particular test of "good" public policy.

While bicameralism can add stability to legislatures that have unstable majority-rule preferences, it can never destabilize a legislature that has stable simple-majority-rule preferences. If an outcome is an element of the simple-majority-rule core, it cannot (by definition) be upset by any simple majority. Consequently, it can never be upset by the subset of simple majorities that are joint majorities. Thus, it must be stable under bicameralism as well.

Limits of Bicameralism

As anticipated by the authors of *The Federalist Papers*, the mutual checks and balances between the House and the Senate can create a core. However, bicameralism does not *necessarily* create a core. Bicameralism creates stability in Figure 6.1 because, for example, the House's majority preference for z over y is counterbalanced by the Senate's majority preference for y over z. The majority preference for z over y (due to H_1, H_2, H_3, and S_1) is thus blocked by a Senate majority with opposing views (S_2 and S_3 both prefer y). If the two chambers had "matched" preferences (e.g., if the preferences of H_1 were the same as those of S_1, those of H_2 were the same as those of S_2, and those of H_3 were the same as those of H_3), then there might always be a joint majority favoring every choice in a simple-majority-rule cycle.

The stability-inducing properties of bicameralism are thus dependent on the existence of distinctly different viewpoints in the two chambers. The idea behind the bicameral Congress, of course, was that the two chambers would indeed have distinct interests and preferences. Madison's analysis of bicameralism in *Federalist* nos. 62 and 63 lays out the conditions under which bicameralism can prevent undesirable policies, and the same observation describes, in surprisingly accurate terms, what is also needed to ensure stability. The Constitution's basic logic, Madison suggested, was that "the improbability of sinister combinations will be in proportion to the dissimilarity in the genius of the two bodies" (no. 62, p. 379). By giving Senators six-year terms, staggering their elections, and allowing state legislatures to select them, it was intended that there would be induced in the Senators preferences which were substantially different from those induced in the Representatives.

The Executive Veto

While bicameralism does not necessarily guarantee stability, stability is guaranteed by the executive veto. Argued Hamilton in *Federalist* no. 73 about the stability inducing properties of the veto (as well as about the veto's role in preventing the adoption of undesirable policies):

> It may perhaps be said that the power of preventing bad laws includes that of preventing good ones; and may be used to the one purpose as well as to the other. But this objection will have little weight with those who can properly estimate the mischiefs of that inconstancy and mutability in the laws, which form the greatest blemish in the character and genius of our governments. They will consider every institution calculated to restrain the excess of lawmaking, and to keep things in the same state in which they happen to be at any given period as much more likely to do good than harm; because it is favorable to greater stability in the system of legislation. (pp. 443–444)

Figure 6.2 provides an illustration of the stability-inducing properties of the veto. For simplicity, we consider only a unicameral legislature facing the executive; when the executive has a veto, bicameralism does not add any "extra" stability (as long as no override is allowed). By itself, the five-member unicameral legislature has no simple-majority-rule core: there is a majority rule cycle which includes all four options.

Assume now that there is an executive, E, who prefers y to w to x to z. (We have, in effect, converted the last legislator in Figure 6.1 into the executive.) In this new game, one alternative dominates another if *both* a majority of this unicameral legislature *and* the executive prefer the first to the second. We now find that y dominates both w and x, and that x dominates z. But since z no longer dominates y, given these new rules, y must be in the core.

Note that y, the executive's most preferred option, is in the core.

FIG. 6.2. Example of an executive veto.

Preference profile for five legislators
and an executive

L_1	L_2	L_3	L_4	L_5	E
z	x	x	z	y	y
y	z	z	y	w	w
w	y	y	w	x	x
x	w	w	x	z	z

Votes each option gets in paired comparisons

x: $L_2,L_3,L_5,$E   w: $L_1,L_4,L_5,$E
z: L_1,L_4 x: L_2,L_3

z: L_1,L_2,L_3,L_4 z: L_1,L_2,L_3,L_4
y: $L_5,$E   w: $L_5,$E

y: $L_1,L_2,L_3,L_4,L_5,$E y: $L_1,L_4,L_5,$E
w: —   x: L_2,L_3

Dominance relationships among options under
simple majority rule (legislators only)

Dominance relationships among options
with an executive veto
if executive prefers y to w to x to z

The reason is that whenever y is compared to any other option, the executive will always vote for y over that other option, thus ensuring that y will remain undominated. In fact, as long as there is no veto override (see the following section), the executive's ideal point will be in the core.

Thus, even when the legislature has no core on its own, creating an executive with a veto will create stability, and this is true no matter what the executive's preferences. We should also note that a core which is due to the executive veto will always be Pareto-efficient, for reasons almost identical to those for why any bicameral core is Pareto-efficient.

It might be argued, on the basis of the historical record, that the veto is of relatively little consequence in relations between President and Congress since it is used so infrequently. However, Hamilton suggested that the veto does not have to be used to be effective:

A power of this nature in the executive will often have a silent and unperceived, though forcible, operation. When men, engaged in unjustifiable pursuits, are aware that obstructions may come from a quarter which they cannot control, they will often be restrained by the bare apprehension of opposition from doing what they would with eagerness rush into if no such external impediments were to be feared. (no. 73, p. 446)

If Hamilton was right, then we can expect the veto power to induce a core even if it is seldom exercised.

The Veto Override

An executive veto guarantees stability, no matter whether the executive faces a unicameral or a bicameral legislature. However, the legislature's veto-override power has the potential for undermining this stability.

For an example, assume that the five-member unicameral legislature in Figure 6.3 can override the executive's veto if at least four of the five members vote to override. The legislators' preferences are the same as in Figure 6.2, and under simple majority rule, there is a majority rule cycle. When there is no override, there is a core consisting of w and y. But with a veto override, both w and y are eliminated from the core, and a cycle reemerges. The reason? Option y is eliminated from the core because an override majority (L_1, L_2, L_3, and L_4) prefers z to y and can overcome E's preference for y. Similarly, w is eliminated because override majorities prefer z to w (L_1, L_2, L_3, and L_4) and y to w (L_1, L_2, L_3, L_4, and L_5), overcoming E's preference for w in each case.

When there is a bicameral legislature facing an executive with a veto, however, an override majority in *each* chamber is needed to override. If the legislators of the two chambers have exactly identical preferences (i.e., if the legislators can be matched across chambers in pairs with identical preferences), then it is as easy for two chambers to override a veto as it is for one.

However, if the chambers have at least somewhat different preferences, then override is more difficult. Something of this sort clearly lies behind Hamilton's argument in *Federalist* no. 73 when he said,

It is to be hoped that it will not often happen that improper views will govern so large a proportion as two thirds of both branches of the legislature at the same time; and this, too, in defiance of the counterpoising

FIG. 6.3. Example of a veto override.

Preference profile for five legislators
and an executive

L_1	L_2	L_3	L_4	L_5	E
z	x	x	z	y	w
y	z	z	y	w	x
w	y	y	w	x	y
x	w	w	x	z	z

Votes each option gets in paired comparisons

x: L_2,L_3,L_5,E w: L_1,L_4,L_5,E
z: L_1,L_4 x: L_2,L_3

z: L_1,L_2,L_3,L_4 z: L_1,L_2,L_3,L_4
y: L_5,E w: L_5,E

y: L_1,L_2,L_3,L_4,L_5 y: L_1,L_4,L_5
w: E   x: L_2,L_3,E

Dominance relationships among options under
simple majority rule (legislators only)

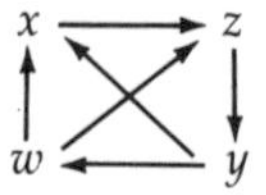

Dominance relationships among options if executive
prefers w to x to y to z and there is no veto override

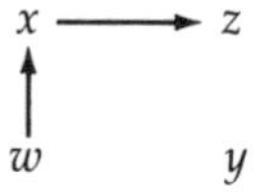

Dominance relationships among options if executive
prefers w to x to y to z and there is a veto override
(override needs 4 votes or more)

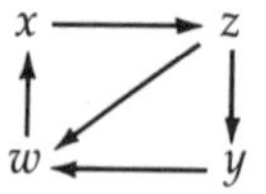

weight of the executive. It is at any rate far less probable that this should be the case than that such views should taint the resolutions and conduct of a bare majority. (p. 446)

For an example, see Figure 6.4. There are five House members and five Senate members, plus an executive. If we treat all ten legislators as a single chamber, there is a simple-majority-rule cycle. With the

FIG. 6.4. Example of a bicameral veto override.

Preference profile for five representatives,
five senators, and an executive

H_1	H_2	H_3	H_4	H_5	S_1	S_2	S_3	S_4	S_5	E
x	z	w	w	x	w	z	w	y	x	y
z	y	x	z	z	x	x	x	w	y	w
y	w	z	y	y	z	y	z	z	w	x
w	x	y	x	w	y	w	y	x	z	z

Votes each option gets in paired comparisons

x: $H_1,H_3,H_5,S_1,S_3,S_5,E$ w: $H_2,H_3,H_4,S_1,S_3,S_4,E$
z: H_2,H_4,S_2,S_4 x: H_1,H_5,S_2,S_5

z: $H_1,H_2,H_3,H_4,H_5,S_1,S_2,S_3$ z: H_1,H_2,H_5,S_2
y: S_4,S_5,E w: $H_3,H_4,S_1,S_3,S_4,S_5,E$

y: $H_1,H_2,H_5,S_2,S_4,S_5,E$ y: H_2,H_4,S_4,E
w: H_3,H_4,S_1,S_3 x: $H_1,H_3,H_5,S_1,S_2,S_3,S_5$

Dominance relationships among options   Dominance relationships among options
under unicameral majority rule   under bicameral majority rule
(legislators only)   (legislators only)

Dominance relationships among options
under bicameralism and executive veto

Dominance relationships among options   Dominance relationships among options
with unicameral veto override   with bicameral veto override
(override needs 8 votes or more)   (override needs 4 votes or more
                                                   in each chamber)

legislators separated into their respective chambers, there is still a
cycle among the options; as previously noted, bicameralism does not
guarantee a core. With an executive veto in either a unicameral or a
bicameral legislature (but with no override), there is now a core which
contains only y, the executive's most preferred option. If we treat all
ten legislators as a single chamber and allow a veto override if

eight or more of the ten legislators can agree, no core exists: there is a cycle including all four options. But with the legislators partitioned into their respective chambers, and at least four votes required from each chamber to override the executive's veto, we find there is again a core consisting of y. The key difference is that, with a unicameral veto override, a coalition of eight legislators (H_1, H_2, H_3, H_4, H_5, S_1, S_2, and S_3) is able to override the executive's veto and enforce z over y, while with a bicameral override, this coalition lacks a necessary Senate vote to override. Hence, z does not dominate y, and y is left as the sole element of the bicameral override core. So while the unicameral legislature can override the veto, thereby destroying the core, the bicameral legislature cannot override the veto. Hence, the stability due to the executive's veto is maintained, and it is due in this case to the bicameralism.

While no formal proof is yet available, we conjecture that the bicameral veto override does not seriously undermine the stability created by bicameralism and the executive veto, as long as there are even just modest differences between the two chambers.

Note here that, as with bicameral cores and executive veto cores, the core (if it exists) of an executive-veto-override game is Pareto-efficient. Consider any alternative in the veto override core. Since the alternative is in the veto override core, this means that there is no joint legislative override majority which can upset it, nor is there an executive-led coalition (consisting of the executive plus a majority of each chamber) which can upset it. If there is no alternative which is preferred by an executive-led coalition consisting of the executive plus a majority of each chamber, this obviously means that there is no alternative which is preferred by the executive and *all* legislators. Hence, we can conclude that an alternative which is in any veto override core is Pareto-efficient.

Conclusion

In *Federalist* no. 37, Madison wrote of the problems of constitutional design:

> Among the difficulties encountered by the convention, a very important one must have lain in combining the requisite stability and energy in government with the inviolable attention due to liberty and to the republican form. . . . Energy in government is essential to that security against external and internal danger and to that prompt and salutary execution of the laws which enter into the very definition of good government. Stability in government is essential to national character and to the advantages annexed to it, as well as to that repose and confidence in

the minds of the people, which are among the chief blessings of civil society. An irregular and mutable legislation is not more an evil in itself than it is odious to the people; and it may be pronounced with assurance that the people of this country, enlightened as they are with regard to the nature, and interested, as the great body of them are, in the effects of good government, will never be satisfied till some remedy be applied to the vicissitudes and uncertainties which characterize the State administrations. On comparing, however, these valuable ingredients with the vital principles of liberty, we must perceive at once the difficulty of mingling them together in their due proportions. (pp. 226–227)

We have not attempted to address all of Madison's concerns, involving not only stability but energy, liberty, and the republican form of government. Nonetheless, our analysis does suggest that the Constitutional Convention designed a set of rules which went far toward creating "the requisite stability." We have also demonstrated that any stable outcomes which might be produced are Pareto-efficient and so meet a plausible test of what constitutes good public policy.

Acknowledgments. We would like to thank Mark Petracca and Brian Humes for their helpful comments on an earlier draft of this chapter.

Notes

1. Page references are to the New American Library edition of *The Federalist Papers*, 1961, Clinton Rossiter, ed.

CHAPTER SEVEN

Why a Constitution?

Russell Hardin

One of the oldest and most honored traditions in political philosophy is the odd claim that a constitution or the very act of forming a government is metaphorically a big contract. There are at least two kinds of force that proponents of "contractarianism" in political theory seem to expect to gain from this persuasive definition. First, there is the descriptive and explanatory force one might get from relating the creation of a constitution to an act of contracting as implied in the commonplace but largely wrong term *social contract*. Second, there is the normative force of using contract theory in the analysis of social institutions to give a justification for them. If we can say that people agreed to certain constitutional arrangements, as they generally do to contracts under which they are obligated, we supposedly can go further and say that they are obligated to abide by these arrangements. I wish here to argue against the first of these theses to show that constitutions are not, even metaphorically speaking, sensibly seen as contracts. I think both these theses are false, but if one can first show that constitutional arrangements are not the simple product of agreement in the sense in which contracts are, even hypothetically, the normative thesis loses most of its interest.[1] I will attempt to establish the first thesis through consideration of the U.S. Constitution and of the understandings of its rationale and role at the time of its writing and adoption, with special reference to *The Federalist Papers* of Alexander Hamilton, James Madison, and John Jay, writing jointly as "Publius."[2]

What is the difference between a contract and a constitution in political life? The latter is prior, in the following sense. We all coordinate in having a practice of promising and a law of contract that make life better for us. A typical contract resolves a prisoner's dilemma, or exchange, problem. But the commonplace view that creating a constitution or establishing a government is equivalent to contracting to cooperate or to live at peace, as though this were similarly an exchange problem, is generally wrongheaded. A constitution does not resolve a particular prisoner's dilemma interaction. It regulates a long-term pattern of interactions. It establishes conventions, in the sociological or strategic sense, that make it easier for us to cooperate and to coordinate in particular moments. Creating a constitution is itself primarily an act of coordination on one of many possible ways of ordering our lives together, not an act of cooperating in a prisoner's dilemma or exchange. In the general case over the long term, roughly speaking, we must have one regime, for example, general enforcement of contracts or no enforcement, general protection of property or no protection. Many of us have an easy choice in this general case: we prefer coordination on a regime of enforcement of contracts and protection of property to coordination on a regime of no enforcement or protection.

It is important to keep clear what is the issue here. One can renege on any given contract and plausibly still keep open the opportunity for mutually beneficial contractual relations with other potential partners. But one cannot will away the whole institution of enforcing contracts and then still expect mutually beneficial contractual exchanges with anyone to work. A constitution is not a contract; indeed, it creates the institution of contracting. Hence, again, its function is to resolve a problem that is prior to contracting. This is the general thesis I wish to explore here.

There are at least three major ways in which a constitution differs fundamentally from a contract. I wish briefly to discuss each below. First, the strategic structures of the modal interactions governed by contracts and constitutions are different: contracts typically govern prisoner's dilemma interactions, and constitutions typically govern coordination interactions. Second, constitutions have a far less significant element of agreement behind them than do contracts. This problem has given rise to a remarkably obtuse and unenlightening literature on tacit consent, hypothetical consent, implied consent, and so forth. In practice, acquiescence is more important than agreement for the working of a constitution, while agreement is crucial if the obligations under a contract are to make sense. Finally, the sources of support for a contract and for a constitution differ radically. Contracts are generally backed by external sanctions; constitutions are more nearly backed by default, by the difficulty of recoordinating on an alternative arrangement. As Caesar, a pseudonymous colleague of Publius, bluntly put it, what is required of most people is that they "proceed without mutiny."[3] The first of these three claims is simply that the strategic structure of the problem resolved by a constitution is not the prisoner's dilemma. The other two claims follow from this fact, but they are of interest in their own right, and their establishment further shows that the interaction at issue is not a prisoner's dilemma.

Despite the differences here, one might still suppose that the contract metaphor is not entirely wrong for constitutions. If constitutions are not strictly analogous to contracts, they might seem to be analogous to contracts by convention, in which a pattern of prisoner's dilemma interactions gets resolved cooperatively through the rise of a convention that regulates behavior. Again, there are elements in common here, but in general, a constitution can be distinctively different from contracts by convention, not least in that it may more typically be created out of whole cloth rather than retrospectively (although the English "constitution" might reasonably be described as a collection of contracts by convention). The most important element that a formal constitution and a contract by convention have in common is that both depend not on sanctions from some external power, as legal contracts typically do, but on sanctions and incentives internal to the group governed by them. Moreover, a constitution may work and be interpreted conventionally, with its content changing over time.

Once we are clear on what a constitution is not, we may then wonder why we want one. I will conclude with a brief discussion of what one might call the strategic functions of a formal constitution.

The Strategic Structure of a Constitution

We may characterize all strategic interactions as being of three types. If preference orderings over outcomes are strictly opposing, a two-party interaction is "pure conflict." If preference orderings over outcomes are identical, an interaction is "pure coordination." All other interactions involve a mixture of both conflict and coordination, with some outcomes in opposing orders and some in identical orders. The prisoner's dilemma is the most studied and discussed of all mixed interactions, largely, no doubt, because it represents the strategic structure of an exchange interaction (Hardin, 1982a).

		Column	
		Cooperate	Defect
Row	Cooperate	2,2	4,1
	Defect	1,4	3,3

Game 1. Prisoner's dilemma or exchange.

The modal purpose of a traditional contract is to regulate an exchange and hence to resolve a prisoner's dilemma interaction. The modal purpose of a constitution is to resolve a coordination interaction. Two-person versions of these two kinds of interaction are represented in Games 1 and 2.[4] In these games, the payoffs to each player are strictly ordinal. That is, the outcome with a payoff of 1 is the player's first choice, or most preferred outcome, that with a payoff of 2 is the player's second choice, and so forth. The resolution of a prisoner's dilemma inherently requires the creation of relevant incentives, usually in the form of threatened sanctions, to get both players to choose their "cooperate" rather than their "defect" strategies. The resolution of a coordination game typically requires little more than signalling, for example, to get both players in Game 2 to choose their strategies I or their strategies II.

It would be wrong to say that there are no similarities between the two kinds of interaction. Obviously, the reason that a prisoner's dilemma is worthy of *joint cooperative* resolution is that it has a large element of coordination within it: all parties to it prefer the all-cooperate to the all-defect outcome. If we analytically define all games for some number of players, we will generally find that most of them include elements both of coordination and of conflict. Moreover, in a time of constitutional creation or revision, one might generally expect to find genuine conflicts of interest over the form of certain of the constitutional provisions. For example, Hamilton objected to the U.S. Constitution that it did not provide for life terms for the Senators and for the chief executive. His opponents, such as Thomas Jefferson, accused him of wanting to impose an aristocracy and a monarchy. Hamilton might have answered that they were right, but that an aristocracy and a monarchy would produce better government than would a relatively free-wheeling democracy with a rapid turnover in the higher offices.[5] But he might also have supposed that, while any strong national government was preferable to a weak national government, still, an aristocracy with a monarchy would better serve *his*

	Column	
	I	II
Row I	1,1	2,2
II	3,3	1,1

Game 2. Coordination.

interests than would a more open democracy. Hence, there was perhaps, in part, merely a disagreement over the facts of how different forms of government would work. But in part, there may also have been a partial conflict of interest, as there is in a prisoner's dilemma.

To the extent that there was a genuine conflict of interest, as between possible coordination outcomes, the interaction was more nearly analogous to that of Game 3 than to that of Game 2. In Game 3, there are two outcomes that both of us prefer to both of the other outcomes. But I prefer one of these, say, (1,2), to the other, (2,1), while you prefer (2,1) to (1,2). Whether we should now see our interaction as essentially one of coordination rather than of conflict turns on how, in our estimations, the differences between 1 and 2 compare with those between 2 and 3. If 1 and 2 are negligibly different while 2 and 3 are radically different for each of us, ours is clearly a coordination interaction. If the converse is true, ours is essentially a conflict interaction. Even if 1 and 2 are substantially different, 2 may still be radically better than 3. In this case we may face a problem of persistent disadvantage for one party if we successfully coordinate one way rather than the other, so that our final coordination may seem exploitative.

Some degree of conflict of interests is inherent in a constitutional arrangement just because the arrangement establishes institutions that can be used for narrow purposes, such as assisting me in securing my interests against you. As Hamilton noted of the U. S. Constitution, it affected many "particular interests" (*Federalist* no. 1). Whether such conflicts are so great as to make the original problem one of a prisoner's dilemma is therefore a factual question, in part. If it is fundamentally a prisoner's dilemma—rather than a coordination interaction with several coordination outcomes, some of which you slightly prefer, others of which I slightly prefer, and so on—then it must be true that some outcomes that are best for some of us are worst for others. There must be outcomes analogous to the (1,4) and

		Column	
		I	II
Row	I	2,1	3,3
	II	4,4	1,2

Game 3. Unequal coordination

the (4,1) outcomes in Game 1 in the view of major groups. If it is fundamentally a coordination interaction, this is not true.

The factual question here for 1787 in the thirteen states is one that *The Federalist Papers* suppose admitted of none but the simple answer that *no one could sensibly have thought it better to have no union rather than some moderately powerful government.* (Of course, many of the anti-Federalists disagreed.) Madison argues that even a strong faction must want the protection of *all* parties (*Federalist* no. 51). Some people clearly preferred a weaker government to the one promised by the Constitution, and perhaps some preferred strategically to block the Constitution in order to get a new negotiation for some other form of government, whether weaker or stronger. Hamilton, perhaps with some exaggeration, argued in the opening *Federalist* that the choice was of "an adoption of the new Constitution or a dismemberment of the Union" (*Federalist* no. 1, final paragraph). There was no general incentive to anyone to enter the agreement in the hope of later cheating and refusing to cooperate, as one might well do with a contract or a promise to resolve a prisoner's dilemma. All of these points would follow from the supposition that the payoff from coordination swamped all other possibilities, a supposition that must have seemed compelling to the Federalists. Although there were different plausible coordination outcomes, with some perhaps preferring one and others preferring another, there was not very likely any major group that could seriously suppose that some outcome was the analogue of the (1,4) outcome of Game 1, with itself getting the most preferred payoff and some other group getting the least preferred payoff instead of both getting some intermediate compromise. For example, Hamilton and other financiers could not have supposed that they would be best off when Jefferson and other agrarians were worst off. Rather, both must have supposed that for either to prosper, the other would also have to prosper. If either were very badly off, the other would also be badly off. The same would be true of Madison's other pairings of conflicting interests in *Federalist* no. 10.

Let us consider this last point at greater length. A contract generally regulates an exchange. What is at stake in an exchange between us is the trading to me of something you have that I value more than I value what I have, and to you of something that I have that you value more than you value what you have. That is a clumsy but full statement. One could say we increase value when we make the exchange, but it is more perspicuous simply to say that we both are made better off. What a stable government that backs contracts, property, various kinds of cooperative organizations, collective decision-making capacity, and other arrangements does is give us the stable expectations to justify longer term efforts to create values, to specialize in ways that would not benefit us except for the strong expectation of being able to trade what we produce for other things that we could not so readily or efficiently produce. It may also create so-called public goods that make virtually all of us more productive, as when it dredges harbors and rivers, maintains roads, or builds bridges, to cite the mundane examples of Adam Smith. Perhaps the most important very early effects of the U. S. Constitution were to eliminate military insecurity between the states (*Federalist* no. 9) and to increase the scale of the market in which entrepreneurs in the states could trade (*Federalist* nos. 11, 23). The Constitution was, in Clinton Rossiter's words, seen as "an open door to prosperity, and a shield to independence" (1965, p. 296). The problem of insecurity was not as idle as it now seems, not least because the states were in severe competition for the control of new territories to the west. Union under a strong national government took away most of the point of such competition and eased the way to development without conflict. The Commerce Clause of the Constitution, whose object had been the early impetus to the Philadelphia Convention,[6] prohibited taxes on interstate commerce, and the national government generally brought about uniformity in certain laws that made trade and other activities easier and more beneficial.

Why then do Hobbes and others seem to think that the problem to be resolved by the creation of government is like that of the prisoner's dilemma, so that its resolution requires something like a contract? At times, Hobbes and many others seem to view our problem as one of merely maintaining what we have, as though it were virtually a problem of pure conflict: I want everything I have plus everything you have—and you do, too. They also clearly enough sometimes see that there are, in a sense, mutual gains to be had (or mutual benefits to be maintained) by securing one allocation rather than another. The combination of these views of the issue makes it appear to be a prisoner's dilemma. What makes the problem of coordination rise above the conflict in my wanting everything and your wanting everything is the tremendous prospect for production and mutual gain when each of us is allowed to keep some of what we have and produce. As Henry Ford is supposed to have recognized, he could profit more if his workers earned enough to buy his cars, so that his well-being depended on theirs.

Thinking of the so-called state of nature is grossly misleading in this respect because it tends to focus our attention on what we already have rather than on what we may produce under the relevant regime of coordination. The central value of government that makes it easy to assent to is that it enables us to coordinate in the production of great gains (also see Hardin, 1988). If government's chief value were to block our conflicts over what we already have from turning violent, its rise would be the mystery that Hobbes tries to solve.

Finally, note that there were plausibly two groups in 1787–88 who saw their interests as essentially opposed to those of the Federalists. Many of the anti-Federalists seemed to prefer the breakup of the union to strong government. And the slaves, who were not party to the constitutional decision, may similarly have seen it in their interest not to have union under a constitution that perpetuated their condition. Hence, both these groups may clearly have preferred the status quo, even if it entailed a collapse of the union, to the creation of a strong national government under the Constitution. If this is a correct view of their interests, it follows, of course, that, from their perspective, the issue of the Constitution was essentially one of pure conflict with the Federalists. They were in neither a prisoner's dilemma nor a coordination interaction with the latter. This must be an accurate account of the position of the relatively anarchistic opponents of the Constitution and of those, like Brutus and Cato, who thought no republic of such size as the thirteen states together could be anything but despotic.[7] Whether it also represents the interests of the slaves turns on what one would have expected to issue from the failure of the Constitution. It is also plausible that some of the anti-Federalists opposed a national government that would diminish their own local power, and that others merely misunderstood their interests through "the honest errors of minds led astray by preconceived jealousies and fears," as Hamilton supposed (*Federalist* no. 1). Both these classes of opponents must then also have seen themselves as being in simple conflict with the Federalists.

Did the Federalists see their problem in resolving the weakness of government under the Articles of Confederation as essentially one of coordination? I think that commonly they did. *The Federalist Papers* are laced with this view, as in Hamilton's opening and closing comments that the issue was union under the Constitution or dismemberment, "the very existence of the nation" (*Federalist* nos. 1 and 85). George Washington strongly advocated a convention to revise the Articles of Confederation and, further, advocated expeditious rather than ideal change. "Otherwise," he wrote, "like a house on fire, whilst the most regular mode of extinguishing it is contended for, the building is reduced to ashes."[8] Caesar wrote explicitly that "Ingenious men will give every plausible, and, it may be, pretty substantial reasons, for the adoption of two plans of Government, which shall be fundamentally different in their construction, and not less so in their operation; yet both, if honestly administered, might operate with safety and advantage" (number 2 in Kurland and Lerner, Vol. 1, pp. 60–61). There might have been other constitutions that could have been defended as cogently as that which the Philadelphia convention proposed. Under the circumstances, however, once many of the most important political leaders of the thirteen states spent a few hot months in Philadelphia hammering out a rescue of the union, they effectively selected one from all plausible points of coordination.[9]

Agreement and a Constitution

Agreement to a contract and to a constitution differ in two important respects: whether one agrees at all and, if one does, what one agrees to. A constitution, to come into being or to be effective, does not require universal or even widespread agreement. Indeed, one of the appeals of proposing a new constitution in 1787 rather than proposing amendments to the Articles of Confederation was that the former could be done without the destructive "absurdity" of the unanimity required by the latter, especially when unanimity could be blocked by tiny but obstinate Rhode Island (*Federalist* no. 40). In many contexts, a constitution does not even require majority "support," it merely needs lack of sufficient opposition.

The U. S. Constitution was adopted in the most grudging of ways. Two of the eventual states first rejected it and only later accepted it after it had taken effect as the result of the ratifications of enough other states. Although Rhode Island's license plates do not proudly proclaim it the last holdout, Rhode Island voters rejected the Constitution in a statewide referendum by the resounding margin of 2,711 to 239; more than two years passed before a Rhode Island state convention ratified the Constitution—after Washington had already been the first President of the new nation for more than a year. North Carolina's first constitutional convention refused to ratify the Constitution; a second convention ratified it more than a year later—again, after Washington entered office as President. Some states ratified the Constitution by large majorities, Delaware, New Jersey, and Georgia even by unanimous consent of their constitutional conventions. But several others voted for it by narrow margins. Of the three crucial large states in the middle of the proposed union—New York, Pennsylvania, and Virginia—only Pennsylvania ratified by a comfortable margin.[10] Despite this grudging acceptance, the U. S. Constitution has had extraordinary impact on social and political relations in North America. In this respect, a constitution is clearly like a convention in the strategic sense: it may not give you the best of all results, but it gives you the best you can expect *given that almost everyone else is following it*. Can one imagine in a like fashion a contract that bound those who had in no sense agreed to it?

Geoffrey Brennan and James M. Buchanan (1985) say that "The rules of political order . . . can be legitimately derived only from the agreement among individuals as members of the polity" (p. 26). The word *legitimately* suggests that this is intended as a normative claim. I do not wish to discuss the normative claim here except insofar as agreement cannot be binding if it is not feasible. It is the implicit feasibility claim that I wish to consider. Or perhaps one should speak of the implicit claim of the meaning of *agreement*. How do we derive the rules of political order from the agreement among individual members of the polity? For a trivial example, consider the rules that govern debate and voting in Congress. These are spelled out in the popularly available version for use in other deliberative bodies in *Robert's Rules of Order* (1951). *Robert's Rules* stipulate that the parliamentarian, whose task is to invoke the relevant rule, should not be elected but appointed by the president of the group: "It is absurd and also embarrassing to elect an advisory officer, when that adviser may know less about the subject than the officer he is supposed to advise" (see inside back cover). What the parliamentarian must know is merely the distillation of past precedents, many of which do not flow from any evident principles and might therefore have been otherwise. That distillation fills about three hundred pages.

Robert's Rules are like the common law. They have grown without a lot of guidance and certainly without a lot of popular control. The polity lets the rules prevail, but it does not often, in any stronger sense, express its agreement to them. If academic deliberative bodies, such as departmental meetings, are typical of the larger society in this respect, many members of the polity must find many of *Robert's Rules* peculiar, unfamiliar, and even quite disagreeable. It is therefore possible for those who master the rules of order, as the late Senator James B. Allen did, to shrewdly manipulate legislative deliberations to their advantage. We let these and many other rules prevail largely because we cannot easily act collectively to influence them. General Robert coordinated us on his version of the congressional system of rules, and we are stuck. We might spontaneously or collectively overturn them, but we can be fairly confident that we will not, as students of the free-rider problem and the logic of collective action know all too well. That we do not is no proof of our agreement with these rules.

Perhaps one could simply alter the terms for what counts as agreement in the case of a *collective* institution that has to govern all of us at once. It is not necessary for all to agree in any meaningful sense; it is only necessary for enough to agree or even merely to acquiesce for us to move ahead with our collective arrangements. Clearly, this is what is done *under* a constitution in most cases: some fraction of those qualified to vote on an issue is all that is required to decide the issue. Those who lose in the vote might be said to suffer an externality. Many who are not signatories to ordinary contracts similarly suffer externalities from the result of others' reaching agreement. But there is much more at stake than this in the formal creation of a constitution. We virtually all benefit from having constitutional regulation of our interactions in a sense that could not plausibly apply to any ordinary contract. Many of the people of Rhode Island presumably only wanted a constitution that would have been more advantageous to themselves than that put to them for a vote. They presumably did not want to refuse union altogether. Hence, after voting against the Constitution relatively early, Rhode Island voted for it when the union was a *fait accompli* that Rhode Island could either join or not join. The vote of the convention of Virginia came after eight of the required nine states had ratified. In the last speech of the Virginia convention on ratification, Edmund Randolph, who had refused to sign the Constitution when it was proposed at the Philadelphia convention, observed that "the accession of eight states reduced our deliberations to the single question of *Union or no Union*" (quoted in Rossiter, 1965, p. 292). Randolph voted for in Richmond what he had refused to sign in Philadelphia. There was no point in not coordinating on what was, by then, the best of likely outcomes. (In fact, in a vote three days before Virginia's, New Hampshire became the ninth state to ratify.)

Eloquent testimony to how little a people must agree to a constitution for it to prevail is the fact that the deliberations of the Constitutional Convention of 1787 were essentially secret and that the secret was maintained until after the death of all the conventioneers (Madison was the last to go, in 1836). It is, as Rossiter (1965) remarks, "one of the intriguing facts of American constitutional history that the people in whose name and by whose power the great charter of 1787 was proclaimed should have had to wait more than half a century to learn how it came to be written" (p. 332).[11] In fact, of course, virtually all of these people had also died by then, so that those by whose power the government was established had little idea how it had been done.

Three centuries of talk about tacit consent and hypothetical agreement notwithstanding, many cannot plausibly be thought to have agreed to the U. S. Constitution on any meaningful account. What is it that they did not agree to that others did? Geoffrey Brennan and James Buchanan (1985, especially ch. 2) claim that a constitution is a social contract that creates rules to commit one's later selves and later generations to various specific things, for example, to the payment of agreed-upon taxes. Clearly, this is the wrong way to put the issue. A constitution does not commit the way a contract does. Rather, it merely raises the cost of trying to do things some other way through its creation of a coordination convention. Moreover, what it commits to is open to evolution and change in a far more expansive way than is the expectation of action under a contract. Signing a contract similarly raises the cost of then going against the agreement, but it does so in a relatively clearly specified, well understood, and predictable way. Typically, in a contract, enforcement and the costs of enforcement come from outside parties, not from the parties to the agreement.[12] And the scope of the sanction that can be applied to one who reneges from fulfillment of a contract is generally well defined.

A constitution involves a much broader gamble than this, as both the advocates and the opponents of the U. S. Constitution recognized (*Federalist* no. 85, final paragraph). One of the major debates of the time was *whether* the presidency would evolve into a virtual monarchy and the Senate into a virtual aristocracy. Even the president as created was "a bad edition of a Polish king," according to Jefferson (quoted in Rossiter, 1965, p. 284). It is only the hubris of retrospect that makes such debates seem misplaced.

Ironically, one of the more grievous issues in the Constitutional Convention in Philadelphia was the supposed conflict between the interests of small states and those of large states. Indeed, Madison wrote that this conflict "created more embarrassment, and a greater alarm for the issue of the Convention than all the rest put together."[13] Rhode Island, the last holdout, was one of the small states fearful of dominance by such states as Massachusetts, New York, Pennsylvania, and Virginia, as was Delaware, the first state to ratify the Constitution. There has not been any significant conflict between small and large states as such since the ratification of the Constitution. One might therefore conclude that either this widely perceived conflict was, in fact, of little or no concern or that the structure of the Constitution resolved the conflict. For example, one might suppose that the constitutional allotment of two Senators to each state, irrespective of population, and the preclusion of ever changing this provision by amendment secured the interests of the small states. It seems more plausible, however, that it was the very general fact of the Constitution that protected the interests of the small states. National union meant that head-to-head conflict between two states ceased to be a major issue, so that inequalities in resources, especially in population, ceased to matter for security. The successful creation of a national government was the best safeguard of the interests of small states. The gamble that the constitutionalists and their opponents thought they were taking on this issue was, in fact, evidently no gamble at all.

We speak of the intentions of parties to a contract and of the intendment of a law. Indeed, as in the secrecy of the debates of the 1787 conventioneers, Lon Fuller (1964/1969) argues that the *intentions* of the law makers are of little or no interest after the law has been in effect for a while (p. 86). Madison agreed, writing in 1821 that, "As a guide in expounding and applying the provisions of the Constitution, the debates and incidental decisions of the Convention can have no authoritative character."[14] The generations that have followed Madison and the other constitutionalists of 1787 have not rewritten much of the original text of the Constitution, but they have surely redefined many of its meanings. Jefferson presciently said of his own time that he feared tyranny not from the presidency but from the legislature, and that the day of presidential tyranny would come in the distant future as the nation grew and its government flourished.[15] Perhaps he was drawing on the analogy of Roman history rather than on keen insight. But either way, he clearly enough sensed that the document would not govern (elected officials would), and that the content of the document would be determined by the electorate and by the people elected to its offices—some of whom these days are blacks and women, contrary to the original intent and words of the conventioneers in 1787. "All new laws," Madison wrote in *Federalist* no. 37, "are considered as more or less obscure and equivocal, until their meaning be liquidated and ascertained by a series of particular discussions and adjudications." How much more must this be true of a new constitution.

The Incentives to Abide by a Constitution

A final crucial difference that shows that the constitutional problem is not generally a prisoner's dilemma is that, once we have settled on a constitutional arrangement, it is not likely to be in the interest of some of us then to try to renege on the arrangement. Our interests will be better served by living with the arrangement. And this is generally true not because we will be coerced to abide if we choose not to but because we generally cannot do better than to abide. To do better, we would have to carry enough others with us to set up an alternative, and that will typically be too costly to be worth the effort.

We abide by a contract, in large part, because there is the shadow of sanctions to be brought against us if we do not, and indeed, we often choose not to abide by a contract when the sanctions are likely to be less costly than fulfillment would be. The sources of the costs of defection in the constitutional and the contract cases are strategically very different. For the contract case, the ultimate source is sanctions from an external body; for the constitutional case, the ultimate source is the internal costs of collective action for recoordination or, in Caesar's word, *mutiny*.

The generally coordinative aspect of the Constitution may be lost in certain fundamentally conflictual contexts, as in that between some of the anti-Federalists and the Federalists and between slave-owning southerners and antislavery northerners in the mid-nineteenth century. An effect of successful coordination can be the creation of great power. Successful coordination of the United States under the Constitution has led to extraordinary power of a kind and a scale that one could not expect in North America without union. This was, of course, a major issue for the anti-Federalists. That their fears were justified, even though their hopes without union may not have been, is suggested by the use of the power that came from coordination to resolve a major conflict through military force in the Civil War. In this instance, the costs of Caesar's mutiny were initially overcome. The tilting of the Congress and the presidency toward a relatively mild antislavery position finally convinced many southerners that their benefits from further coordination with the North were outweighed by the potential costs of conflict. Hence, they saw the interaction as no longer essentially one of coordination but one of conflict, as though the differences in the 1 and 2 preferences in Game 3 far outweighed those between the 2 and 3 preferences. This made the interaction not more nearly like a prisoner's dilemma, but more nearly like a pure conflict. Many Federalists shared the fear that such conflicts could arise and would be settled forcibly, even tyrannously, but saw the balance in favor of coordination nevertheless.

Contract by Convention and a Constitution

Note that the establishment of a constitution, as in the United States in the two years 1787–1788, is a relatively singular act in the way that the establishment of a convention often is not. Much of its import is, of course, open to interpretation over time, but there is a certain fixedness in the creation itself. When we are involved in a repeated interaction of the form of the prisoner's dilemma, we commonly discover a convention for cooperation that resolves the instances of the interaction well rather than letting them all, one after the other, end in a failure of cooperation. It makes sense to call this process of the emergence of a convention a *contract by convention* because it resolves prisoner's dilemma interactions, as contracts do, but it does so by the happenstance creation of a convention, that is, by coordination on a pattern for resolving the interactions, rather than by a literal contract that is externally enforceable (Hardin, 1982b, chaps. 10–14). This process can be spontaneous and not regulated. Deliberate creation of a constitution is clearly different from this and yet, in some ways, strategically similar. It is neither a formal contract nor a spontaneous convention.

A major difference between contract by convention and the creation of a constitution is this: The latter is a very general move made very much in ignorance about the future range of choices that it will help to govern. It is, as noted above, a large gamble. A contract by convention grows piecemeal out of a very clear class of interactions. It is unlikely to gain anything approaching general scope, although it may serve as an example that will influence the way other, similar patterns of interaction get resolved. By contrast, a constitution is little more than a commitment to go on to resolve various interactions that involve some conflict as well as some that perhaps do not, that are virtually pure coordination problems in which little more than centralized signaling is required for successful coordination.

This is the truth in the common view that we can often agree on the procedure for deciding an issue even when we cannot so readily agree on what decision to make on the issue itself. This view is even more compelling for establishing a procedure well in advance of addressing any specific issues.[16] Indeed, one of the most compelling considerations in defense of a particular procedure is merely that it has been in use for a while already. This is often the persuasive force of, say, *Robert's Rules of Order*, which may be invoked to settle debate in some peculiar circumstance. People who strongly disagree on how to proceed typically desist from debate immediately when shown some arcane rule in this tedious book born of long experience.

In formally adopting a constitution, we can agree to coordinate one way rather than another. But we may still not have full control over what happens because we may steadily fall into doing what works instead of what we agreed to do. This is one of the beauties of conventions as devices for social regulation: they need not be constrained by mistaken ideal conceptions; they can accommodate a far wider input of understanding and experience than would be available to a particular group of constitution drafters such as that in the State House (now Independence Hall) in Philadelphia in 1787. The range of likely uncertainty in most contracts is therefore radically less than that in what one should expect from a new constitution. Taking a gamble on such uncertainty will seem worthwhile if we suppose that the gains from coordination that we might achieve will outweigh the stakes in the conflicts that we might face. One may sensibly read as the lesson of economic progress that this is commonly true.

So Why a Written Constitution?

It would be wrong to think of constitutional procedures as simply devices for conflict resolution. They are far more profoundly devices for enabling us to act. This is also true of the devices that make contracting useful. What I do when I contract is to bind myself in certain ways, but I bind myself in order to be free to accomplish certain things.[17] More generally, what it means to commit oneself to action a is to block oneself from taking actions $b, c, d, \ldots$ It is through constraint that we are enabled in our strategic interactions with others to achieve outcomes that require joint action. (Indeed, it is trivially true that even in order to act alone, one must forgo other actions.) The point of a constitution is to tie our hands in certain ways in order to discipline them to more productive use. This point was considered "paradoxical" by no less an authority than Publius in *Federalist* no. 63. There, it was argued that too quick a response of elected officials to changes of view among the electorate would lead to inefficient changes in policy. Therefore, legislators should not have too short terms in office because short terms, not to speak of constant referenda, would not be in the interest of the electorate.

This view is sometimes supposed to imply that Publius, in this case apparently Madison, distrusted the electorate and was somewhat antidemocratic. On the contrary, the view seems merely to reflect common sense. Even in one's individual decision-making, the power to make a decision and then to get on with life rather than to keep the issue permanently open is beneficial. Decision costs can be made so high as to leave no benefit from deciding. Hence, that constraints are enabling is not a logical paradox even though it may seem odd on first statement. Anyone who has come to understand the modern economist's view that virtually everything is a matter of trade-offs should no longer view it as odd or paradoxical; it is the heart of learned good sense. To put it negatively, the point of establishing a constitution and of creating particular institutions is to put obstacles in our way in order to force us to move along certain paths and not others. It enables us the more readily to organize ourselves for progress, rather than to dissipate our energies in random directions.

Suppose one grants the central claims in the previous sections above. Still, one may wonder: Why go to the trouble of creating a constitution if there were not something vaguely like a contractual purpose? Clearly, we can live by conventions for which no one has ever voted. Indeed, one might say that the English Constitution is only a constitution so-called: it is really a set of conventions that have developed over time and that now seemingly prevail,[18] just as the peculiar rules of the English road prevailed in England before they were made the law of the road. Moreover, the law of contracts and their enforcement preceded the U. S. Constitution through the conventions of common-law courts. So why a written constitution? Obviously, in order to hasten the establishment of relevant con- ventions and to direct them in certain ways rather than others by getting people to commit themselves immediately rather than bumbling through to a result, a result that might have been the rise of a tyrant by force.

But one cannot simply commit oneself and then have it stick. This is the whole point of Hobbes's ridiculing the possibility that a sovereign can be governed by the laws that the sovereign passes and enforces. One cannot bootstrap oneself into doing what, when the time comes, one would not want to do. Contract works not because I say today that I will pay tomorrow but because I submit today to an authority who can force me to pay tomorrow. The sovereign cannot submit to the sovereign in the same external sense but must bootstrap future action from present commitment. Neither can one's signature on a document or one's vote for it thereby generally make stick one's commitments under or to it.

Is Hobbes's argument somehow beside the point here? Yes. What one can do is commit oneself and then *arrange* to have it stick. That is what Ulysses did when he wished to hear the sirens and yet survive, and that is what we all do frequently. Indeed, many—most?—of us arrange to have some of our commitments stick in just the way the precitizens of the United States arranged to have their commitments stick. We set ourselves up in public to be made fools or worse if we do not follow through on our supposed commitments. If enough of the states had not ratified the Constitution two centuries ago, conventions and perhaps other formal arrangements would still have regulated their relations, or life in the states would have become nastier and shorter. Once enough of them did ratify, however, reneging became difficult—and increasingly difficult as time passed and the convention of coming under the governance of the Constitution became stronger. Eventually, the southern states discovered during the Civil War just how difficult reneging might be. Today, one need not "love it," but if one wishes to renege, one must "leave it" or become criminal.

Arguments about commitment in this context are often framed as though they were individual problems, as in the problem of Hobbes's sovereign, who supposedly cannot self-commit. Pascal wrote of devices that one could individually use to bring about one's commitment through a kind of psychological habituation. Ulysses used external, nonpsychological devices in having himself tied to the mast. The forms of commitment that are especially important for constitutional and even for conventional social choice, however, are those that derive from the difficulties of collective action and of recoordination from one coordination outcome to another. These are not merely problems of internal psychological discipline, and they can be powerfully effective in securing a system because they typically make the costs of changing the system radically higher than the costs of simply abiding by or even submitting to it. They may occasionally be overcome, as they were in 1787–1788 when the Constitution was substituted for the Articles of Confederation in the United States and as they have been in many revolutionary contexts. But they can be a grand block to taking certain roads rather than others. Moreover, they can apply to one whom Hobbes might have thought sovereign in his sense of being able to change one's mind at a whim and to have the power to back the whim (Hardin, 1985).

The Constitution of 1787 worked in the end because enough of the relevant people worked within its confines long enough to get it established in everyone's expectations that there was no point in not working within its confines. The agreement of certain people to it may have been important for those people to work within the Constitution, but agreement was not the only motivator. Many must have worked within the Constitution simply because it was the most useful thing for them to do in their own interests. They might as soon have continued to work within the Articles of Confederation and their respective state constitutions. There were frequent efforts to undermine the Constitution in minor ways from the very beginning, and such efforts seem likely to continue so long as some group has interests that could be furthered somewhat better by a slightly different constitutional order. There have even been what one could reasonably call unconstitutional efforts to strengthen the reach of that Constitution, as when Thomas Jefferson, avowedly one of the most democratic of the early constitutionalists, so democratic that he was ill at ease at the adoption of the Constitution, chose autocratically to overreach his authority as President to purchase the Louisiana Territory. No group of serious political consequence today appears to think its interests better served by a radical overthrow of the order that has grown out of the Constitution of 1787, although the southern states after the election of 1860 and various other groups at other times have wanted and even attempted such an overthrow, and there may be others to come.

One could easily give a normative justification or criticism of the Constitution or of other constitutions from the perspective of various moral theories. One cannot sensibly give such a justification from the supposed agreement of people to such a constitutional order, however, without grossly simplifying away the problems of coordination and collective action that make for an acquiescence that cannot meaningfully be called agreement. That fact does not make the Constitution bad, but neither would agreement make it good. For most of us in the United States most of the time, the order that the Constitution brings about is a part of the necessity of the world in which we live. Benjamin Franklin remarked that "Our Constitution is in actual operation; everything appears to promise that it will last; but in this world nothing is certain but death and taxes."[19] It has since lasted two centuries, and to some extent, that fact makes it seem virtually certain in our lives. But the more impressive implication of that survival is its role in explaining our incentives under the Constitution. The long survival of the Constitution gives force to the expectations we have that it will continue to survive, and the strength of those expectations is perhaps the chief of the reasons that it probably will continue to survive. Hence, it generally makes sense for us individually to coordinate on the order that the Constitution has helped to bring about. This suggests the strategic basis for the conservative dogma that what is is good, at least sometimes and to some extent (Hardin, 1987).

It is the failure to grasp the self-enforcing quality of a successful constitution that makes the vision of the constitution of government as a contract—as though our fundamental problem were to overcome a prisoner's dilemma—so exasperating to those who hold to that vision. Because it is not a contract but a convention, a constitution does not depend for its enforcement on external sanctions or bootstrapping commitments founded in nothing but supposed or hypothetical agreement. Establishing a constitution is a massive act of coordination that creates a convention that depends for its maintenance on its self-generating incentives and expectations. Given that it is a mystery how contracting could work to resolve our constitutional problem, we should be glad that the problem is such that we have no need of a social contract.

Acknowledgments. I am grateful to many colleagues for their comments on an earlier draft of this paper, especially to Stephen Elkin, Bernard Grofman, Edwin T. Haefele, Don Herzog, Jane Mansbridge, Jack Nagel, and Donald Wittman, and to participants at a conference of the Committee on the Foundations of Democratic Government at the University of Pennsylvania.

Notes

1. One might wish to argue, as some contractarian moral theorists do, that we are bound by those morals that we rationally would assent to. See, for example, David Gauthier (1986).
2. References to *The Federalist Papers* will be by number in the text. Any standard edition should suffice for reference.
3. Caesar, no. 2, 17 October 1787, in Kurland and Lerner (1987), Vol. 1, pp. 60–61.
4. One should beware of generalization from two-person games to the interactions of whole societies or even larger groups. I will generally be concerned with interactions between large groups, so that the two-person analogy should not be misleading.
5. He declared as much at the Convention on 18 June 1787 (Kurland and Lerner, Vol. 1, pp. 255–256).
6. The Annapolis Convention of September 1786 was called by several states to consider ways to regulate trade and commerce more harmoniously. Attended by too few states, the convention merely recommended a further convention to consider the broader range of problems with the Articles of Confederation (Kurland and Lerner, Vol. 1, pp. 185–187; also see accompanying documents, chapter 6 in ibid.) It may be unfair to note that two of the twelve commissioners in Annapolis were Hamilton and Madison and unfairer still to recall Madison's claim that the Commerce Clause of the new Constitution was really the only new power that that document gave to the new government (*Federalist* no. 45).

7. See essays by Brutus and Cato, in Kurland and Lerner, Vol. 1, pp. 124–127. Hamilton goes far toward demolishing their claims in *Federalist* no. 9, and Madison addresses them further in *Federalist* nos. 10 and 63, and, I think less persuasively, in the famous number 51.

8. George Washington, Letter to Henry Knox, 3 February 1787, in Kurland and Lerner, Vol. 1, p. 188.

9. To this extent, James Wilson's claim before the Pennsylvania ratifying convention that the drafters of the Constitution "exercised no power at all" is surely false (speech excerpted in Kurland and Lerner, Vol. 1, p. 202). They forced the selection of a particular constitutional order to stand as the sole effective alternative to Hamilton's dismemberment. In the concluding number of *The Federalist Papers*, no. 85, Hamilton observed, with eminent plausibility, that the prospect of "assembling a new convention, under circumstances in any degree so favorable to a happy issue, as those in which the late convention met, deliberated, and concluded" was nil.

10. New York, indeed, elected to its state convention a majority of delegates opposed to ratification. Hamilton privately threatened that New York City would secede from the state if the state refused to join the union. Perhaps this threat turned the convention, as Rossiter supposes, by convincing enough of the conventioneers of the opposite of their belief that there would be no union without New York, namely, that there would be no New York without union (Rossiter, 1965, p. 294). For a summary record of the ratification, see Michael Kammen (1986, pp. xxviii–xxix). For a more discursive account, see Chapter 14 of Rossiter (1965). Of the eleven states that ratified in time to participate in the formation of the new government, Rossiter supposes that at least four could easily have been lost, thereby killing the Constitution, but for the shrewdness of the Federalist advocates (Rossiter, 1965, p. 296) and some accidents of timing.

11. Madison's extensive notes on the convention were first published in 1840. Quite fragmentary bits from other participants had appeared earlier.

12. Those who deal with each other repeatedly or who depend on their reputations may successfully enforce their own agreements by contract by convention. See further below, "Contract by Convention and a Constitution."

13. James Madison, Letter to Thomas Jefferson, 24 October 1787, in Kurland and Lerner, Vol. 1, p. 647.

14. James Madison, Letter to Thomas Ritchie, 15 September 1821, in Kurland and Lerner, Vol. 1, p. 74.

15. Thomas Jefferson, Letter to James Madison, 15 March 1789, in Kurland and Lerner, Vol. 1, p. 479.

16. Brennan and Buchanan say that "The scope for potential agreement on rules is *necessarily* wider than that for agreement on outcomes within specified rules" (1985, p. 29, italics added).

17. As Thomas Schelling notes, it is by constraining oneself to be subject to suit under various contingenices of one's own actions that one can enter beneficial contracts (1960, p. 43).

18. This is, of course, an old thesis. For a recent account of the state of the conventions that govern England, see Geoffrey Marshall (1984). A reading of Marshall should suggest just how much of the American and any other constitutional system is similarly a matter of convention.

19. Benjamin Franklin, Letter to Jean Baptiste Le Roy, November 13, 1789 (in Smyth, 1907, pp. 68–69).

Part III

Power: Checks and Balances

Introduction

There are two standard power indices, that of Shapley and Shubik (1954) and that of Banzhaf (1965; see also, Coleman, 1971). Each makes similar assumptions about the equiprobability of certain coalitions: one assumes all coalitional permutations to be equiprobable, and the other assumes all coalitional combinations to be equiprobable. Calculations performed by Brams involving the Banzhaf index support the assertion that the House will be advantaged relative to the Senate.[1] Calculations using the Shapley–Shubik index lead to the opposite conclusion, but Brams argues that the coalition formation model underlying this index seems less plausible than the coalition-disintegration model underlying Banzhaf. Moreover, Brams shows that empirical evidence confirms the superiority of the House "in getting bills, veto override attempts, and amendments that it initiates accepted more frequently by the Senate than vice versa," thus suggesting that of the two indices, in the legislative context, Banzhaf comes closer to corresponding to other indices of relative influence. Brams also explores the power of the President vis-à-vis Congress using the Banzhaf measure.

Of course, as Brams is careful to point out, the analysis he offers is only preliminary. It is "a first attempt to wed a rigorous formal analysis of . . . power and empirical evidence on the effectiveness of actors in getting their way." Future work might well make use of power calculations based on more realistic coalitional probabilities, for example, those which recognize the existence of partisanship and ideology and are conditioned by the existence of national electoral tides which affect the partisan and ideological makeup of both chambers as well as the presidency.

Chamberlin's essay provides a nice complement to that of Brams. It expands the framework of analysis to include the Supreme Court as well as Congress and the President. In his simplified model of the federal government, passage of legislation "requires the formation of one of the following coalitions:

1. The President and at least a simple majority of the other three bodies, or
2. At least a two-thirds majority of both houses of Congress and a simple majority of the Supreme Court."

Using the Banzhaf index, Chamberlin's conclusion is that "the Supreme Court is somewhat more powerful than the President but considerably less powerful than either house of Congress." However, Chamberlin is careful to distinguish between the power of the Constitution and the power of the Supreme Court. As he points out, "the constitution is a powerful constraint on the actions of all branches of government, and it was intended to be." Moreover, Supreme Court Justices are constrained by precedent. Thus, Chamberlin suggests, "in much of the everyday legislative process," the Supreme Court "is much less powerful" than the Banzhaf analysis would suggest.

In chapter 10, Schwartz brings together the themes of efficiency, power, and principal-agent representation in looking at the mechanisms by which Congress is able to impose its will on the federal bureaucracy. Schwartz is concerned to rebut the claim that Congress, in delegating sweeping authority to administrative agencies, "has neglected its oversight responsibility, allowing administrative excesses to go unchecked." His analysis draws upon the principles of analysis found in *The Federalist Papers*, most importantly the nature of institutional incentives for both members of Congress and bureaucrats.

Schwartz finds delegation efficient for members of Congress because it reduces their decision-making load and permits those with expertise and information to draft the detailed rules and administer them. Moreover, Congress is able to control the behavior of bureaucrats through its power of the purse and ultimate oversight—which provide the necessary incentives to bureaucratic agents to behave as their principal (Congress or, perhaps more precisely, particular congressional committees) would have them behave. Schwartz, following up the analysis of McCubbins and Schwartz (1984), also shows that the most efficient type of congressional oversight is by means of what he and McCubbins call "fire-alarms," rather than by continuous monitoring (a type of oversight, they refer to as "police-patrols"): "Under a fire-alarm policy, a member of Congress does not address concrete violations unless someone has complained about them, in which case he or she can receive credit for intervening, so a unit of time spent on oversight is likely to yield more benefit for a member of Congress under a fire-alarm policy than under police-patrol policy."

Petracca's critique of the application of formal models of power is based on a concern that the abstract analysis of decisive votes misses completely the real (and quite complex) institutional structure. For example, Petracca calls attention to more subtle checks on the power of the courts, such as congressional control of jurisdictional assignments and the power of appointment. Also, the focus on formal measures of power misses the fact that influence may derive from control of resources external to the institutional setting, as well as from an ability to persuade.

Bernard Grofman

Notes

1. For a more complete description of the similarities and differences between these two power indices see Straffin (1977). For a discussion of power indices based on assumptions other than equiprobability see Wittman (1976) and Owen and Grofman (1984).

CHAPTER EIGHT

Are the Two Houses of Congress Really Coequal?

Steven J. Brams

In *Federalist* nos. 63 and 58, Madison argued that the House and Senate would be "co-equal branches" (p. 388), but that the House would have "no small advantage" (p. 358);[1] Hamilton echoed this sentiment in no. 66. In this chapter, I shall show that the apparent premonitions of Madison and Hamilton about the greater power of the House are borne out by the application of the Banzhaf voting-power index to the federal system comprising the House, the Senate, and the President in the passage of ordinary legislation, and the House and Senate in the proposal of constitutional amendments.

This result is not just theoretical. Empirical data confirm the predominance of the House in getting bills, veto override attempts, and amendments that it initiates accepted more frequently by the Senate than vice versa. A revised Banzhaf power calculation for the President suggests that he is *primus inter pares*, which is consistent with the overall success of Presidents in having their vetoes sustained. Alternative game-theoretic formulations of voting power are considered, and suggestions are offered for extending and refining the empirical analysis.

Federalist Premonitions and Modern Political Analysis

In *Federalist* no. 63, Madison, discussing the possible spread of corruption from the Senate to the House of Representatives, referred to the House as that "co-equal [with the Senate] branch of the government" (p. 388). In no. 58, Madison asked, rhetorically, "Would not the one [house] be as likely to yield as the other?" (p. 359). But also in no. 58, Madison averred that

> the House, composed of the greater number of members, when supported by the more powerful States, and speaking the known and determined sense of the majority of the people, will have no small advantage in a question on the comparative firmness of the two houses. (p. 358)

Under certain conditions, then, the House may have the upper hand. In no. 66, Hamilton agreed with the latter judgment:

> The most *popular* branch of every government partaking of the republican genius, by being the general favorite of the people, will be as generally a full match, if not an overmatch, for every other member of government. (p. 403; italics in original)

Earlier in no. 66, Hamilton had noted that the "prerogatives" of the Senate—ratification of appointments and treaties and the trying of government officials impeached by the House—may make it seem that there is an "undue accumulation of power in that body [Senate] . . . that will give a decided predominancy to senatorial influence" (pp. 402–403). However, he countered this claim with an observation as astute as any one might find in a contemporary treatise on the conceptualization and measurement of power:

> To an objection so little precise in itself it is not easy to find a very precise answer. Where is the measure or criterion to which we can appeal for estimating what will give the Senate too much, too little, or barely the proper degree of influence? Will it not be more safe, as well as more simple, to dismiss such vague and uncertain calculations, to examine each power by itself, and to decide, on general principles, where it may be deposited with most advantage and least inconvenience? (p. 403)

In this and a subsequent passage, Hamilton had his finger on what I believe to be the central philosophical and methodological issue in constitution writing: By what "general principles" can we both assess power and determine how to apportion it among the different branches or institutions of government to avoid "the hypothetical danger of . . . too great weight" (p. 403) being invested in any branch—specifically, in this instance, in either the House or the Senate?

The purpose of this chapter will be to specify formally, and to test empirically, the views of Madison and Hamilton that the two houses of Congress are coequal or, if there is a bias, that it is one that favors the House. Indeed, in no. 66, Hamilton felt bold enough to advance a hypothesis: "It would not perhaps be rash to predict, that as a mean influence it [the House] will be found to outweigh all the peculiar attributes [i.e., the heretofore mentioned prerogatives] of the Senate" (p. 404).

Two hundred years after this prophecy, a combination of formal analysis and empirical evidence lends support to the Madison–Hamilton hypothesis. Formally, as I shall show, a game-theoretic concept of voting power suggests that the House may be nearly twice as influential as the Senate in the passage of ordinary legislation (by simple majorities of both houses plus the concurrence of the President) and the override of presidential vetoes (by two-thirds majorities of both houses). In addition, the House is still more influential in the proposal of constitutional amendments (by two-thirds majorities of both houses). Empirically, the predominant influence of the House is confirmed by its ability to get ordinary bills, veto overrides, and amendments that it *originates* affirmed by the Senate more frequently than the Senate is able to get the House to accede to its prior judgment on each of these three measures of congressional activity.

I want to emphasize that I did not set out to "prove" that Madison and Hamilton were right, or at least extraordinarily prescient, in foreseeing the possible predominance of the House. In fact, the formal and empirical analyses of this paper were carried out before *The Federalist Papers* were examined for the views of their authors on the distribution of legislative power under the bicameral system they helped to create. Also, though I consider the formal analysis and the empirical data favoring the House quite compelling, they are, even in tandem, not conclusive.

For one thing, an alternative notion of formal voting power reverses the power ranking of the two houses. For another, the aggregate data analyzed herein mix, even in the three different categories of legislative activity considered, vastly different kinds of bills and amendments. More refined empirical analysis, especially, is called for to establish precisely the conditions under which the House (or perhaps the Senate on occasion) tends to prevail over the other body.

I shall not undertake such a detailed analysis here, which is well beyond the scope of this chapter. Instead, I shall describe and apply one plausible concept of formal voting power to the decision rules of the federal system (and briefly consider alternative formulations), compare the theoretical power values with aggregate data on the relative success of each house in getting its collective judgment accepted by the other house, comment on the role of the President in the federal system, and conclude with some remarks on the contributions of the *Federalist* authors.

Banzhaf Voting Power

We commonly attribute "influence" or "power" to actors who can control outcomes, although other definitions of influence and power stress the effect that actors can have on each other.[2] For the purpose of defining the power of actors in voting situations, however, an outcome-oriented measure is preferable to an actor-oriented measure. In large voting bodies (or even in the electorate, where the influence of each person on every other person is generally small and often nonexistent), an actor-oriented measure would suggest that few, if any, actors have significant power. In fact, if each person has one vote, each person would have an equal chance to influence the outcome, which seems a more reasonable way to view power in voting situations.

This view is not compatible with defining the voting power of an actor as being proportional to the number of votes he or she casts, because votes per se may have no bearing on outcomes. For example, in a three-member weighted voting body $\{a,b,c\}$, where a has 4 votes, b 2 votes, and c 1 vote, members b and c are powerless if the decision rule is a simple majority (4 out of 7). Since the fact that members b and c together control $3/7$ of the votes is irrelevant to the selection of outcomes by this committee, call these members *dummies*. Member a is a *dictator*, on the other hand, by virtue of having enough votes alone to determine the outcome.

A weighted voting body can have only one dictator, whose existence renders all other members dummies, but there may be dummies and no dictator. For example, if a has 5 votes, b 5 votes, and c 2 votes, and the decision rule is a two-thirds majority (8 out of 12), member c is a dummy: c's addition to or absence from the winning coalition of $\{a,b\}$, comprising 10 votes by itself, has no effect on the outcome. Moreover, if c formed a coalition with either a or b, the pair would still be 1 vote short of the required 8 votes, so c in this case, too, would have no effect on the outcome.

It is worth noting in this example that both a and b have a *veto*: each is necessary, but neither is sufficient by itself, to form a winning coalition. Like the President and both houses of Congress in the passage of ordinary legislation, each must give its approval for action to be taken. By contrast, in the federal system, if the President vetoes a bill passed by both houses, it is not an absolute veto: two-thirds majorities of both houses can override this veto, rendering the President's veto ineffective and instead giving these qualified majorities in each house a kind of ultimate veto. Yet, because the Supreme Court can overturn any legislation enacted by Congress, there are limits on what even both houses of Congress can accomplish by themselves. And, of course, a ruling by the Supreme Court can be overturned by a constitutional amendment.

As a measure of voting power, Banzhaf (1965) defined the power of a member of a voting body as being equal to the number of its critical defections in minimal winning coalitions (MWCs) as a proportion of the total number of critical defections of all members combined. A *critical defection* is one that transforms an MWC into a losing coalition; an *MWC* is a winning coalition in which at least one member's defection is critical, that is, can render it losing. Thus, in the first example, dictator a is the only MWC. Its defection is obviously critical, and since this is the only critical defection, a has voting power of 1. In the second example, $\{a,b\}$ is the only MWC. Because a and b have one critical defection each, making the total number of critical defections two, each has voting power of ½, which I indicate by voting power vector $(\frac{1}{2},\frac{1}{2},0)$ for $\{a,b,c\}$.

These calculations are trivial but do illustrate basic concepts that help one bracket the minimal (dummy) and maximal (dictator) amounts of power that actors can possess in voting situations. A vetoer falls in between these extremes and may additionally, like the President, have its veto circumscribed.

To facilitate the more complex calculations for Congress and the President that take account of such subtleties, some notation from combinatorial mathematics is useful (see Appendix). With this notation, I shall illustrate the voting power for a hypothetical voting body of four members, just slightly larger than the two bodies just analyzed. This will set the stage for comparing the voting power of the two houses of Congress in different legislative activities.

Consider a voting body of four members whose five votes are distributed $\{1,1,1,2\}$. If the decision rule is simple majority (3 out of 5), each of the 1-vote members will cast a critical (third) vote—indicated by parentheses—when joined by the two other 1-vote members (shown to its left in the sequence below),

$$1\ 1\ (1)\ 2; \qquad \tbinom{2}{2} = 1 \text{ combination,}$$

or when joined by the 2-vote member,

$$2\ (1)\ 1\ 1; \qquad \tbinom{1}{1} = 1 \text{ combination.}$$

In the former sequence, there is exactly one way of choosing the two (out of two) noncritical 1-vote members to form an MWC with the critical 1-vote member (in parentheses); likewise, in the latter sequence, there is exactly one way of choosing the one (out of one) 2-vote member to form an MWC with the critical 1-vote member. In sum, there are two combinations in which *each* of the three one-vote members is critical: its defection would cause the above MWCs, comprising the critical member and those to its left, to be losing.

The 2-vote member will be critical in two sequences,

$$1 \ (2) \ 1 \ 1; \ \binom{3}{1} = 3 \text{ combinations,}$$
$$1 \ 1 \ (2) \ 1; \ \binom{3}{2} = 3 \text{ combinations,}$$

wherein it casts a critical (third, or third and fourth) vote. In the former sequence, there are three possible ways of choosing one of the three 1-vote members to form an MWC with the critical 2-vote member; likewise, in the latter sequence, there are three possible ways of choosing any two of the three 1-vote members to form an MWC with the 2-vote member—or, equivalently, excluding any of the three 1-vote members [shown to the right of (2)] from this MWC. In sum, there are six combinations in which the 2-vote member is critical.

It is worth pointing out that in the second sequence for the 2-vote member, each of the two 1-vote members who form an MWC with it are not critical: neither's defection would cause the three combinations that this sequences comprises to become losing. This example illustrates that an MWC may be *minimal* winning with respect to the defection of one but not other members—in this case, the 2-vote member but not the 1-vote members. Generally speaking, larger members (with more votes), mirroring their greater voting power, will be critical in MWCs in which smaller members are not.

In the present example, there are three 1-vote members critical in two combinations each and one 2-vote member critical in six combinations. Altogether, there are twelve critical defections that the members may cast, with the proportions of critical defections of $\{1,1,1,2\}$ giving voting power vector $(\frac{1}{6},\frac{1}{6},\frac{1}{6},\frac{1}{2})$. Thus, the 2-vote member has Banzhaf power equal to that of the other three members combined. But note that he or she does not have a veto, because there is one combination (the first for the 1-vote members) in which he or she is never critical, establishing that his or her presence is not necessary in every MWC.

In the next section, I shall be analyzing not weighted voting bodies but institutions connected by various decision rules. These rules may have a substantial impact on voting power. As a case in point, suppose that the three 1-vote members in the voting body {1,1,1,2} form a caucus—or constitute a committee or even a separate voting body—that reaches its decisions on how to cast its 3 votes according to majority rule (2 out of 3). Patently, this 3-vote subset of members would reduce the 2-vote member in the larger body (with a decision rule of 3 out of 5) from the weightiest member with half the voting power to a dummy, for the 3 votes of the MWC (1,1,1) are always decisive in the larger body. Each member of this MWC, because all have the same weight, would have $\frac{1}{3}$ of the voting power.

In the next section, I shall turn to the question of whether the House and the Senate are coequal. The simple answer to this question is that they are, for the House and Senate *as voting bodies*—or at least, a simple majorities of their members—each have the same veto power over legislation.

This answer, however, glosses over the fact that it is not the voting bodies themselves that are critical in the passage of legislation but the members that compose them. Whether the voting power of the members of the House and the Senate can be simply summed will be addressed shortly. First, though, I shall indicate how the voting power of members of each house can be calculated for different kinds of legislative activity. In each case, empirical data on the success of each house in getting its collective will accepted by the other house will be compared with the Banzhaf power values.

Passage of Ordinary Legislation

The President, the Senate, and the House are interconnected by constitutional decision rules that allow for the enactment of bills if supported by at least a simple majority of Senators, a simple majority of Representatives, and the President, or by at least a two-thirds majorities in both the Senate and the House without the support of the President (i.e., in order to override a presidential veto). (For simplicity, I shall not include in the subsequent analysis the role of the Vice-President in breaking Senate ties.)

To be sure, this conceptualization ignores the fact that a majority of the Supreme Court can, in effect, veto a law by declaring it unconstitutional, and that Congress (and the states) have the countervailing power to amend the Constitution and thereby to nullify Supreme Court rulings. Nevertheless, although other actors may affect the outcome, it seems useful to abstract those relationships among that set of actors having the most immediate impact on the enactment of bills into laws. Consider next the combinations, in which the defection of the President, a Senator, or a Representative is critical.

1. *President.* For the President's defection from an MWC to be critical, the MWC must include the President, at least a simple majority of Senators, and at least a simple but less than a two-thirds majority of Representatives (i.e., between 218 and 289)—in order that the President can prevent the override of a presidential veto in the House—which can occur in the following number of ways:

$$\binom{1}{1} \left[\binom{100}{51} + \binom{100}{52} + \ldots + \binom{100}{100} \right] \left[\binom{435}{218} + \binom{435}{219} + \ldots + \binom{435}{289} \right]$$

or it must include the President, at least a two-thirds majority of Representatives (simple majorities were counted in the previous calculation), and at least a simple but less than a two-thirds majority of Senators (i.e., between 51 and 66)—in order that the President can prevent the override of a presidential veto in the Senate—which can occur in the following number of ways:

$$\binom{1}{1} \left[\binom{435}{291} + \binom{435}{292} + \ldots + \binom{435}{435} \right] \left[\binom{100}{51} + \binom{100}{52} + \ldots + \binom{100}{66} \right]$$

2. *Senator.* For a Senator's defection to be critical, a MWC must include exactly 50 of the 99 *other* Senators (so that his or her defection would kill action by the Senate), the President, and at least a simple majority of the House, which can occur in the following number of ways:

$$\binom{99}{50} \binom{1}{1} \left[\binom{435}{218} + \binom{435}{219} + \ldots + \binom{435}{435} \right]$$

or it must include exactly 66 of the 99 *other* Senators (so that his or her defection would kill action by the Senate in an override attempt), no President, and at least a two-thirds majority of the House, which can occur in the following number of ways:

$$\binom{99}{66} \binom{1}{0} \left[\binom{435}{290} + \binom{435}{291} + \ldots + \binom{435}{435} \right]$$

3. *Representative.* For a Representative's defection to be critical, an MWC must include exactly 217 of the 434 *other* Representatives (so that his or her defection would kill action by the House), the President, and at least a simple majority of the Senate, which can occur in the following number of ways:

$$\binom{434}{217} \binom{1}{1} \left[\binom{100}{51} + \binom{100}{52} + \ldots + \binom{100}{100} \right]$$

or it must include exactly 289 of the 434 *other* Representatives (so that his or her defection would kill action by the House in an override attempt), no President, and at least a two-thirds majority of the Senate, which can occur in the following number of ways:

$$\binom{434}{289} \binom{1}{0} \left[\binom{100}{67} + \binom{100}{68} + \ldots + \binom{100}{100} \right]$$

Note that in counting combinations in which a Senator or a Representative is critical in an override attempt, I implicitly assumed that the way he or she voted initially (i.e., in the nonoverride vote) does not change. Indeed, for the purposes of this calculation, there is only one vote: a Senate or a House member's power accrues from being critical in his or her house either when the President assents or when the President dissents (i.e., casts a veto)—but not both. For if a Senator or a Representative could be critical in both a simple majority on the first vote and a two-thirds majority on the override attempt, this would imply that at least $\frac{2}{3} - \frac{1}{2} = \frac{1}{6}$ of the members of his or her house changed their votes in favor of passage in the override attempt. Although it is conceivable that this change could occur, it is predicated on the assumption that a President can simultaneously sign a bill (making a member of a simple majority in one house critical) and veto a bill (making a member of a two-thirds majority in one house critical), which is obviously impossible. In counting critical defections, therefore, I assume, in effect, that all actors vote the same way on both the original bill and, if this fails, an override attempt, which is equivalent to assuming that only one vote is taken.

The Banzhaf power of a President, based on critical defections, is unambiguous, but what meaning can be attached to the power of the Senate and House as a whole? I contend that it is reasonable to conceptualize their power as proportional to the sum of the numbers of critical defections of *all* their individual members—or majorities of their members, which gives essentially the same proportions vis-à-vis each other (but not the President, as I shall show later). This is equivalent to saying that, considering all MWCs in which the President, a Senator, or a Representative is critical, the Senate and House's formal voting power is proportional to the total number of ways their respective members can, by defecting from the MWCs, render them losing.

These numbers for each house, as Dubey and Shapley (1979, pp. 102–104) demonstrated, are proportional to the expected number of critical members in each house, based on a different normalization of the Banzhaf index. Presumably, the greater the expected number of members who are critical in a house, the greater its power in the federal system.

My contention that the power of an entity like the Senate or the House resides ultimately in its members is, of course, not the only way to view the federal system. An alternative view is that these

TABLE 8.1 Banzhaf Voting Power for Passage of
Ordinary Legislation

Actor	Individual	Collectivity
President	0.03803	0.03803
Senator/Senate	0.00329	0.32881
Representative/House	0.00146	0.63316

entities can be thought of as blocs, but this view violates much that we know about the behavior of the Senate and House: they are not monoliths. Thus, to treat the federal system under consideration as a three-actor voting body, $\{P,S,H\}$, wherein each actor has a veto and consequently the same power, seems too simple.

To be sure, conceptualizing the voting power of the Senate and the House as the sum of the voting power of their members needs to be tested against some empirical reality. Consider the figures of Banzhaf voting power for individual members and the entire voting bodies, based on the previous calculations, that are shown in Table 8.1. Putting aside the case of the President for now, a Senator is more than twice as powerful as a Representative (0.0033 versus 0.0015), but because there are more than four times as many Representatives as Senators, the House as an entity is nearly twice as powerful as the Senate (0.63 versus 0.33).

To try to test which house might, in fact, be the more powerful, I hypothesized that the more powerful house would be more success-ful in getting bills which it first passed accepted by the other house. Beginning with the Eightieth Congress (1947–1948)—when data on bills passing one house but not the other were first compiled—and running through the First Session of the Ninety-ninth Congress (1985), the Senate concurred with 76.4% of the 18,664 bills introduced and first passed in the House, but the House concurred with only 60.7% of the 12,658 bills introduced and first passed in the Senate.[3] These figures sustain the hypothesis that the House is more effective in getting its way than the Senate, a finding that tends to support qualitatively, if not quantitatively, the Banzhaf attribution of greater power to the House. (The Table 8.1 power values change very slightly when, before 1959, there were 48 states.)

Veto data provide further support for this ranking. There were (through 1984) 105 instances in which one house voted by a two-thirds or greater majority to override a presidential veto one day or more before the other house acted.[4] In these cases of conflict between the President and one house, I hypothesized that the house which, after voting to override a presidential veto, more frequently gains the subsequent support of the other house is the more powerful institution.

In fact, the Senate concurred with the override judgment of the House in 66.2% of the 65 cases in which the House acted first, whereas the House concurred with the override judgment of the Senate in only 45.0% of the 40 cases in which the Senate acted first. Thus, as previously, the judgment of the House is more often decisive in the Senate than vice versa, a finding lending further empirical support to the Banzhaf ranking.

Proposal of Constitutional Amendments and the Power of the President

The Constitution prescribes that at least two-thirds majorities of both the Senate and the House can propose constitutional amendments (or the legislatures of two-thirds of the states can call a convention to propose constitutional amendments, a condition which has never occurred), which then require the ratification of three-quarters of the state legislatures (or of state conventions called to act upon a proposed amendment, a condition which has occurred only once). What is the power of individual Senators and Representatives, and the Senate and House as a whole, in the proposal of constitutional amendments?

For a Senator's defection from an MWC to be critical, the MWC must include exactly 66 of the 99 other Senators and at least a two-thirds majority of the 435 Representatives (i.e., 290), which can occur in the following number of ways:

$$\binom{99}{66} \left[\binom{435}{290} + \binom{435}{291} + \ldots + \binom{435}{435} \right]$$

For a Representative's defection from an MWC to be critical, the MWC must include exactly 289 of the 434 other Representatives and at least a two-thirds majority of the 100 Senators (i.e., 67), which can occur in the following number of ways:

$$\binom{434}{289} \left[\binom{100}{67} + \binom{100}{68} + \ldots + \binom{100}{100} \right]$$

The Banzhaf values for individual Senators and Representatives, and for the Senate and House as a whole, are shown in Table 8.2. With the requirement of two-thirds majorities, the power of individual Senators and Representatives are almost on a par, making the House—more than four times as large an institution as the Senate—more than four times as powerful.

TABLE 8.2. Banzhaf Voting Power for Proposal of Constitutional
Amendments

Actor	Individual	Collectivity
Senate/Senator	0.00195	0.19529
House Representative	0.00185	0.80471

Following the line of reasoning offered earlier, I hypothesized that the power of a house is a function of the proportion of times its initial action in proposing a constitutional amendment by at least a two-thirds majority is subsequently affirmed by at least a two-thirds majority of the second house. Although there have been over 6,000 proposals to amend the Constitution that have been introduced in Congress since 1788,[5] almost all have died in committee. Of those that saw floor action, only 31 were ultimately adopted by at least two-thirds majorities in both houses of Congress, and 26 of these were subsequently ratified by the states.

Information on action taken by Congress on all proposals to amend the Constitution is available for the period from December 6, 1926, to January 3, 1963. Of the 2,340 proposed amendments introduced in Congress during this period, 4 received the initial support of at least a two-thirds majority in the House, and 8 received the initial support of at least a two-thirds majority in the Senate.[6] Four additional amendments have been proposed by both houses (one passed just one house) since 1964, two of which have been ratified. These two were passed initially by the Senate, whereas of the two not ratified, one was passed initially by the House and the other by the Senate.

Altogether, the Senate affirmed its support of five of the six amendments (83%) initially proposed by the House; the House affirmed its support of three of the eleven amendments (27%) initially proposed by the Senate. Once again, not only does the House appear to be the more powerful institution but, in this case, by a magnitude that reflects its substantially greater Banzhaf value.

So far, I have focused on the relative power of the House and the Senate—and have ignored the President—in two different legislative areas: the passage of ordinary legislation (with and without a presidential veto) and the proposal of constitutional amendments. Clearly, the legislative data support the Banzhaf finding that the House is the more powerful institution. Are there any data that would allow one to assess the relative power of the President vis-à-vis Congress?

Consider the Banzhaf value of 0.04 for the President (Table 8.1), which seems inordinately low, even for "weak" Presidents.[7] On the other hand, if one sums the power values of simple majorities of Senators (51) and Representatives (218)—on the presumption that these minimal majorities are sufficient to control the outcomes in their respective bodies—and assumes that the remaining power in the federal system accrues to the President, then the collective Banzhaf values become President, 0.515; House, 0.317; and Senate, 0.168. (The President would have still greater power—about 67%—if the President were presumed to have power approximately equal to that of the two-thirds majorities of Congress necessary to overturn a presidential veto.)

Now the President, with more than half the power by the first calculation and two-thirds by the second, is the dominant actor in the system—as seems often to be the case, especially when the President is reputedly "strong." The House and the Senate maintain their same relative standing, so these new calculations do not contradict the earlier analysis supporting the greater power of the House over the Senate: the revised power values of these houses are in the same ratio as in Table 8.1.

Some empirical data, in the vein of the data previously assayed, bear on the power of the President in the federal constellation. Excluding "pocket vetoes" (41.3% of all presidential vetoes that have been cast)—whereby a President, by taking no action, prevents the passage of a bill if Congress adjourns within ten days after the bill is sent to the President—which cannot be overridden, the forty Presidents from George Washington (1789–1797) to Ronald Reagan (through 1986) have cast a total of 1,406 vetoes. Only 98, or 7.0%, have been overridden by Congress in this almost two-hundred-year span of time, suggesting that Congress's constitutional authority has not increased its effective power—at least to override vetoes—very significantly (Roberts, 1986).

True, one or both houses of Congress made the attempt to override only 256, or 18.3%, of all the nonpocket vetoes cast by Presidents through 1984 (1,398). Of these, Congress was successful in overriding 40.6%. Moreover, while even this is not a fantastic success rating, it would appear that the bills on which an attempt was made to override a presidential veto were among the most important passed by Congress.[8]

Overall, however, it seems fair to say that Congress's constitutional authority to override presidential vetoes has not dramatically augmented its influence over the passage of legislation. In fact, almost half of all Presidents (nineteen) never had a veto overturned, including John F. Kennedy (1960–1963) and Lyndon B. Johnson (1963–1969).

In short, Presidents cast a large shadow, but a quantitative comparison with Congress is difficult to justify, since the acceptance of each's judgment by the other does not have the symmetry of Senate-House legislative comparisons, in which each house may initiate legislation. On the other hand, this symmetry is not perfect, for revenue bills must start out in the House. Yet, the House still prevails more often in areas where this prerogative is not material (veto overrides and proposals of constitutional amendments), so its sway over the Senate seems not to be an artifact.

Conclusions

The answer to the question raised in the title of this chapter now seems evident: at least a qualified "no," as Hamilton and Madison almost two hundred years ago seem to have suspected might turn out to be the case, even while proclaiming the coequality of the two houses. Why this is so seems rooted, at least in part, in the greater "criticality" of House members *in toto*, whether one aggregates the power of all, or a simple or a two-thirds majority of their members, and compares these aggregated values with comparable power values for the Senate.

More generally, Banzhaf power in bicameral legislatures follows roughly a "square-root law": the members of the larger house will have less power as individuals, but this decrease is more than offset by the increased size of the body, with the net effect being that the power of the larger (with n members) house relative to that of the smaller (with m members) house is approximately $\sqrt{n/m}$ (Brams, 1975, pp. 260–263). Thus, for example, this ratio for Congress is $\sqrt{435/100} = 2.08$, which is close to the exact Banzhaf power ratio of $0.63316/0.32881 = 1.93$.

But, of course, there is a plenitude of other possible explanations for the House's apparent predominance, including its sheer size; the proximity of its members to their constituents; the shorter electoral terms of Representatives, which put them in closer touch with public opinion than Senators; their greater specialization and expertise, which make them more persuasive with their Senate colleagues; their higher probability of reelection (at least recently), which makes them more independent; and so on. These and other reasons could certainly be marshaled to explain particular successes, but what I seek here is a more general explanation embedded in the constitutional decision rules.

The Banzhaf index is not the only game-theoretic measure of formal voting power. Shapley and Shubik (1954) proposed another measure, based on equiprobable permutations rather than combinations, but the coalition-formation model underlying it (Riker and Shapley, 1968) seems less plausible than the coalition-disintegration model underlying Banzhaf (Brams, 1975, pp. 167–171), at least in the context of legislative bargaining.

This is because a legislator's threat to defect from a coalition is probably his or her most potent weapon for extracting concessions or payments from a coalition leader. It therefore seems a proper basis on which to gauge formal power in the federal system. Furthermore, because the Shapley–Shubik index reverses the Banzhaf ranking of the House and the Senate, attributing greater power to the Senate (Brams, 1975, pp. 192–193; Dubey and Shapley, 1979, pp. 103–104) in the passage of ordinary legislation (their power is virtually the same in the proposal of constitutional amendments), the empirical data presented here cast doubt on the validity of this index as a measure of power in the federal system.

These data, however, beg for more refined analysis than that given here. Lumped together are public bills, resolutions, and joint resolutions over a host of disparate issues—from trivial to momentous, from vehemently partisan to blandly nonpartisan—with such parameters as the size of majorities (except in the veto override cases) ignored in the analysis.

In partial defense of analyzing such highly aggregated data, I would make two points: (1) this is a first attempt to wed a rigorous formal analysis of federal power and empirical evidence on the effectiveness of the actors in getting their ways; and (2) with the possible exception of revenue bills, which must originate in the House, the mix of bills and amendments starting out in the House and the Senate is probably similarly heterogeneous—and therefore comparable, at least for spotlighting overall trends.

Not surprisingly, the House has initiated more bills and veto override attempts than the Senate. More surprising is that it has been considerably more successful, despite the larger numbers, in getting the Senate to acquiesce in its judgment than vice versa. Moreover, this greater influence extends to its success in obtaining Senate support for constitutional amendments that it first proposes.

The President's formal power is harder to assess against the data because, except when there are veto override attempts by Congress, the President exercises this power last, and the President's decision may be anticipated by Congress. However, the overall success of

Presidents in having their vetoes sustained argues for their dominant role in the system, consistent with the revised theoretical calculations of a President's formal power proposed in the preceding section.

If the Federalists did not quite succeed in making the two houses of Congress coequal, and if the President stands *primus inter pares* in the federal setup, these deviations from any egalitarian intentions that the Federalists professed can hardly be called an intellectual or ethical failure on their part. I am still impressed by Madison's and Hamilton's remarkable understanding of the system they helped to create— and especially their anticipation of its effects (before it became operative), including the possible advantages that the House might enjoy. Two hundred years later, the President, the Senate, and the House do not seem seriously out of kilter, even if one institution occasionally seems to run roughshod over another, for usually this seeming dominance is redressed or even reversed a few years later.

Acknowledgments. Portions of this chapter are adapted from an unpublished paper coauthored with Lee Papayanopoulos, "Legislative Rules and Legislative Power," presented at the Seminar on Mathematical Models of Congress, Aspen, Colorado, June 16–23, 1974. I thank Paul J. Affuso and Douglas Muzzio for research assistance on the original paper and Ellen Carnaghan and Julie K. Glynn for research assistance on the present chapter. The comments of Barry Nalehuff, D. Marc Kilgour, Philip D. Straffin, Jr., and participants of Irvine conference on *"The Federalist Papers* and the New Institutionalism" are gratefully acknowledged, but none of these people should be held responsible for the analysis or conclusions herein.

Notes

1. *The Federalist Papers,* Clinton Rossiter, ed., 1961. Page references are to this edition.
2. For a good collection of readings on the concept of power, see Bell, Edwards, and Wagner (1969).
3. Computed from data given in the final editions of *Calendars of United States House of Representatives and History of Legislation* (1949–1986).
4. These figures and some of the veto data given in the following section were computed from data given in U.S. Senate (1978, 1985).
5. *The Constitution of the United States.* Virginia Commission on Constitutional Government, 1967, p. ix.
6. Computed from data given in U.S. Senate (1963).
7. See Brams, Affuso, and Kilgour (1989) for a modification of the Banzhaf index, which gives more realistic power values for the President that are also less ad hoc than those discussed later in the paragraph.
8. For details, see Jackson (1967).

Appendix

The standard notation for the number of combinations is $_n^m$ which denotes the number of combinations that can be formed from m objects taken n at a time, or $m!/n!(m-n)!$. The exclamation point (!) indicates a factorial and means that the number it follows is to be multiplied by every positive integer smaller than itself (e.g., 4! = 4·3·2·1 = 24).

As an illustration of the meaning of combinations with a simple example, suppose one wishes to calculate the number of ways of choosing a subset of three voters from a set of four, designated by $\{a,b,c,d\}$. Clearly, any of the four voters can be excluded from any subset of three voters that is chosen, yielding four different subsets of three voters: $\{a,b,c\}$, $\{a,b,d\}$, $\{a,c,d\}$, and $\{b,c,d\}$. This number, found by complete enumeration of all the subsets, can be calculated directly as the number of combinations of four objects taken three at a time:

$$\binom{4}{3} = \frac{4!}{3!1!} = \frac{(4\cdot3\cdot2\cdot1)}{(3\cdot2\cdot1)(1)} = 4$$

CHAPTER NINE

Assessing the Power
of the Supreme Court

John R. Chamberlin

Disputes about the power of the U.S. Supreme Court have been commonplace in American history, beginning with the debate between the Federalists and the anti-Federalists following the Constitutional Convention, and have included FDR's "court-packing" scheme, criticism of the activist Warren Court, and more recent debates about the meaning and coherence of the doctrine of strict constructionism. The unavailability of an objective interpretation of the Constitution, combined with an appointed judiciary insulated from electoral forces, probably insures that controversy about the Court's power and role in American politics will be forever with us. This prospect should not deter us, however, from trying to reach analytical conclusions about the power of the Supreme Court, and in this chapter, I use the analytical apparatus of game theory to provide one perspective on this issue. My goal is to assess the power of the Court relative to that of the other branches of the national government. My analysis can be viewed as a extension of Steven J. Brams's in chapter 8. I too begin with a quote from *The Federalist Papers*, in this case Alexander Hamilton's assessment of the power of the judiciary:

> . . . the judiciary is beyond comparison the weakest of the three departments of power. (*Federalist*, no. 78, pp. 465–466).[1]

Like Professor Brams, I pursue an answer to the question of the

Court's power using a power index approach. This analysis shows the Court to be an intermediate power between the President and the houses of Congress. In subsequent sections I comment on the extent to which this approach may mislead us about judicial power and conclude that, were it not for the insulation of the Court from electoral forces, Hamilton's assessment would not be far off the mark.

The Power Index Model

The power index approach focuses on the process of coalition formation and dissolution. The basic structure of the model is explained by Brams in chapter 8, so I will not repeat it here. The Banzhaf model, which Brams uses and I will follow here, identifies *critical* members of minimal winning coalitions. In this model, the power of a political actor is proportional to the number of minimal winning coalitions in which the actor's defection would be critical (i.e., change the coalition from a winning coalition to a losing coalition). I propose to treat the Supreme Court as just another player in the legislative game, for that is what its formal powers permit it to be. Like the House and the Senate, it has a veto over ordinary legislation that cannot be overriden by any coalition of actors in the national government. This may strike some as a curious way to model the Court, since it is conventionally viewed as standing aside from the legislative struggle and entering only at the final moment to rule on the constitutionality of legislation. One might also object to such an analysis on the grounds that the Supreme Court is fundamentally different from the other branches because, unlike the other branches, its decisions reflect judgments about constitutionality rather than policy preferences. I will comment on these matters later in the chapter, but for the time being, I will treat the Court as just another political actor and assess its power under this assumption. I will then adjust this assessment in light of my later comments. If we include the Supreme Court in Brams's model, it means that we have four political bodies with different numbers of members: the President (1), the Supreme Court (9), the Senate (100), and the House (435). Passage of legislation requires the formation of one of the following coalitions:

1. The President and at least a simple majority of the other three bodies;
2. At least a two-thirds majority of both houses of Congress and a simple majority of the Supreme Court.

In order for the President, a Senator, or a Representative to be a critical member of a minimal winning coalition in this case, it is

TABLE 9.1. Banzhaf Voting-Power Values for Passage of
Ordinary Legislation

Actor	Individual	Collectivity
President	.03477	.03477
Senator/Senate	.00301	.30065
Representative/House	.00133	.57901
Justice/Supreme Court	.00907	.08557

necessary to add to the requirements stated by Brams the requirement
that a majority of the Supreme Court also be members of the coalition.
There are nine justices, any five or more of whom must be members
of a minimal winning coalition, so we must add to each of the
products of combinatorial expression in Brams's paper an expression
showing the number of ways in which five or more justices can be
selected from the Court. Thus, we need to multiply each of Brams's
expressions by

$$[\binom{9}{5} + \binom{9}{6} + \binom{9}{7} + \binom{9}{8} + \binom{9}{9}]$$

We must also derive an expression for the number of minimal
winning coalitions in which a Supreme Court justice is a critical
member. For this to occur, the other members of the coalition must
include one of the following groups:

1. The President, a simple majority of both houses of Congress, and four
    other Supreme Court justices.
2. At least a two-thirds majority of both houses of Congress and four
    other justices.

The number of ways in which each of these can occur is given by

$$\binom{8}{4} \binom{1}{1} [\binom{100}{51} + \ldots + \binom{100}{100}] [\binom{435}{218} + \ldots + \binom{435}{435}]$$

and

$$\binom{8}{4} \binom{1}{0} [\binom{100}{67} + \ldots + \binom{100}{100}] [\binom{435}{290} + \ldots + \binom{435}{435}]$$

This leads to the assignment of the power indices shown in Table
9.1. According to this analysis, a Supreme Court justice is more
powerful than a Senator or a Representative but less powerful than
the President. If we follow Brams in assessing institutional power by
multiplying the power of an individual actor by the number of actors
in that political body, then the Court is seen to be less powerful than
either house of Congress but more powerful than the presidency.

This occurs because, other things being equal, a body with a veto will be more powerful than a body without one, and bodies for which a veto override requires a special majority (i.e., the houses of Congress) will be more powerful than bodies for which a simple majority is sufficient to override (i.e., the Court).[2] The addition of the Supreme Court to the analysis does not change the relative power of the other three bodies: their power decreases proportionately when the Court enters the picture.

It is often claimed that the Supreme Court is weak relative to the other branches because its power is passive in that the Court can only react to the legislation that results from the interplay of the executive and legislative branches. It is said that the Court is limited to acting as a *blocking* coalition, vetoing the actions of others but unable to act on its own to upset the status quo. The power index approach to modeling decision making suggests that such claims are mistaken; the claim may have merit for the reasons I note below, but such differences in power do not arise in the game under consideration. Interestingly, Shapley and Shubik (1954) claim that a blocking power index aimed at capturing this difference either will be equal to the power index they define or will violate at least one of a set of seemingly desirable logical properties of such an index (p. 789). One effect of modeling the Court in this fashion, then, is that it enables us to take a fresh look at some of the conventional wisdom about the Court's power.

According to the game-theoretic analysis presented here, the Supreme Court is somewhat more powerful than the President but considerably less powerful than either the House or the Senate when it come to the passage of ordinary legislation. So Hamilton's claim is not substantiated to the extent that Federalist claims about Congress are supported in chapter 8. However, there are still some important issues that must be considered.

Caveats Concerning the Power Index Approach

The power index approach treats the Supreme Court as just another legislative body operating under majority rule, a view that is at considerable variance with the conventional view of the Court. In addition, the interaction of the branches of the national government is considerably more complex than is pictured by the theory of simple games that underlies the power index approach. As I indicate below, it seems to me that most of the "corrections" to the power assessments given above that would follow from consideration of these matters act to lower our assessment of the power of the Court from that given in Table 9.1.

It is useful to distinguish between the power of the Constitution and the power of the Court. The Constitution was intended to be and is a powerful constraint on the actions of all branches of government. It seems to me that we risk conflating the power of the Court with the power of the Constitution itself. If there were an objective interpretation of the Constitution, and if there were a straightforward algorithm for obtaining such an objective interpretation, then we would view the Court as having little power on its own; it would simply be the actor that turned the handle on the algorithm and produced the answer. In such a case, the power would reside in the Constitution, not in the Court. However, since there is little to recommend such a view of the Constitution, the matter is more complicated, and this complication raises the first issue I want to consider.

Game-theoretic models of legislative behavior, including the power index approach, typically assume that actors will act in pursuit of their own interests (however they define them: interests of the nation, interests of their constituents, interests in reelection, etc.). Such assumptions are standard in public choice theory, but they conflict with the conventional view of how justices ought to behave and with many views about how they do behave. According to most theories of the Court, including those adhered to by both Federalists and anti-Federalists, Supreme Court justices are supposed to render judgments based on what the Constitution says, not on the basis of their own policy preferences.[3] The Court is thus supposed to approve all legislation that passes constitutional muster, not legislation that passes such muster *and* accords with the policy preferences of the justices. The principal effect of this in the game-theoretic model presented above is that, although a Supreme Court justice might be a critical member of a minimal winning coalition, he or she would be constrained by judicial duty from defecting from the coalition solely on the basis of his or her policy preferences. If the expectation that justices will refrain from exercising their individual policy preferences is borne out in practice, then Supreme Court justices will, in fact, be critical members much less often than the calculations underlying the power index suggest. The extent to which this occurs is difficult to pin down with any confidence, but the greater the extent to which it happens, the more we ought to discount the power attributed to the Court in Table 9.1. To delve into this matter here would take me too far afield, so I simply note that in my judgment, this issue by itself erodes most of the difference in relative power between the President and the Supreme Court as reported in Table 9.1.

The difference between judging constitutionality and exercising policy preferences would be highlighted if legislation were studied through a spatial model rather than the model of simple games underlying the power index approach, for the decision then becomes not a "yes or no" decision but a "how much" decision. In recent years, there has been a burst of productive activity in the field of public choice that shows the effects of institutions and rules on decision making in a spatial setting. Consider how the Court would fit into such an analysis in a particular case, say, a proposed increase in the federal minimum wage. If the Court is constrained by precedent from declaring a federal minimum wage unconstitutional, then it has little power in the legislative bargaining that would go on in such a case, even though the justices themselves might have quite strong preferences concerning various policy alternatives. In the case of federal legislation affecting wages and working conditions, the Supreme Court once exercised great power, holding a broad range of such legislation to be in conflict with the Constitution. But once the Supreme Court shifted its interpretation (after the election of 1936 and the court-packing fight), it relinquished power over the matter. Its power in the current legislative game would be viewed as limited to establishing very loose constraints on what Congress and the President might choose to do. So long as the justices are constrained by precedent, they cannot act the way the model supposes a critical member of a coalition to act—bargaining for a more preferred outcome. In much of the everyday legislative process, then, the Supreme Court is much less powerful than Table 9.1 would suggest.

There is, of course, no formal prohibition that prevents the Court from reversing itself and thus exercising real power once again on such an issue. Nevertheless, it is unlikely that the Court will do so with great frequency. Not only do the norms of judicial duty make such behavior less likely; in addition, the number of issues the Court can attend to in a session is much smaller than the number the other branches regularly deal with. The nature of the judicial process is such that fewer issues can receive active consideration, and this means that the Court is an implicit cooperator in most legislative activity and therefore unable to exercise its potential power. Thus, even if the Court wishes to exercise its policy preferences in its decisions, it will not be able to do so with the frequency that the model assumes.

These considerations suggest that the power index approach over estimates the power of the Supreme Court. There is one obvious argument that leads in the other direction. This is that the Supreme Court is by far the most independent of the four bodies. The elected branches are subject to periodic checks by the electorate, and their decisions are thus subject to being overridden at regular intervals by external forces. The Court, on the other hand, can be overridden only by a constitutional amendment, a check that is, without doubt, much weaker. This is a genuine source of power for the Court that is not captured by the model presented above. This power is illustrated, for instance, by the length of time the Court was able to hold out against the elected branches on the example mentioned above: federal wage and working-conditions legislation. The case of the Court's blocking progressive legislation seems not to have been given much consideration in the debate about the judiciary that followed the Constitutional Convention. Most of the Founding Fathers were not given to thinking of government as an engine of progress, so one finds little concern in the ratification debates about the possibility of the Court's blocking actions of the elected branches that have broad public backing; concern was focused instead on the prospect that runaway legislatures might act in opposition to the "public interest." Although the possibility of amendment was intended to be an important check on an independent judiciary, there was doubt from the very beginning about the extent to which this could be an important constraint. Consider the remarks of Patrick Henry at the Virginia Ratification Convention, in which he exhibited considerable insight into the problem of coalition formation:

> Let us consider the consequences of this. . . . Two-thirds of the Congress, or, of the State Legislatures, are necessary even to propose amendments: If one-third of these be unworthy men, they may prevent the application for amendments; but what is destructive and mischievous is, that three-fourths of the State Legislatures, or of State Conventions, must concur in the amendments when proposed: In such numerous bodies, there must necessarily be some designing bad men: To suppose that so large a number as three-fourths of the States will concur, is to suppose that they possess genius, intelligence, and integrity, approaching to miraculous. It would indeed be miraculous that they should concur in the same amendments, or, even in such as would bear some likeness to one another. For four of the smallest States, that do not collectively contain one-tenth part of the population of the United States, may obstruct the most salutary and necessary amendments: Nay, in these four States, six tenths of the people may reject these amendments; and suppose, that amendments shall be opposed to amendments (which is highly probable) is it possible, that three-fourths can ever agree to the same amendments? A bare majority in these four small States may hinder the adoption of amendments; so that we

may fairly and justly conclude, that one-twentieth part of the American people, may prevent the removal of the most grievous inconveniences and oppression, by refusing to accede to amendments. A trifling minority may reject the most salutary amendment. Is this an easy mode of securing the public liberty? It is, Sir, a most fearful situation, when the most contemptible minority can prevent the alteration of the most oppressive government. . . . If, Sir, amendments are left to the twentieth or the tenth part of the people of America, your liberty is gone forever. (Ketchum, 1986, pp. 204–205)

Conclusion

There is no straightforward way to use these considerations to adjust the power indices in Table 9.1, so each of us must make our own subjective judgment. My own conclusion is that Hamilton's judgment about the Court would hold only if the problem of the independence of the Supreme Court from electoral control could be dealt with satisfactorily. If it could, the other arguments in the last section would lead me to agree with Hamilton that the Court is the least powerful branch. Hamilton's own argument on the independence issue is not one of his strongest, however, for it required him to diverge from the usual assumption that those entrusted will use their power to their own advantage and to argue that it will be possible to appoint as justices individuals whose personal character and commitment to the Constitution will triumph over human nature (as viewed by Federalists, anti-Federalists, and public choice theorists alike).

Notes

1. Page references are to the New American Library edition of *The Federalist Papers*, 1961, Clinton Rossiter, ed.
2. Shapley and Shubik (1954) note, "Raising the majority in one chamber (say from one-half to two-thirds) increases the relative power of that chamber" (p. 790). This advantages the House and the Senate relative to the Court in those situations in which the President exercises a veto.
3. The Constitutional Convention explicitly rejected proposals that the Supreme Court be permitted to reject legislation (by itself or in concert with the President) on the basis of its policy preferences. In *Federalist* no. 78, Hamilton carefully distinguished between the *judgment* of the Court and its *will*, insisting that only the former should be exercised.

CHAPTER TEN

Checks, Balances, and Bureaucratic Usurpation of Congressional Power

Thomas Schwartz

Congress, we are continually told, has relinquished much of its power to the federal bureaucracy: besides delegating sweeping authority to administrative agencies, Congress has neglected its oversight responsibility, allowing administrative excesses to go unchecked. That would surprise a time traveler from 1787: the authors of *The Federalist Papers* expected the legislative branch not only to provide a counterweight to the executive branch and to check its excesses but to be the dominant branch (Madison, *Federalist*, nos., 48, 49, and 51). Its own potential excesses—factionalism, sectional tyranny, usurpation of state sovereignty—were to be prevented chiefly by frequent elections, extensive territory, and bicameralism (Madison, no. 10). So constructed, however, the legislative branch was expected to wield most of the power of the national government. What has gone wrong?

Nothing. Congress has not relinquished power to the bureaucracy. I defend this thesis on the basis of the *Federalist*'s principles of political analysis, outlined in chapter 2.

Delegation and the Neglect of Oversight

The contention that Congress has relinquished much of its constitutional power to the bureaucracy rests on two observations.

Delegation: Congress has delegated to executive agencies many of the legislative powers assigned to Congress by Article I of the Constitution (Clarkson and Muris, 1981; Dodd and Schott, 1979; Hess, 1976; Lowi, 1969; Wilson, 1980; Woll, 1977).

Neglect of Oversight: Congress has neglected its oversight responsibility: it has done little to detect and remedy administrative violations of legislative goals (Bibby, 1966, 1968; Dodd and Schott, 1979; Fiorina, 1977a,b, 1982; Hess, 1976; Huntington, 1973; Lowi, 1969; Mitnick, 1980; Ogul, 1976, 1977; Pearson, 1975; Ripley, 1978; Scher, 1963; Seidman, 1975; Woll, 1977).

Both observations are the impressions of experienced observers supported by considerable, widely available anecdotal evidence: the first observation is supported chiefly by a reading of authorization bills, the second chiefly by observing the infrequency of oversight hearings. Neither observation has, to my knowledge, been rigorously operationalized (apart from a book in progress by Joel Aberbach).

My thesis is that the first observation is true but irrelevant by itself to the hypothesis of bureaucratic usurpation, that the second is flatly false, that there has been no significant bureaucratic usurpation of legislative power, and that *Federalist* principles enable us to demonstrate these points.

The Federalist Position

What would Publius have said? What would a modern heir to the *Federalist* style of analysis—a public choice scholar—say about delegation, oversight neglect, and bureaucratic usurpation? Six things.

Thing 1. Because legislators cannot avoid all ambiguity or anticipate all contingencies, those who administer laws must perforce enjoy some latitude (Madison, no. 37). Thus, some measure of delegation is required by human cognitive limits. Although the *Federalist* authors did not even dimly foresee the size and complexity of the present federal government ("The number of individuals employed under the Constitution of the United States will be much smaller than the number employed under the particular states"—Madison, no. 45), they would have examined government growth (had they foreseen it) in terms of institutional incentives: the current size and complexity of the federal government affords congressmen an incentive to delegate a great deal of legislative authority to the bureaucracy because delegation saves congressmen time and reduces the cost to them of acquiring the information and expertise needed to legislate. In short, delegation is predictable.

Thing 2. Delegation does not gainsay congressional control so long as Congress has an effective oversight system—an effective system for detecting and remedying administrative violations of legislative goals, including goals hard to make precise in advance of concrete applications. For the exercise of authority is always limited by institutional incentives, which an effective oversight system would provide. Employers delegate considerable authority to employees, whose actual discretion is limited (well or poorly) by their incentives to produce results ultimately pleasing to their employers. In general, it is fallacious to infer lack of control by principals of agents from delegation alone.

Thing 3. Usurpation of power is best prevented not by "parchment barriers against the encroaching spirit of power" (Madison, no. 48) but by a system of countervailing incentives—by making ambition counteract ambition. Therefore, the best way to ensure bureaucratic policy compliance (to oversee the bureaucracy) is neither by legislating in detail nor even, necessarily, by minutely supervising the bureaucracy, but by structuring the executive branch so that tendencies to act contrary to congressional goals—tendencies not to do what congressmen themselves would have done had they taken the time and acquired the information and expertise to decide the case at hand—are effectively challenged by those whose interests are harmed thereby.

Thing 4. Because congressmen are chosen by voters, whose interests are likely to be harmed by administrative violations of legislative goals, it is in the interests of the congressmen to devise such an oversight system: elections provide the institutional incentive to do so.

Thing 5. Because administrative agencies are the creatures and wards of Congress, Congress has the power to enforce administrative compliance with legislative goals by means of incentives. In a republic, the legislative branch is inevitably the dominant branch (Madison, no. 48).

Thing 6. Policy outcomes are equilibria, or balances, of interests that not only are institutionally selected but clash within an institutional framework. Checks—counteracting interests—preserve the balance: they restore momentarily upset equilibria. But for that very reason, their operation cannot be observed in equilibrium. Therefore, the fact (if fact it be) that Congress infrequently discovers and penalizes administrative violations of legislative goals does not prove that Congress does a poor job of oversight. What it proves is that Congress does *either* a poor job *or* an excellent job. An empty jail is evidence not that the sheriff is doing a poor job but that he is doing either a poor job or an excellent one.

From a *Federalist* point of view, then, congressmen have an incentive to delegate much of their Article I authority to the bureaucracy, but they also have the power and incentive to check excesses by instituting an oversight system in which bureaucratic interests in violating congressional goals are counteracted by the interests of those hurt thereby. Congress has, I shall now argue, instituted just such a system.

Police Patrols and Fire Alarms

Matthew McCubbins and I (1984) have distinguished two forms or techniques of oversight, two types of oversight policy, available to Congress.

1. *Police-patrol oversight.* Analogous to the use of real police patrols, police-patrol oversight is comparatively centralized, active, and direct: on its own initiative, Congress examines a sample of executive-agency activities with the aim of detecting, remedying, and discouraging violations of legislative goals. An agency's activities might be surveyed by any of a number of means, such as reading documents, commissioning scientific studies, conducting field observations, and holding hearings to question officials and affected citizens.

2. *Fire-alarm oversight.* Analogous to the use of real fire alarms, fire-alarm oversight is less centralized and involves less active and direct intervention than police-patrol oversight: instead of examining a sample of administrative decisions, looking for violations of legislative goals, Congress establishes a system of rules, procedures, and informal practices that enable individual citizens and organized interest groups to examine administrative decisions (sometimes in prospect), to charge executive agencies with violating congressional goals, and to seek remedies from agencies, courts, and Congress itself. Some of these rules, procedures, and practices afford citizens and interest groups access to information and to administrative decision-making processes. Others give them standing to challenge administrative decisions before agencies and courts or help them bring violations to the attention of congressmen. Still others facilitate collective action by comparatively disorganized interest groups. Congress's role consists in creating and perfecting this decentralized system and, occasionally, intervening in response to complaints. Instead of sniffing for fires, Congress places fire-alarm boxes on street

corners, builds neighborhood fire houses, and sometimes dispatches its own hook-and-ladder in response to an alarm.

In the literature on congressional control of the bureaucracy, it was police-patrol oversight whose neglect was observed and decried: the chief evidence of neglect was the infrequency of oversight hearings. Yet, it is fire-alarm oversight that best meets the *Federalist* specifications for an oversight system: it is fire-alarm oversight that makes ambition counteract ambition, ensuring a clash between the interests of wayward bureaucrats and those of aggrieved citizens.

Congress might adopt an oversight policy containing both police-patrol features, such as the requirement of sunset review, and fire-alarm features, such as the requirement of public hearings by regulatory agencies. But fire-alarm features are likely to predominate because fire-alarm oversight has a fourfold advantage for congressmen.

First, congressmen engaged in police-patrol oversight inevitably spend time examining a great many executive-branch actions that do not violate legislative goals or harm voters, at least not enough to occasion complaints. They might also spend time detecting and remedying arguable violations that nonetheless harm no voters. For this they receive scant credit: their time is wasted. But under a fire-alarm policy, a congressmen does not address concrete violations unless someone has complained about them, in which case he can receive credit for intervening. So a unit of time spent on oversight is likely to yield more benefit for a congressman under a fire-alarm policy than under a police-patrol policy. As a result, a fire-alarm policy enables congressmen to spend less time on oversight, leaving more time for other profitable activities, or to spend the same time on more personally profitable oversight activities—on addressing complaints. Justly or unjustly, time spent putting out visible fires gains one more credit than the same time spent sniffing for smoke.

Second, under a realistic police-patrol policy, congressmen examine only a small sample of executive-branch actions. As a result, they are likely to miss violations that harm voters and so miss opportunities to take credit for redressing grievances, however fair the sample. But under a well-designed fire-alarm policy, citizens and interest groups can, in most cases, bring to congressmen's attention any violations that harm them and for which they have received no adequate remedy through the executive or judicial branch.

Third, although fire-alarm oversight can be as costly as police-patrol oversight, much of the cost is borne by the citizens and interest groups who sound alarms and by administrative agencies and courts rather than by congressmen themselves. A congressman's responsibility for such costs is sufficiently remote that he is not likely to be blamed for them.

Finally, legislative goals often are stated in such a vague way that it is hard to decide whether any violation has occurred unless some citizen or group registers a complaint. Such a complaint gives Congress the opportunity to spell out its goals more clearly, much as concrete cases and controversies give the courts the opportunity to elucidate legal principles that would be hard to make precise in the abstract.

Evidence

Owing to the dual incentive, congressmen have to delegate authority while preventing bureaucratic excesses, and owing to the comparative cost-effectiveness to congressmen of a fire-alarm system of oversight—one in which ambition is made to counteract ambition—we should expect to observe an oversight policy in which fire-alarm features predominate. We do.

Complaints against administrative agencies are often brought to the attention of congressional subcommittees by lobbyists for organized groups and to the attention of administrative agencies by congressional subcommittees. The functioning of this "subgovernmental triangle" has been well documented (Dodd and Oppenheimer, 1977; Fenno, 1966, 1973a,b; Goodwin, 1970; Huitt, 1973; Matthews, 1960; Ornstein, 1975; Ripley, 1969; Ripley and Franklin, 1976).

Congress has passed legislation to help comparatively disorganized groups voice their grievances against the federal government. McConnell (1966) shows how the Agriculture, Labor, and Commerce Departments act as lobbyists for farm, labor, and small-business interests. Congress has also created new programs, such as the Legal Services Corporation, to organize and press the claims of comparatively voiceless citizens.

Constituent-service activities are not limited to untying procedural knots. As part of the fire-alarm system, district staff and casework help individuals and groups—some of them otherwise powerless—to raise and redress grievances against decisions by administrative agencies. This casework component of legislative policymaking has been examined only recently, with a primary focus on the electoral connection (Cain, Ferejohn, and Fiorina, 1979a,b; Fenno, 1978; Fiorina, 1977a; Mayhew, 1974a; Parker and Davidson, 1979) and a secondary focus on policy consequences (Fiorina and Noll, 1978, 1979a,b).

Often the fire-alarm system allows for the redress of grievances by administrative agencies and courts; Congress itself need not get involved. To facilitate such redress, Congress has passed several laws—notably the Administrative Procedures Act of 1946 and the Environmental Procedures Act of 1969—that have substantially increased the number of groups with legal standing before administrative agencies and district courts regarding bureaucratic controversies (Lowi, 1969). Congress has also, as in sections 4–7 of the Toxic Substances Control Act of 1976, increased the courts' powers to issue injunctions in response to alarms and has required administrative agencies to hold hearings, to publish information, and to invite public comment on agency decision-making. (On this aspect of fire-alarm oversight, see Ferejohn, 1986; McCubbins, 1982; McCubbins, Noll, and Weingast, 1986.)

There have been numerous cases in which violations of legislative goals were brought to the attention of Congress, which responded with vigorous remedial measures. For example, Congress dismantled the Area Redevelopment Administrative (ARA) in 1963, even though it had been authorized in 1961. The ARA was encouraging industries to relocate in redevelopment areas despite clear provisions in the law to the contrary (Ripley, 1971). Congress can also redefine or reaffirm its goals by redefining or explicating the jurisdictional authority of an administrative agency. This happened when the Federal Trade Commission sought to regulate cigarette advertising, children's television, and funeral parlors. Sometimes congressional intervention is legislatively mandated. Before taking action on a pending case, for example, the National Labor Relations Board must consult with the appropriate congressional committees.

The point of this sketch is that elaborate procedures have been established whereby individuals and groups hurt by bureaucratic excesses can fix responsibility and ring alarms and that alarms, when rung, have been answered. That alone—not the frequency of oversight hearings or sanctions—is evidence of an effective oversight system and therewith the absence of extensive bureaucratic usurpation.

Conclusion

Far from having relinquished its Article I powers to administrative agencies, Congress has found a particularly effective way to exercise those powers: delegate broadly to bureaucrats, but devise a system of counteracting ambitions—of fire-alarm oversight—to check bureaucratic violations of congressional goals.

With its powers of authorization and appropriation, Congress is near sovereign among the three branches. If it infrequently chastises bureaucrats, that is compatible with an effective oversight system no less than with an ineffective one: in equilibrium—when interests are in balance—checks are not observed. Evidence of effective oversight consists in the elaborate system that affords affected citizens representation before agencies, courts, and Congress itself. Those who reason from the magnitude of delegation and the infrequency of sanctions to bureaucratic usurpation might as well say that producers determine prices because they have the legal authority to do so and because, in equilibrium, we observe no queues or uncleared inventories, no adverse behavior by consumers.

Acknowledgments. The third and fourth sections of this chapter borrow heavily from McCubbins and Schwartz (1984). Some of the themes of those sections are nicely developed by Calvert, McCubbins, and Weingast (1986). I thank Mathew McCubbins for invaluable discussions of my topic over several years. This research was supported by NSF grant SES 8612120.

CHAPTER ELEVEN

The Distribution of Power in the Federal Government: Perspectives from *The Federalist Papers*—A Critique

Mark P. Petracca

No topic in American history has attracted as much attention as the question of how power is and should be distributed in the federal government. This topic evokes both empirical and normative analysis. Indeed, in the current political epoch, frequently defined by stalemate, gridlock, and immobilism, no topic is more worthy of continued debate, investigation, and analysis. As a result, it comes as no surprise that we return to the political rhetoric and principles set forth in *The Federalist Papers* on this subject for guidance, inspiration, explanation, and theory. The two chapters by Steven J. Brams and John R. Chamberlin take up this important issue directly.

This essay is a critique of their efforts. My analysis will consider (1) how Brams and Chamberlin fail to delineate and understand the important contextual aspects of statements made by Madison and Hamilton; (2) how they fail to justify the applicability of their particular methodology to the determination of "power values" for all four bodies of the federal government; (3) how their empirical data and subsequent commentary do not always support their intended conclusions; and (4) why their attempt to make public choice theorists out of the Federalists is seriously suspect. I offer this critique in the spirit of the vigorous and pointed arguments which occurred during the ratification debates between the Federalists and the anti-Federalists.

The Federalists on Institutional Power

Professors Brams and Chamberlin utilize premonitions and predictions from *The Federalist Papers* as inspirations for very similar analyses of the distribution of political power in the federal government. Unfortunately, each fails to understand the full meaning of various positions taken by James Madison and Alexander Hamilton and, as a result, seriously undermines the impact of their respective analyses. Indeed, it should be clear to even the most casual reader that neither chapter is dependent upon nor fundamentally linked to the principles of republican government discussion either at the Constitutional Convention or during the ratification debates.[1] In this sense, the results and implications of their analyses are not actually dependent upon their interpretations of *The Federalist Papers*. However, since this book is supposed to be about *The Federalist Papers* and the principles of government they espoused, a more extensive analysis of Madisonian and Hamiltonian positions is completely justified.

Brams begins by suggesting that Madison and Hamilton believed the two houses of Congress to be coequal or, if there was a bias, that it would be one that favored the House of Representatives. This assessment is reached by an extremely selective reading of *Federalist Papers* nos. 58 and 63 by Madison and no. 66 by Hamilton. The positions attributed to Madison and Hamilton are largely taken out of appropriate historical context. We should not forget that *The Federalist Papers* were written mainly to persuade various delegates to state ratifying conventions to adopt the proposed constitution *and* to refute the many charges lodged against that document by the anti-Federalists. The barrage of criticism began immediately after the conclusion of the Constitutional Convention in September of 1787. *The Federalist Papers* are efforts at political persuasion, sophisticated and principled to be sure, but persuasion nonetheless. This does not diminish their brilliance or significance.[2] Rather, it compels the reader to be particularly careful about what was said, what was not said, and why—a commendation not well followed by either Brams or Chamberlin.

With regard to claims made by Brams, what are the focal points of Madison's and Hamilton's responses? In general, they are reacting to the numerous arguments by anti-Federalists that the Senate, as proposed, was too powerful and undemocratic. The three *Federalist Papers* cited by Brams are intended to answer some very specific attacks by the anti-Federalists.

In *Federalist* no. 58, Madison disputes the charge that the size of the House may not be appropriately increased as the population of the nation increases, thus rendering it increasingly undemocratic. In October of 1787, the best known and most prolific of the anti-Federalist essayists, Centinel (Storing, 1985, p. 19), expressed great dissatisfaction with the proposed means of constituting the supposedly popular House of Representatives:

> Thus we see, the house of representatives, are on the part of the people to balance the senate, who I suppose will be composed of the better sort, the well born, etc. The number of the representatives (being only one for every 30,000 inhabitants) appears to be too few, either to communicate the requisite information, of the wants, local circumstances and sentiments of so extensive an empire, or to prevent corruption and undue influence. . .

During the same month, Federal Farmer (Storing, 1985, p. 44) also criticized the small size of the House and its limited democratic nature:

> As to the organization—the house of representatives, the democrative branch, as it is called, is to consist of 65 members: that is, about one representative for fifty thousand inhabitants, to be chosen biennially. . . . The people of this country, in one sense, may all be democratic; but if we make the proper distinction between the few men of wealth and abilities, and consider them, as we ought, as the natural aristocracy of the country, and the great body of the people, the middle and lower classes, are the democracy, this federal representative branch will have but very little democracy in it, even this small representation is not secured on proper principles.

Beyond the expression of significant disappointment with the House, the anti-Federalists also charged that, by comparison, the Senate was too powerful and aristocratic. Federal Farmer (Storing, 1985, p. 47) argued that, "The formation of the senate, and the smallness of the house, being, therefore, the result of our situation, and the actual state of things, the evils which may attend the exercise of many powers in this national government may be considered as without remedy." Likewise, Centinel (Storing, 1985, p. 19) lamented that the Senate is "the great efficient body in this plan of government" and that it "is constituted on the most unequal principles." Cincinnatus (Storing, 1981a, p. 49) summed up the critique quite well: "We have seen powers, in every branch of government, in violation of all principle, and all safety condensed in this aristocratic senate: we have seen the representative or democratic branch, weakened exactly in proportion to the strengthening [of] the aristocratic."

It is plausible that, in an effort to counter such penetrating criticisms, both Hamilton and Madison sought to allege coequality, if not the slight dominance, of the House. Hamilton's remarks in *Federalist* no. 66 are directed against the charge that the impeachment power is inappropriately located in an already powerful Senate.[3] Madison's commentary in *Federalist* no. 63 is similarly directed against the charges that the Senate would be an independent and aristocratic body capable of great infringement on liberty.

Madison, however, was not content simply to offer a declarative defense of apparent House superiority. Unlike Professor Brams, who fails to offer a theory of or an explanation for the more powerful position of the House vis-à-vis the Senate, Madison suggests that the House would be an effective check on the Senate because of its popular electoral base, not because of its relative size. In *Federalist* no. 63, Madison displays a rich knowledge of ancient and modern history to prove that there is an "irresistible force possessed by that branch of a free government [i.e., the House], which has the people on its side" (p. 389).[4] As a result, he concludes that "the House of Representatives, with the people on their side, will at all times be able to bring back the Constitution to its primitive form and principles" (ibid.).

This was Madison's public explanation for why state convention delegates could safely trust the democratic nature of the House to keep the slightly aristocratic Senate in check. However, in more private settings, Madison took a significantly different position. During the Convention debates, Madison (Farrand, 1966, Vol. 1, p. 151) suggested, as a matter of political principle, that the power of a legislative chamber was inversely related to its size, so that the Senate was the more powerful branch of government:

> The use of the Senate is to consist in its proceedings with more coolness, with more system, & with more wisdom, than the popular branch. Enlarge their number and you communicate to them the vices which they are meant to correct. He [Madison] differed from Mr. D. [Dickenson] who thought that the additional number would give additional weight to the body. On the contrary it appeared to him [Madison] that *their weight would be in an inverse ratio to their number.* (italics added)

This proposition and the subsequent defense of the Senate in light of experience with Roman tribunals raises the question of whether or not Madison's position in *Federalist* no. 63 was authentic or simply a well-made persuasive response to anti-Federalist critics. It is, of course, impossible to know for certain. However, in private correspondence with Thomas Jefferson shortly after the conclusion of the Convention, Madison (Kammen, 1986, p. 67) described the Senate to the absent diplomat as "the great anchor of the government." Such revelations are not consistent with the assessment that Madison believed the two houses to be coequal or that the House was slightly more powerful.[5]

One final note, given Madison's explanation in *The Federalist Papers* for the apparent superiority of the House over the Senate (that being its popular base), we might suspect that with the passage of the Seventeenth Amendment in 1913 (which made Senators subject to popular election), a more vigorous argument could be made for their coequality in the federal government. The absence of an explanation of why the Federalists (i.e., Madison and Hamilton) took this position in defense of the House over the Senate means that Brams also misses the opportunity to speculate on the effect of the Seventeenth Amendment on the relative power of the two branches of government.

Professor Chamberlin utilizes Hamilton's assertion, in *Federalist* no. 78, that the U.S. Supreme Court is the weakest branch of government, to begin an analysis of judicial power. Like Professor Brams, Chamberlin offers no explanation or analysis of the specific or general context within which this argument is set forth by Hamilton. The specific focus of Hamilton's position in *Federalist* no. 78 is the charge that tenure during good behavior among members of the Court results in a judiciary beyond any popular control. Brutus (Storing, 1985, p. 183) offered a stern warning about the power of the Court in March 1788 (two full months before the publication of no. 78 in May 1788):

> The supreme court under this constitution would be exalted above all power in the government, and subject to no controul. . . . I question whether the world ever saw, in any period of it, a court of justice invested with such immense powers, and yet placed in a situation so little responsible. . . . There is no power above them, to controul any of their decisions. There is no authority that can remove them, and they cannot be controuled by the laws of the legislature. In short, they are independent of the people, of the legislature, and of every power under heaven. Men placed in this situation will generally soon feel themselves independent of heaven itself.

Hamilton's response to this attack (*Federalist Papers*, Rossiter ed., p. 466) regarding the weakness of the Court refers to its capacity to pose a danger to the political rights invested in the Constitution. It was "liberty" which had nothing to fear from the judiciary, not necessarily the other branches of government (although Hamilton does concede the limits of judicial enforcement powers).

When it came to an assessment of power among the three branches of the federal government, Hamilton and other Federalists were willing to portray the Court as "the least dangerous branch." Why? It is clear that many members of the Constitutional Convention—for example, Wilson, Madison, Gouverneur Morris, King, Gerry, Mason, and Luther Martin—had supported the notion that the judiciary would have the power to declare null and void laws that were inconsistent with the Constitution (Farrand, 1913, p. 157). Attempts to diminish the apparent power of the Court should thus be viewed as a direct response to criticisms by anti-Federalists about the power of the Court in relationship to the states and other branches of the federal government. George Mason (Kammen, 1986, p. 256), a Convention delegate, refused to sign the Constitution because of many objections, one of which concerned the judiciary:

> The Judiciary of the United States is so construed and extended, as to absorb and destroy the Judiciarys of the several States; thereby rendering Law as tedious[,] intricate and expensive, and Justice as unattainable, by a great part of the Community, as in England, and enabling the Rich to oppress and ruin the Poor.

Beyond destroying state judiciaries, anti-Federalists claimed that the Court would subvert state governments and generally lead to the uninhibited expansion of the central government. Again, Brutus (Kammen, 1986, p. 335) put this point most vehemently:

> The judicial power will operate to effect, in the most certain, but yet silent and imperceptible manner, what is evidently the tendency of the constitution:—I mean, an entire subversion of the legislative, executive, and judicial powers of the individual states. Every adjudication of the supreme court, on any question that may arise upon the nature and extent of the general government, will affect the limits of the state jurisdiction. . . . That the judicial power of the United States, will lean strongly in favour of the general government, and will give such an explanation to the constitution, as will favour an extension of its jurisdiction, is very evident from a variety of considerations.

According to Brutus (Kammen, 1986, p. 359), "nothing better could have been conceived to facilitate the abolition of the state government than the constitution of the judicial." While anti-Federalists were more concerned about the loss of state autonomy in the hands of the judiciary, they did express concern that the Court could pose a serious danger within the federal government as well. Federal Farmer (Storing, 1981a, p. 50) warned that "we are more in danger of sowing the seeds of arbitrary government in this department [the judiciary] than in any other."

By calling attention to the Court's obvious lack of enforcement power—possessing neither sword nor purse—Hamilton hoped to diminish the persuasive effect of these various anti-Federalist claims. This is not to suggest that Hamilton's claims were insincere. Unlike Madison's case regarding the House and Senate, I could find no evidence to suggest that Hamilton really thought the Court was extremely powerful, despite claims to the contrary. However, it is worth keeping in mind that the lengths to which Hamilton seems willing to go in an attempt to discount the power of the Court are probably in proportion to the perceived severity of the anti-Federalist attacks. This cautions against taking Hamilton's commentary in *Federalist* no. 78 *too* literally.

The Applicability of Method

Brams and Chamberlin utilize the same method to calculate a power index for the President, the House, the Senate, and, in Chamberlin's case, the Supreme Court. Banzhaf's index proposes that an actor's political power is proportional to the number of minimum winning coalitions from which the actor's defection would be critical. Unfortunately, the authors do not explain why the Banzhaf index is a particularly appropriate or useful measure for the analysis of institutional power. There is an air of unreality to the entire application of this method. The Banzhaf index is designed to explain legislative voting "games," not the process by which a President, the House, and the Senate (to say nothing of the Supreme Court) engage in the complicated process of lawmaking within a system of separate institutions with shared powers (see Neustadt, 1976).

On the one hand, the process of lawmaking obviously entails far more than can be captured by a legislative-voting-game model. Even the activities which occur in either house of Congress entail processes which are not reducible to voting games. The importance of party leadership, committee chairpersons, and professional staff stands as an obvious example. In addition, it is not entirely clear that the zero-sum assumptions of the Banzhaf index are applicable to the interactions of institutions as opposed to individuals. It would seem that there are few institutional situations, even actual legislative votes, which are truly zero-sum games. To be fair, Brams and

Chamberlin do allude to the inherent limitations of their approach. However, without further explanation or justification, they proceed undaunted to conduct their analysis. On the other hand, it is a surprise to see the Banzhaf index being utilized to measure power in a nonweighted voting game. In an earlier work, Brams (1976) suggested that this index is designed "to measure an actor's ability to control the selection of outcomes in a weighted voting body" (p. 190). Surely, some explanation is required to persuade the reader—even the most knowledgeable—that such a shift in application is both permissible and productive.

A special note is needed about the applicability of a legislative-voting-game model to the Supreme Court. While Chamberlin devotes considerable attention to the obvious inapplicability of this method, the case is not made as explicit as it should be. The Court is not "just another player" in a legislative game. First, the Court is not in any real sense a required actor in the legislative process, as are the other two branches of government. A reading of Article III, section 2, of the Constitution shows that the Court has original jurisdiction in only a few matters. It takes less than 10% of its cases on appeal, while all other cases reach the Court's calendar through the discretionary process of granting *writs of certiorari*. Indeed, empirically, the Court infrequently and ever so carefully interacts with the other branches of the federal government. Through the 1978–1979 session, the Supreme Court had struck down only 122 pieces of legislation as unconstitutional and had ruled against presidential actions in only a handful of cases. On the contrary, when it came to the states, during the same time period the Supreme Court had ruled against 950 state laws on the grounds of constitutionality (see Abraham, 1980).[6] Second, the Court's decision-making calculus is entirely different from that of a President, a Representative, or a Senator. In an excellent study of Supreme Court case selection, Marie Provine (1980) shows that the justices are neither constitutionally mechanical nor entirely political in their decision-making processes:

> The view that downplays the individuality of judgment and treats case selection as a mechanical screening process . . . ignores, for example, the selectivity of justices concerning the types of cases they believe deserve review. . . . It [also] does not take account of individual differences among justices. . . . To accept the importance of individual judgment in Supreme Court decision making is not, however, to embrace the view that equates judicial decision making with decision making by a nonjudicial political body. . . . Supreme Court justices are not ordinary political decision makers, because members of the Supreme Court share a conception of their

role which prevents them from using their votes simply to achieve policy preferences. (pp. 173–174)

For these and other reasons, it just does not make sense to analyze the Supreme Court's decisions as part of some larger legislative voting game.

The Potency of Analysis

Given what Brams and Chamberlin are willing to assume away, when completed the voting-power values are fascinating. Once the individual power values for institutional members have been added, it turns out that for Brams, the House is most powerful, followed by the Senate and then, well behind, the President.[7] Not surprisingly, for reasons which will become apparent momentarily, Chamberlin discovers that the House is most powerful, followed by the Senate, the Court, and then the President.

In both Banzhaf power-value calculations for the passage of ordinary legislation, the President turns out to be the *least powerful* actor in the American political system—and by quite a bit! Surely, such a finding would constitute a major breakthrough in our understanding of American national government, if only it were accurate. In both accounts, it seems clear that the major factor contributing to this peculiar relative distribution of power is the size of the particular institution. Brams claims that the reason the House is more powerful than the Senate "seems rooted, at least in part, in the greater 'criticality' of House members *in toto*." Unfortunately, this is the only explanation offered and probably the only one possible, given the particular method of analysis. House members are not more powerful than Senators or Presidents as individuals. The House becomes more powerful only when the individual power value of its members is multiplied by their total number of 435. Interestingly, Chamberlin shows that, as individuals, members of the Court are more powerful than Representatives or Senators but significantly less powerful than Presidents. Collectively, however, the Supreme Court falls well behind the House and the Senate and only tops the President.

An explanation of relative power based on size, if one were made in either chapter, would not be insignificant. It would certainly cast doubt on Madison's asserted proposition at the Constitutional Convention and would also suggest that anti-Federalist concerns about the relatively small size of the House have been put to rest by historical developments. There are many implications which could stem from the potential redistribution of representatives between the houses of Congress. However, it is unlikely that the Supreme Court could grow to be competitive with either house, nor is it likely that we will see a plural executive in the near future (although the New Jersey plan at the Constititional Convention did call for one). If relative size is the major explanatory variable for the relative distribution of power in the passage of ordinary legislation, then there is little left to be said from either an explanatory or a normative perspective.[8] The fact that, over time, the relative size of both bodies has changed is not a product of either a constitutional principle or an institutional characteristic. Rather, it is a product of U.S. territorial expansion (for the Senate) and population growth (for the house).

However, Brams and Chamberlin do not place much explanatory weight on size. Rather, they claim that decision rules determine the Banzhaf power values. This may be accurate for the values, but not for their relative distribution, and it is the distribution which is claimed to be most significant. I fail to see why this is not largely attributable to size, especially since the relative distribution remains the same in Brams even when the decision rule changes. Even if decision rules were responsible for the distribution, it is not clear how such a revelation constitutes an institutional explanation for that distribution.

Professor Brams courageously attempts to support the Banzhaf voting power values for the House, the Senate, and the President with empirical data. The method of confirmation is dependent upon the comparative timing of the action by an institutional actor. If a decision taken by Institution A is followed by a similar decision taken by Institution B, then Institution A is credited with "having power."[9] As applied to the House and the Senate, this assumes that the order of decision making in either house is nearly random. Of course, that is not the case at all. For example, while not constitutionally prescribed, it is customary for all appropriations bills to originate in the House (as all bills for raising revenue must constitutionally originate in the House). In addition, certain kinds of legislation—for example, public works—tend more often to originate in the House than in the Senate. The impact of these requirements, traditions, and patterns is to diminish the higher percentage of bills apparently passed by the Senate which originated in the House rather than vice versa. In general, when comparing the difference between Senate passage of House bills and House passage of Senate bills, we should remember that the House has greater difficulty passing legislation. For the period 1947–1983, on average the House was able to pass only 11.7% of its bills, while the Senate was able to pass 37.3%.[10] What accounts for such a difference in institutional capacity? Unfortunately, Brams does not offer a theory of institutional power to explain why the House might be in a better institutional position to influence the Senate rather than the other way around. The "more general explanation embedded in constitutional decision rules" certainly does not explain the empirical data. Indeed, I am hard-pressed to find a "general explanation" in this chapter which has anything to do with the internal organization of either house or their constitutional relationship to the executive.

Chamberlin in chapter 9 does not attempt to support the Banzhof voting-power values for the Supreme Court with empirical data. Rather, he spends the better part of his chapter attempting to discount the surprising finding that, as a collectivity in the passage of ordinary legislation, the Supreme Court is more powerful than the President. A number of these arguments merit final consideration. Chamberlin argues that the Court's power is diminished by the sense of constraint it feels in rendering judgments about the Constitution. Fair enough. However, the same logic of institutional, to say nothing of ideological, constraint is equally applicable to the executive branch and Congress. The demands for party unity, for example, can frequently be quite compelling for a member of Congress. It is curious that neither Brams nor Chamberlin takes the effects of party very seriously when discussing their respective branches of government.[11] Presumably, each branch experiences its own sense of constraint, which has emerged from the historical traditions and practices inhering in it, as well as the general constraints under which all American public policy is made (see Hartz, 1955; Katznelson, 1986; Lindblom, 1982). This is yet another reason that the legislative-voting-game approach of the Banzhaf index challenges one's analytic toleration.

Like Brutus, Chamberlin suggests that the judiciary is "by far the most independent of the four bodies." As a result of its independence from electoral control, the Supreme Court may, in fact, possess a great deal of institutional power. Many years ago, Robert Dahl (1957) suggested that the Court merely followed shifts in the electoral majorities as represented in the other branches of government. While this argument has been adequately critiqued and revised by Jonathan Casper (1976) and Richard Funston (1975), a number of serious checks on the Court's independence beyond amendment (the only one mentioned by Chamberlin) continue to lend support to the crux of Dahl's point—a point in clear opposition to this final supposition by Chamberlin. Presidents can check the Court by refusing to abide by decisions, by failing to enforce court decisions, and through the process of appointment. The Congress can check the Court through reversal by legislation, by limiting the Court's appellate jurisdiction, by changing the size of the Court, by the confirmation process, by impeachment, and by the control of judicial salaries. While many of these devices are infrequently used, they do set forth a context within which the Court must operate. The Court's power in American society probably rests less in its ability to play the legislative game than in its capacity to constrain institutional actions through the process of anticipated reactions and to raise important issues for public debate through the vehicle of agenda building (see Page and Petracca, 1983, pp. 278–316).

The Federalists and Public Choice Theory

These chapters and the entire volume are premised on the assertion that the Federalists were really early public-choice theorists. This is an assertion which is extremely difficult to accept. I conclude with a number of arguments in support of this difficulty. The Federalists, even in their efforts at political persuasion, were theorists of the first rank. They diagnosed problems, offered theories to explain their existence, and as a result were then able to propose potential solutions. Madison's diagnosis of faction in *Federalist* no. 10 is a classic example, but there are many others. In these two chapters, the theory, such as it is, driving the analysis is of a low-octane variety. Neither Brams nor Chamberlin has a theory of institutional power or interbranch decision-making to explain the results of their analysis.

Unlike the claims of many public-choice theorists, the Federalists were interested in far more than the effects of institutional decision rules. *The Federalist Papers*, as well as various notes from the Convention and other period-specific writing, are filled with dozens of references to human nature—in complicated and theoretically interesting ways—not always consistent, but there nonetheless. These various theories of human nature were the main, albeit not the exclusive, motivator for the creation of particular institutions. On the one hand, the Federalists believed that certain institutions were made necessary as the result of a particular understanding of human nature. Surely, it is the institutional response of the inevitability of human nature which captures the brilliance of Madison's *Federalist* no. 10 and no. 51. On the other hand, like John Stuart Mill's *Considerations on Representative Government* (1862/1962), the Federalists understood that certain institutions could be put into place in order to induce particular behaviors. Like Mill, some believed that the progressive potential of human beings could be attained through proper institutional constructions—what Mill would call the capacity for personality valuation and the enhancement of moral character. For others, like John Adams (see Peek, 1954), institutions were an essential check against the inherently wicked and irredeemable nature of humankind.

The attempts by Brams and Chamberlin, as well as by some of the other authors in this volume, to assert a comaradarie between the Federalists and public choice theorists need to be directly sustained. The use of game-theoretic and empirical techniques when appropriate can be extremely suggestive. We ought not to assume, however, that such methods are necessarily applicable or that they render a truthful portrayal of reality. As Claude Levi-Strauss (1979) suggests, "What we as social scientists are trying to do is only to offer better explanations—which cannot be said to be true or false—than those accepted before" (p. 16). But of course, the Federalists were already savvy about the inherent limitations of "political science." Apropos of this entire venture, Madison's analysis in *Federalist* no. 37 provides the final caveat:

> Experience has instructed us that no skill in the science of government has yet been able to discriminate and define, with sufficient certainty, its three great provinces—the legislative, executive, and judiciary; or even the privileges and powers of the different legislative branches. Questions daily occur in the course of practice which prove the obscurity which reigns in these subjects, and which puzzle the greatest adepts in political science. (p. 228)

Notes

1. Brams honestly concedes this point early in chapter 8.
2. An excellent interpretation of *The Federalist Papers* can be found in Epstein (1984).
3. Federal Farmer (Storing, 1985, p. 47) selected the Senate's impeachment power as one of the instances where the House would lose out to the Senate: "All officers are impeachable before the senate only—before the men by whom they are appointed, or who are consenting to the appointment of these officers. No judgment of conviction, on an impeachment, can be given unless two thirds of the senators agree. Under these circumstances the right of impeachment, in the house, can be of but little importance; the house cannot expect often to convict the offender; and, therefore, probably, will but seldom or never exercise the right."
4. All citations to *The Federalist Papers* are to the 1961 edition edited by Clinton Rossiter.
5. It is interesting to note that in a letter to John Adams in November of 1787, Jefferson (Kammen, 1986, p. 84) expressed concern that "The house of federal

representatives will not be adequate to the management of affairs either foreign or federal."

6. In this respect, the concerns of the anti-Federalists were right on target.

7. Later in the chapter, when Brams attempts to reconcile the obviousness of presidential power in the American political system against these relative rankings, he decides to "recalculate" presidential power by subtracting the power values of simple Senate and House majorities from an assumed power value of 100. This has the effect of giving the President a "majority" of power in a simple-majority decision-rule and nearly two thirds of the power when a two-thirds majority of both houses is necessary to overturn a presidential veto. While mathematics may be compelling here, the deployed logic leaves much to the imagination. What Brams would need to explain is why the Banzhaf figure is so low relative to the other branches in the first place, beyond the obvious explanation regarding differential size. To his credit, Chamberlin, while adopting the Banzhaf index, does not replicate this exercise in an effort to reempower the presidency in his analysis.

8. There have, of course, been important historical changes in the distribution of power between the House and the Senate based on changes in size. Following Brams's suggested "square-root law" for bicameral legislatures, the ratios for Congress from 1789 to 1986 were calculated. When these ratios are taken to be close to the Banzhaf power values (according to Brams), it turns out that the House was most powerful in 1810 (with a ratio of 2.31), when there were 181 Congressmen and only 34 Senators, and least powerful in 1789 (with a ratio of 1.58), when there were 65 Congressmen and 26 Senators. We can say that the high point of House power was reached early in the development of the republic. Since 1810, House power has been as low as 1.88 in 1860 and, in the twentieth century, as high as 2.17 in 1910.

9. There are serious problems in conceptualizing power as an institutional (or individual) attribute and in asserting that power is best viewed in relationship to outcomes. As an attribute, power becomes a possession rather than, more appropriately, a relation. When we look to political outcomes in order to assess power, we fall into the trap of limiting the analysis of power to a subset of causal relations. "Power-as-cause-or-outcome" assertions narrow the research possibilities in at least two ways. First, they make the form of the power relationship unidirectional. Second, they limit the location of power to overt and observable individual (or group) behavior. (See Petracca, 1986.)

10. Data collected from Ornstein, Mann, Malbin, Schick, and Bibby (1984, pp. 143–146).

11. Considering the effects of party loyalty and cohesion on legislative voting patterns might significantly alter the calculations of the Banzhaf power index, which assumes that individuals act to maximize preferences (see Clausen, 1973; Hinckley, 1978; Kingdon, 1981).

Part IV

The Ratification Debate

Introduction

Constitutions allocate power which, in turn, affects the distribution of political and economic wealth. Other things being equal, those who would be better off under the federal Constitution *vis-à-vis* the Articles of Confederation would be more likely to be in favor of its ratification. The first two chapters in this section seek to determine who the winners and losers would be under the proposed Constitution and to test the hypothesis that the groups identified as winners actually had a greater probability of voting for the Constitution.

Before discussing the particular chapters, it is important to discuss what such an investigation does and does not say about the role of economic interests in the design and ratification of the Constitution. To have economic interests does not mean that these are the only interests, that they are paramount, nor that people can be divided into simple classes. Rather, they show how, *on the margin*, the probability of voting for the Constitution changed when certain economic characteristics of the voter or representative changed. Furthermore, these studies are designed to find the differences between voters, not their similarities, so that shared values will at best appear as part of an intercept term.

The U.S. Constitution and the Articles of Confederation allocated power and wealth differently, and hence, some groups would be hurt and others benefited by a change in the regime. Using a sample of over twelve hundred delegates to the various ratifying conventions (perhaps the most methodologically sophisticated study of ratification to date), McGuire and Ohsfeldt find that delegates with merchant interests or representing areas with merchant interests, delegates from western lands (which needed federal forces to protect them from Indians), and delegates who owned private or public securities (which would be protected under the Constitution) tended to be in favor of the Constitution, while delegates who were in personal debt, owned slaves (or represented areas with slave-holding interests), or were in the back-country areas (where interstate commerce was less important) were opposed.

Eavey and Miller argue that the different state constitutions under the Articles of Confederation allocated power differently. To the extent that the U.S. Constitution affected the state constitutions and the resulting distribution of power, similar economic groups in different states might react differently to the proposed Constitution. For example, under the Articles of Confederation, if in State A, frontierspeople were in a majority and had control of the state legislature, then they might be less inclined toward the proposed Constitution, which would alter the balance of power within the state, than in State B, where the frontierspeople did not have control of the government and therefore were hoping for an improvement when the states became less influential under the proposed Constitution. Thus, the pattern of support and opposition to the proposed U.S. Constitution stemmed in large part from the variations in the allocation of power across the states. In a nutshell, opposition to the proposed Constitution came from those groups whose economic and political position within the state would be threatened by the new order.

Why did the Federalists win so strongly (the Constitution was ratified by 11 of the 13 states)? Fink and Riker first go through the conventional explanations and show them to be wrong (e.g., overwhelming support for the Constitution, gerrymandering, and disenfranchisement of the anti-Federalists). They then argue that the Federalists won by agenda control. The national convention was dominated by the Federalists. They changed the method of ratification, from approval by state legislators to approval by state constitutional conventions, in order to make their campaign easier. The Constitution was ratified state by state. The Federalists made sure that the states strongly in favor voted first while they delayed votes in those states where the people were opposed. Fink and Riker also document how the Federalists controlled the voting agenda in some state constitutional conventions, even though the Federalists were initially in a numerical minority.

Donald Wittman

CHAPTER TWELVE

Public Choice Analysis and the Ratification of the Constitution

Robert A. McGuire and Robert L. Ohsfeldt

This chapter presents the results of a theoretical and statistical analysis of the relationship between self-interest and the voting behavior of the delegates to the special state assemblies that convened between 1787 and 1790 to consider the adoption of the U. S. Constitution. The delegate's self-interest is defined broadly to include personal and constituent economic and ideological characteristics. We use an expected utility model of self-interest to guide our statistical analysis of delegates' voting behavior. We found that many of the delegates' personal economic interests and the economic and ideological interests of their constituents affected their voting behavior in a manner consistent with the predictions of our self-interest paradigm. The statistical results show that merchants, western landowners, financiers, and large public-securities holders, *ceteris paribus*, supported the new Constitution, whereas debtors and slave owners, *ceteris paribus*, opposed the Constitution. The findings generally confirm Charles Beard's (1913/1935) conclusions about the division of interests on the ratification of the Constitution. This chapter does not, however, presume a dichotomous class-interest motivation for the division of interests. Our self-interest paradigm analyzes the partial effects of different interests on voting and does not suggest, for example, that all slave owners opposed the Constitution; rather, it shows that slave owning significantly decreased the probability of a favorable vote, *ceteris paribus*.

In 1913, the noted historian and political scientist Charles A. Beard proposed a view of the formation of the U.S. Constitution that remains a much discussed yet unresolved interpretation of the behavior and motives of the men who drafted and ratified the document. Since Beard's classic book, *An Economic Interpretation of the Constitution,* first appeared, literally hundreds of articles and books have been written concerning the making of the Constitution.[1] Surprisingly, the continuing controversy among historians and political scientists concerning the Beard thesis has been virtually ignored in the economics literature and has never been addressed in a convincing empirical manner.[2] The oversight is even more surprising given the fundamental nature of the Beard thesis. The Beardian view of the Constitution is that the stance taken on the Constitution by delegates at the Philadelphia Convention of 1787, who drafted the Constitution, and by those at the state ratifying assemblies, who eventually adopted it, was affected by their own economic interests. As long ago as 1913, Charles Beard was emphasizing the importance of economic considerations and self-interest in understanding the formation of political institutions.[3]

Concern about combining economic motives with political actions has been of interest to economists recently. James M. Buchanan and Gordon Tullock (1962) use economic theory to analyze political behavior. Lance Davis and Douglass C. North (1971) develop an economic model to explain secular changes in political institutions in the United States. Numerous economists have developed economic models of voting behavior, suggesting that economic interests contain significant explanatory power.[4]

We suggest that the current view of the formation of the American Constitution is not well founded and needs a thorough revision because the existing literature lacks explicit theoretical models and the necessary empirical analysis of voting behavior. Also, it is naive to regard our Founding Fathers as disinterested individuals. This chapter employs econometric procedures and both primary and secondary data to statistically test what has come to be regarded as Charles Beard's fundamental thesis, that the formation of the Constitution, which strengthened the national government, was a response to the economic interests represented at the several conventions. The chapter contains both a theoretical and a statistical analysis of the relationship between the voting behavior of the delegates to the thirteen state conventions over ratifying the Constitution and the delegates' economic and other interests. It is important to note that Charles Beard stated long ago that an investigation of the contest over ratification was the ultimate test of an economic interpretation.

This chapter analyzes voting at the ratification stage and uses a sample of more than twelve hundred delegates, allowing for a much stronger test of the factors influencing voting behavior than at the Constitutional Convention of 1787, which consisted of only fifty-five delegates. A greater variety of economic interests were present at the state ratifying conventions. Also, because voting at the state conventions was either for or against the Constitution as drafted, we avoid most empirical problems related to strategic voting behavior inherent in an analysis of the Constitutional Convention held in Philadelphia.[5] This chapter not only addresses an important and controversial historical issue (the role of economic interests in the ratification of the Constitution), it advances our general understanding of political behavior, particularly regarding the process of constitutional change.

The Issue in Historical Perspective

Some of the earliest scholarly treatments of the formation of the American Constitution are by the post–Civil War historians, who said there was conflict over economic interests. But economic interests influenced only the opponents of the Constitution (the anti-Federalists). The Founding Fathers, who wrote this "most wonderful work ever struck off at a given time by the brain and purpose of man," are considered "to have risen to the heights of prophecy" and were not motivated by economic interests.[6] Conversely, during the Progressive Era (the first two decades of the twentieth century), the Constitution came under attack. The Founding Fathers and their eighteenth-century supporters (the Federalists) were now considered to have foisted the Constitution on their democratic opponents. Selfish interests now motivated the Founding Fathers, whereas the anti-Federalists were made to "seem embattled champions of the public good" (Hutson, 1981, p. 342).

Charles Beard challenged these views in 1913. He argued that the making of the Constitution was a struggle based on economic interests—interests of both the opponents and the proponents. Beard's view suggests that the delegates who supported the Constitution—supporters of a strong, centralized government—were individuals whose major economic interests were tied to personal property. He claimed that the Federalists were mainly merchants, shippers, bankers, speculators, and holders of private and public securities (pp. 149–151). The anti-Federalists—the opponents of the

Constitution and supporters of a highly decentralized government—were individuals whose major economic interests were tied to real property. This group representing "landed interests" consisted mainly of farmers (usually debtors) and some northern planters (pp. 26–30). Beard argued that because southern planters held as much of their wealth in personal property as the northern "commercial interests," they should be included as supporters of the Constitution (pp. 29–30).

Beard (1913) suggested that the primary beneficiaries under the proposed Constitution would be individuals with financial and commercial interests—particularly holders of public securities, whom he considered to be the dynamic element at the Constitutional Convention. The Constitution included a clause requiring the assumption of all existing federal debt by the new central government. These individuals would also benefit because of more certainty in the rules of commerce, trade, and credit markets under the Constitution (pp. 31–51). Farmers, the northern planters, and debtors would be the primary beneficiaries under the status quo and, therefore, were likely opponents of the Constitution. They would have greater ability at the state level with decentralized government to avoid heavy land taxation—used to pay off the public debt—and to promote "soft" money and debt moratorium issues (pp. 26–30).

Contemporary academic reviewers generally looked favorably upon Beard's work. William Dodd (1913) suggested that Beard "has looked beneath the surface of things and brought to light many new facts, or old facts long overlooked" (p. 163) and concluded that his book "is one of the most important works of recent times" (Dodd, 1916, p. 495). Another scholar argued that Beard "made a distinct contribution to knowledge of the financial circumstances and presumable motives of the leaders of 1787" (Levermore, 1914, p. 118). Still another added that "none will deny that new light has been thrown upon this important question and that to a limited extent at least his position is unassailable" (Hall, 1913, p. 408). Harold Faulkner, the author of a major economic history text at the time (1924), concluded that Beard's book "is the most authoritative study of the economic phases of the movement for the Constitution" (p. 186). On the other hand, John Latané (1913) accused the author of reducing "everything to a sordid basis of personal interest" (p. 700). Edward Corwin (1920) suggested that Beard had "Socialistic sympathies" and had no basis for implying "that the Convention of 1787 was governed by unworthy motives" (pp. iv–v). Nicholas Murray Butler (1923), the president of Columbia University (Charles Beard's employer in 1913), stated that "It is a travesty to dignify so unscholarly an adventure by the title of an economic interpretation of history" (p. 96).

Although Beard's thesis was the standard historical interpretation by the 1930s, it began to face serious academic challenges during the 1950s. The challenges include empirical examinations of the state ratification conventions in New Jersey, North Carolina, and Virginia. The authors suggest that their results indicate voting behavior almost antithetical to Beard's view.[7] Cecelia Kenyon (1955) suggests that Beard has misinterpreted the motives of the anti-Federalists, who, she claims, supported stronger protections of property rights from popular majorities, not weaker, as Beard argues. Others question the logical consistency of Beard's thesis, suggesting that the Constitution had little, if any, influence on the economy (Commager, 1958). But the most detailed and influential critiques are by Robert Brown (1956) and Forrest McDonald (1958).

Brown's (1956) critique is concerned primarily with attacking Beard's conclusions that eighteenth-century America was not very democratic, that the wealthy were staunch supporters of the Constitution, and that the Constitution was generally opposed by the propertyless masses (farmers and debtors). His empirical evidence is qualitative data on voting rights and attitudes toward the Constitution. Brown, however, presents no statistical analysis of whether the voting behavior of any delegates was influenced significantly by their economic interests.

In contrast, McDonald (1958) quantifies the economic interests of the delegates at the Constitutional Convention and the state ratifying conventions, a quantification that Beard never completed. McDonald's study contains a detailed account of the delegates' wealth positions—approximately twelve hundred economic biographies— and a record of each delegate's vote. Similarly to Brown, McDonald presents no statistical analysis of the voting behavior of any delegates. His analysis of the data is limited to "eyeballing" for "obvious" voting patterns related to economic interests. Both Brown and McDonald conclude—based on their very casual analyses—that the Beardian view of the making of the Constitution is not valid because they find no obvious voting patterns.

Despite their lack of modern rigor, Brown (1956) and McDonald (1958) are generally credited with offering a definitive debunking of Beard.[8] But Brown and McDonald have also faced some criticism. Lee Benson (1960) suggests that neither Brown nor McDonald possesses a sufficient understanding of Beard's thesis to criticize it successfully. Jackson Main (1960) and Robert Schuyler (1961) contend that some of

McDonald's data do not support his conclusions. In another study, Main (1961) finds important voting patterns related to economic interests in the state ratifying conventions. E. James Ferguson (1961) finds widespread support among public creditors for the Constitution, contrary to McDonald. Unfortunately, neither Benson, Ferguson, Main, nor Schuyler base their conclusions on any statistical analyses.[9]

Literature on the Ratification Process

Numerous studies of the details of the ratification process in individual states have been completed in the last thirty years. The state-level literature is best characterized by its lack of a consensus concerning the division of economic interests in the contest over ratification. The state-level literature generally examines voting patterns at a particular state ratifying assembly or voting patterns at several ratifying assemblies, with each examined individually. Although differences in institutional structures and economic conditions across states provide some justification for the methodology, analyzing each ratifying assembly separately tends to obscure generalities in the voting patterns across states.[10] The literature is also marred by an absence of formal hypothesis-testing, which contributes to inconsistencies among the various studies.

Some of the most detailed empirical studies examine voting at ratifying conventions in states regarded as divided over the Constitution (New Hampshire, Massachusetts, Pennsylvania, and South Carolina). With respect to the delegates at the Pennsylvania ratifying assembly who owned public securities, different studies find that they were more likely to have favored the Constitution (Brunhouse, 1942), were more likely to have opposed the Constitution (McDonald, 1958), or were divided on the Constitution (Main, 1961). Most studies find that public-security holders at the Massachusetts and New Hampshire assemblies favored the Constitution (Main, 1961; McDonald, 1958; Rutland, 1966). In the South Carolina ratifying assembly, Nadelhaft (1981) and Schuyler (1961) find that voting for ratification was positively related to public-security holdings, but McDonald (1958) concludes that public-security holders in South Carolina opposed the Constitution. Three studies find no geographic pattern in the vote at the ratifying assemblies of Massachusetts, New Hampshire, and South Carolina (Handlin and Handlin, 1944; McDonald, 1958, 1963), while four other studies find delgates from coastal areas more likely to have favored the Constitution than delegates from inland areas in the three states (Daniell, 1970; Hall, 1972; Main, 1961; Rutland, 1966).

Much attention has also been directed to the contest over ratification in the states generally opposed to the Constitution (New York, North Carolina, Virginia, and Rhode Island). The most thoroughly studied is Virginia. Main (1961) argues that public-security holders at the Virginia assembly favored the Constitution, while McDonald (1958) suggests that they were divided. Slave owners appear to have supported the Constitution, according to Main (1961) and Risjord (1974), but they were divided according to Thomas (1953) and McDonald (1958). There is a similar lack of agreement concerning geographical voting patterns. McDonald (1958) finds no geographic pattern in Virginia, while Main (1961) and Thomas (1953) suggest that delegates from coastal areas were more likely to have favored the Constitution than other delegates.

With respect to the states that generally favored the Constitution (Connecticut, Delaware, Georgia, Maryland, and New Jersey), there is comparably less analysis of the contest over ratification. In fact, three of the states (Delaware, Georgia, and New Jersey) ratified the Constitution unanimously. Still, there is a lack of consensus in the literature over the influence of economic interests at their ratifying assemblies. Delegates in Connecticut who owned public securities were overwhelmingly supporters of the Constitution (Main, 1961; McDonald, 1958), but in New Jersey, they were either more likely to have favored the Constitution (Main, 1961; McCormick, 1950) or less likely to have favored it (McDonald, 1958). In Maryland, Crowl (1943, 1947) finds that delegates who owned a large number of slaves favored ratification, and that paper-money advocates opposed it. But Main (1961) concludes that paper-money advocates in Maryland were divided, and McDonald (1958) finds that slave owners were divided.

Such inconsistencies across the state-level studies result in part because few employ formal statistical techniques to analyze their data. For example, Pool (1950) concludes that there was no pattern in the vote at the North Carolina ratifying assembly related to the slave holdings of the delegates. But by use of the data contained in Pool's summary tables, a simple test of association reveals a statistically significant positive relationship between voting for the Constitution and the number of slaves owned. It may be the case that, because of the lack of formal hypothesis-testing and explicit theoretical paradigms, scholars predisposed to find an absence of voting patterns related to economic interests conclude that any differences in voting indicated by the data are "too small" to be important, while those otherwise predisposed find almost any difference significant.[11]

The absence of formal statistical analysis in the state-level and the

Constitutional Convention studies should not be surprising. Traditionally, historical analysis has not been quantitatively oriented, or at least not oriented toward statistical analysis. At the time many of the studies were conducted, most scholars in the social sciences were unfamiliar with statistical techniques other than simple mean comparisons or tests of association. What is surprising is that political scientists and the new economic historians with training in statistical analysis have uncritically accepted the findings of several of the studies.[12]

Analytical Framework

In the economics literature, the voting behavior of elected officials (politicians) is generally analyzed in the context of a simple principal-agent model (for recent examples, see Kalt and Zupan, 1984; Peltzman, 1984, 1985). The legislator is said to be the agent of the principal (the constituent) who elects or supports him or her. Because the agent can be fired (i.e., not reelected), it is in the agent's self-interest to satisfy his or her constituents' desires. Peltzman (1984) argues that the economic theory of political voting is not well developed and that the empirical strategy used to test the principal-agent model usually takes on a "fishing-expedition" character. According to him, most studies incorrectly conclude that noneconomic variables are centrally important in understanding politicians' voting behavior (pp. 182–83).

The primary controversy in the literature concerns the relative role of economic interests (the constituents') versus ideologies (the legislators') in explaining the voting behavior of elected officials (see Kalt and Zupan, 1984; Kau and Rubin, 1979, 1982; Peltzman, 1984, 1985). Peltzman (1984, 1985) presents empirical evidence supporting the notion that politicians are primarily faithful agents of the constituents' economic interests. He concludes that ideology is not an exogenous variable and is often interest-determined. Kau and Rubin (1979, 1982) and Kalt and Zupan (1984), on the other hand, provide evidence supporting the notion of ideological shirking, in which the agent bases his or her votes partly on a personal ideology (or his or her view of the public interest).

In other contexts, it has been argued that public officials may be more accurately characterized as maximizers of their own interests than as maximizers of their constituents' interests (see Alchian and Demsetz, 1972; Barro, 1973; Tollison, 1982; Welch and Peters, 1983; Wittman, 1973, 1983). The literature on property rights, public choice, and rent-seeking behavior suggests that politicians may be personal-utility maximizers and rent seekers, pursuing rent through their decision-making authority, particularly because they face attenuated property rights to any residual from their decisions. In addition, when the costs of monitoring and policing agents' behavior are positive, a positive amount of appropriating and rent seeking on the part of politicians may take place. Because of institutional constraints and the large-group nature of the situation, the principals (citizen-owners) cannot easily recognize and capture the net gains from efficient political decisions, even though they are legally the residual claimants in a democratic society.

The preceding suggests there is little basis for a hypothesis that political voting behavior is determined only by a perfectly monitored demand for legislation. Because of the agency problems inherent with political decision makers (nonresidual claimants), we argue that the suppliers are active participants in the production of legislation. Moreover, substantial evidence exists to suggest that individuals, including politicians, possess ideologies (sets of beliefs about the correct social relations to be followed), and that among other interests, they act on those beliefs (see Higgs, 1986).

There is strong reason to believe that the monitoring costs in the 1780s were high enough to permit substantial shirking by political agents. Communication technology was relatively undeveloped. As Gary Walton and Ross Robertson (1983) have observed, "At the time of the Revolution, it took about three weeks for news of any importance to spread to the chief settlements throughout the colonies. Those who lived on the frontier often waited much longer to learn of major events and were almost completely isolated from reports on . . . mundane matters" (p. 87). Delegates to the state ratifying conventions were elected to attend a one-time convention and were not subject to reelection to that position; thus, constraints on the delegates' voting behavior were lessened further. Many delegates, however, were elected officials and possessed future political ambitions. Two states actually had second conventions because, in the case of New Hampshire, the first convention adjourned without a vote and, in the case of North Carolina, the first convention voted against ratification. Monitoring of the delegates' voting behavior, therefore, was not zero.

We suggest that the most appropriate assumption about voting behavior at the thirteen ratifying conventions is that a delegate's expected utility would have been a function of the anticipated effects of the vote on *both his personal interests and his constituents' interests.* We further assume that a delegate's personal interests would have

depended on his personal economic interests and his personal
ideology, both determined independently of his constituents. A
delegate's constituents' interests would have depended on his constituents' economic interests and his constituents' ideologies. A
delegate would have voted in favor of the Constitution if he perceived
that his expected utility would have been greater if the Constitution
was ratified. We assume that a delegate expected to receive utility
from satisfying each of the four sets of interests.[13]

In voting on ratification, a delegate's personal economic interests
may have been in conflict with his constituents' economic interests,
with his constituents' ideologies, or with his personal ideology. It is
still possible to determine conceptually the partial effects of each of
the economic interests and ideologies on voting behavior through
their marginal impact on a delegate's expected utility. A single partial
effect on the probability of voting, of course, does not predict a
delegate's actual vote. The overall effect of adoption of the Constitution on a delegate's total expected utility (the aggregate of the partial
effects of all his interests) would have determined his actual vote.
With respect to the relative magnitudes of the influence of personal
interests versus constituent interests, the issue is essentially an
empirical question—a question we attempt to answer in this chapter.

Our theoretical foundation follows the basic framework of James
Buchanan and Gordon Tullock's *Calculus of Consent* (1962). The
ratification of the U.S. Constitution, however, does not correspond
directly to Buchanan and Tullock's general economic theory of
constitutions (1962, chap. 6). Buchanan and Tullock argue that the
consequences of self-interest are quite different at the "constitutional" level than at the "operational" level. The individual's interest
at the constitutional level is in choosing voting rules, given perceptions regarding the operation and the consequences of the rules.
Buchanan and Tullock (1962) suggest that, at the constitutional level,
an individual "will not find it advantageous to vote for rules that may
promote sectional, class, or group interests because, by presupposi-
tion, he is unable to predict the role that he will be playing in the
actual collective decision-making process at any particular time in the
future (p. 78).[14]

It is more accurate to argue that the ratification process is a situation
closer to Buchanan and Tullock's "operational" level of collective
choice. It is here that individuals are making collective choices within
certain agreed-on rules. At the operational level, the individual
calculus is similar to deciding on the allocation of resources within a
well-defined time period where the individual knows his or her

interests and location relative to others. As Buchanan and Tullock (1962) state about the rational individual at the operational level of public choice, "he is assumed to be motivated by a desire to further his own interest, to maximize his expected utility, narrowly or broadly defined. In this stage . . . the individual's interest will be more readily identifiable and more sharply distinguishable from those of his fellows than was the case at the constitutional level of decision" (p. 120).[15]

The rules under which state assemblies voted on the Constitution stated that the Constitution would be considered adopted when nine of the thirteen state assemblies had, by a majority vote of the assembly delegates, ratified the Constitution. Given this decision rule, the outcome in a particular ratifying assembly often affected the vote in subsequent assemblies. The impact of timing considerations complicates an analysis of voting across state assemblies. (The issue of timing considerations is discussed in detail in our empirical analysis.) There is no evidence of any explicit vote-trading among the delegates at different state assemblies. Indeed, with the exception of the compromise over a "bill of rights" in several states (ratification with a call for a "bill-of-rights" amendment or suggested amendments instead of no ratification), there is little evidence of significant strategic voting behavior in the ratification process.[16]

The assumption that delegates acted in their self-interest by maximizing their individual utilities, of course, does not suggest that the political principles or moral philosophy of the delegates had no impact on their voting behavior. Rather, the assumption suggests that an individual delegate whose political or moral preference was to support the Constitution would have been less likely to do so if he perceived that his economic interests (including his constituents') were directly and adversely affected by the adoption of the Constitution. Nor do we assume that the rhetoric in the debates or in the campaign prior to the ratifying assemblies had no impact on voting behavior. Those factors are assumed to have affected the ideologies of the delegates and their constituents. As a practical matter, however, the impact on voting of rhetoric, polemics, and pamphlets in the ratification campaign would be very difficult to determine empirically. We attempt to control for such factors by incorporating several rough proxies for ideological preferences in our empirical analysis.

With respect to the ratification of the Constitution, to determine which delegates expected to benefit on the margin from the change and which delegates expected to lose on the margin it is necessary to examine the economic conditions and institutional structure existing under the Articles of Confederation and the perceived changes in the conditions attributable to the Constitution. According to Gordon Wood (1980, p. 8), during the 1780s the "state assemblies were abusing their extraordinary powers." Because annually elected legislatures were subject to intense pressures by various special-interest groups, "more laws were enacted by the states in the decade following independence than in the entire colonial period." Charles Beard (1912, pp. 80–81) states that "holders of the securities of the Confederate government did not receive the interest on their loans." Western landowners "chaffed at the weakness of the government and its delays in establishing order on the frontiers." And merchants "found their plans for commerce on a national scale impeded by local interference with interstate commerce." As Stanley Lebergott (1984) concludes, "Year after year the Confederation failed to meet the demands for protection or payment. It did not lack good intentions; it lacked money" (p. 53).[17]

The adoption of the Constitution dramatically altered conditions, according to Gary Walton and James Shepherd (1979, ch. 9). Under the Constitution, the power to tax was delegated firmly to the central government, along with the authority to settle past federal government debts. Walton and Shepherd argue that the assurance that public debts would be honored was a cornerstone in the development of a sound capital market. The Constitution also improved the capital market by assigning the sole right to mint coinage and to regulate its value to the central government. With respect to interstate trade, Walton and Shepherd note that "no substantial barriers to interstate commerce developed," but they also suggest that "the possibility of such barriers loomed as a threat until the Constitution specifically granted the regulation of interstate commerce to the federal government" (p. 188; also, see Shepherd and Walton, 1976). Walton and Shepherd conclude that the most important changes in institutions associated with the movement to the Constitution "were those changes that strengthened the framework for protection of private property and enforcement of contracts" (p. 188).

Because of the existing economic conditions and expectations in the 1780s, we have the following priors about the partial effect of each economic interest on the voting behavior of the delegates: We expect creditors—especially public creditors—to have favored the new government because of provisions in the proposed Constitution for the national government to assume previous federal credit obligations, provisions emphasizing the sanctity of private contracts, and a prohibition on *ex post facto* laws. We expect debtors to have opposed

the new government because of the emphasis on contractual obligations, the prohibition on state paper-money issues, and the ban on *ex
post facto* laws, which was expected to make state stay laws (debt
moratoria) unconstitutional. Debtors expected the costs of influencing debtor relief measures and soft money policies to be lower at the
state level than at a national level (see McDonald, 1965, pp. 289,
321–325).

To the extent that provisions in the new Constitution concerning
tariff policy, trade regulation, and national security encouraged
interstate and international trade through a decrease in the costs of
trade activities, we expect merchants engaged in such activities to
have favored the Constitution. Delegates classified as farmers (individuals whose primary economic interests are in localized, noncom-
mercial activities) would have opposed the Constitution because of a
perception that trade provisions in the Constitution strongly favored
national interests at the expense of local interests, which could have
been more fully satisfied at the state level (Wood, 1980, p. 8).

We expect western landowners to have favored the proposed
Constitution, because it represented the foundation of a stronger
national government, included specific provisions for providing
national security to western lands by the central government, and
included provisions allowing for uniform rules for the disposal of
public land that encouraged settlement. Contemporary perceptions
were that western land values would rise under the new government
(Hughes, 1983, pp. 94–101).

Finally, slave owners are expected to have opposed the adoption of
the Constitution because of their fear of a truly national government
controlled by a future northern majority and its consequent restrictions upon the sovereignty of the states. Slave owners were afraid
that a strong national government might impose restrictions on the
use of slaves and the expansion of slavery, adversely affecting the
value of slaves or the ability to produce slave-based products.[18] They
also feared the imposition of navigation acts that would allow
northern merchants to monopolize the southern staples trade and
reduce its value.[19]

Estimation and Data

Voting patterns are estimated using the general specification

$$V = f(P,E,I,T) \tag{1}$$

where V is a dummy variable representing a delegate's vote on the

Constitution, P is a set of personal interest variables, E is a set of measures of constituents' economic interests, and I is a set of measures of constituents' ideology (see Table 12.1). Because of a lack of data, we do not include measures of the delegates' ideologies in the empirical estimation. Even though the theoretical model includes delegate ideology as an explanatory variable, its exclusion causes no severe problems to the extent the omitted variable is not strongly correlated with the included variables.[20] The variables in the set T measure the impact of the timing of the state ratifying assembly in the ratification process and other institutional or political factors on voting behavior.

Because the dependent variable in our analysis is limited (the delegate could vote only "yes" or "no" on the Constitution), we use logit analysis rather than ordinary least-squares regression to estimate voting patterns. The advantages of logit for models of this type are well known. The assumption of homoscedasticity implied by the use of ordinary least-squares (OLS) regression is untenable with dichotomous dependent variables (Hanushek and Jackson, 1977, p. 181). It follows that hypothesis-testing is more precise with logit than with OLS. Furthermore, the fact that a delegate's true probability of voting for the Constitution must lie between 0 and 1 suggests a nonlinear relationship between the vote (V) and the independent variables (P, E, I, and T). Logit assumes a more realistic functional form than is generally possible with OLS (Hanushek and Johnson, 1977, p. 183). Logit techniques have also been shown to be consistent with an expected-utility-maximization postulate (McFadden, 1974).

Data Sources

A major source of data on the votes and the personal economic interests of the delegates employed in our study is McDonald (1958), which contains economic biographies of over twelve hundred of the 1,648 delegates to the state ratifying assemblies along with their vote on the Constitution. The assets owned by the delegates recorded by McDonald are the value of public-security holdings, the number of slaves owned, and, in some instances, acres (or value) of land owned, and the quantity of horses, livestock, ships, warehouses, mills, foundries, carriages, and other belongings. McDonald also includes several nonquantitative economic interests. The qualitative data are the delegates' principal occupations, a determination from the available records of whether the delegates possessed private-security interests (i.e., owned bank stock, held private notes, or were other-

TABLE 12.1. Description of Variables

Dependent Variable

VOTE	= 1 if the delegate to the ratifying assembly voted to ratify the Constitution (0 otherwise).

Measures of Delegates' Personal Interests (P)

DMERC	= 1 if the delegate's principal occupation was a merchant (0 otherwise).
DWLAND	= 1 if the delegate owned western lands (0 otherwise).
DFARM	= 1 if the delegate's principal occupation was farming (0 otherwise).
DDEBT	= 1 if the delegate was in deep personal debt (0 otherwise).
DPRIV	= 1 if the delegate owned private securities (0 otherwise).
DSLAVE	= 1 if the delegate owned slaves in 1790 (0 otherwise).
VSLAVE	= value (in $000's) of slaves owned in 1790.
DPCSLAVE	= difference between delegate's slave ownings and constituents' slave ownings in 1790.
DPSECR	= 1 if the delegate owned public securities (0 otherwise).
DLPSECR	= 1 if the delegate owned more than $1,000 in public securities (0 otherwise).
VPSECR	= value (in $000's) of the delegate's public-security holdings.
DPCSECR	= difference between delegate's public securities ($) and constituents' public securities ($)

Measures of Constituents' Economic Interests (E)

CSLAVE	= slaves per 100 whites in the delegate's home county or township in 1790.
NPSECRPC	= per capita net public credit at funding in 1793.
NWEALTH	= net physical wealth per probate-type wealth-holder in 1774.

Measures of Constituents' Ideology (I)

POPW	= total white population (000's) in the delegate's state in 1790.
DISTN	= distance from the delegate's home county or township to the nearest navigable water (in miles).
ENGANS	= percentage of population in the delegate's home county or township of English ancestry.

Measures of Timing Factors

ORDER	= order of each state's ratifying assembly in the ratification process.
MOOT	= 1 if the assembly voted on the Constitution after nine states had approved the Constitution (0 otherwise)

Other

PAPER	= 1 if the state issued paper money during the Confederation period (0 otherwise).
AMENDR	= 1 if the assembly ratified the Constitution with recommended amendments (0 otherwise).
AMENDC	= 1 if the assembly ratified the Constitution with strong declarations and recommended amendments, implying more conditional ratification (0 otherwise).

Source: See text.

wise private creditors), whether the delegates were deeply in debt, and whether they owned western land. McDonald seldom included the dollar value for private securities, debts, or western landholdings (land on the frontier). Gaps in McDonald's data for delegates economic interests are filled with information contained in Main (1973), Lynd (1962), and Pool (1950).[21]

The completeness of McDonald's (1958) data varies considerably across states. For all states, McDonald reports the principal occupation and the public-security holdings of virtually all the delegates for whom he reports any economic information, and includes his determination of the other three qualitative characteristics (private creditor status, debtor status, and western land status) for many delegates. Data on the number of slaves owned are reasonably complete for all southern states, except Georgia, when Pool's (1950) data are included. The value or amount of nonwestern land holdings and the quantity of the other types of assets are reported very sporadically. The data on land and other assets are, in fact, so sporadic that they are not used here. Overall, the best data are for Virginia, South Carolina, and Maryland. The worst data are for Delaware and New York.

McDonald's occupational groupings number about one dozen, but most delegates fall into one of four major occupations (merchant, farmer, planter, and lawyer). Merchant and farmer are used in the empirical model. Because McDonald did not distinguish clearly between farmer and planter, we classify all small planters (delegates whom McDonald classified as planters who owned three or fewer slaves) as farmers. The remaining planter category is not used because it is almost perfectly correlated with slave owning. The lawyer occupation is probably overrepresented. Most delegates classified as lawyers were also classified under another occupation. Many college-educated men in the eighteenth century studied the law yet were not primarily practicing attorneys. Additionally, the primary interests of the clients of delegates who were practicing attorneys is not known, and thus, voting expectations cannot be determined readily. The lawyer category was also not used. Delegates who were not farmers, merchants, or slave owners are the excluded category and may have been, for example, shopkeepers, frontiersmen, ministers, or lawyers.

Data from the 1790 Census are used to provide several measures of constituents' economic interests and ideologies.[22] The census data are slave holdings, population, and the ancestry of the population. As noted, ownership of slaves was a major economic interest during the late eighteenth century. Constituents' slave interests, as measured by their slave holdings, are expected to influence the voting behavior of the delegates in the same direction as the delegates' personal slave interests. Population is included because it is commonly claimed that citizens of the more populous states were more likely to have favored the Constitution for two reasons (for recent statements of this, see Jillson, 1981; Jillson and Eubanks, 1984). Citizens of large states expected to dominate a new national government, and they possessed a more worldly view than citizens of the less populous and less urban states. Delegates representing more populous states were thus more likely to have favored the Constitution. Finally, ancestry is included because Main (1961) argues that individuals of English ancestry also possessed a greater sympathy for strong central governments. Their cultural background and heritage of a strong central government influenced them to be more likely to have supported the Constitution than individuals of Scottish or Irish ancestry. This hypothesis predicts that delegates representing English descendants were more likely to have voted for the Constitution.

Given that funding the public debt was a major part of the debate over the Constitution, the public-security holdings of citizens may have been an important factor in voting at the ratifying conventions. We expect constituents' holdings to have influenced the delegates in the same (positive) direction as the delegates' personal holdings. A rough measure of constituents' public-security interests is obtained from James E. Ferguson (1961). It is the net public-securities credit per capita for each state at the funding of the national debt in 1793. It is at best only a rough proxy for constituents' public-security interests. But better measures of constituents' public-security interests are not consistently available for all the states.

Because the traditional Beardian view is that supporters of the Constitution were generally men of wealth, a rough measure of average state wealth is taken from Alice Hanson Jones (1980, pp. 377–379). We calculated population-weighted averages of her county wealth estimates for each state.[23] In addition, we compiled measures of the distance from each delegate's home to the coast, to navigable water, and to major commercial cities. The measures serve as proxies for the lack of commercial orientation of each delegate's constituents. Many scholars, following Libby (1894), suggest that individuals from coastal areas were more likely to be sympathetic to a strong central government because they possessed a "cosmopolitan" ideology—a commercial orientation that was national in scope. Individuals farther from coastal areas were more likely to have opposed the new government because they possessed a "localist" ideology—a non-commercial, self-sufficiency orientation that was limited in scope.[24]

A dummy variable for the states that had issued paper money during the Confederation period (see McDonald, 1958, pp. 387–388) is included to account for the possible influence of direct experience with paper money among the delegates within a state's ratifying assembly. The political history of paper money may have intensified creditor-versus-debtor conflicts in the ratification process in states where paper-money issues had been used as a means of debtor relief. States that issued paper money were often accused of abusing their authority. This suggests that delegates in states with paper money were more likely to have opposed the Constitution because the state's adoption of paper money indicates a desire by the state to utilize monetary policy instruments and proxies a strong antinational sentiment within the state.

Two dummy variables are included in the specification of the model to incorporate differences across states in the nature of the ratification of the Constitution. Several states ratified the Constitution with various nonbinding declarations and recommendations for amendments (Elliot, 1836, vol. 1, pp. 318–338). Two sets of states are defined according to the strength of their nonbinding conditions of ratification: states that included only recommendations for amendments and states that included stronger declarations of constitutional interpretation and recommendations for amendments, implying more conditional ratification. Because both represented compromise proposals, we expect their coefficients to be positive. A delegate was more likely to have voted for ratification if the vote represented a compromise between supporters and opponents of ratification.

The specific measures of delegates' personal interests (P), constituents' economic interests (E), constituents' ideology (I), and timing considerations (T) are listed in Table 12.1. For reasons noted earlier, we expect delegates who were merchants, western landowners, and private- or public-security owners to have been more likely to vote for the Constitution, *ceteris paribus*. We expect delegates who were slave owners or farmers or who were in deep personal debt to have been more likely to oppose the Constitution. Delegates who represented slave owners are expected to have been more likely to vote no, while those who represented public creditors, coastal areas, or constituents of English ancestry are expected to have been more likely to vote yes. Finally, we expect delegates in ratifying assemblies held later in the ratification process to have been more likely to vote no, while delegates in assemblies held after the Constitution had been adopted

TABLE 12.2. State Ratifying Conventions

State	Vote	Date	Order
Connecticut	128 – 40	01/09/88	5
Delaware	30 – 0	12/07/87	1
Georgia	26 – 0	01/02/88	4
Maryland	63 – 11	04/26/88	7
Massachusetts	187 – 168	02/06/88	6
New Hampshire[a]	57 – 47	06/21/88	9
New Jersey	38 – 0	12/18/87	3
New York	30 – 27	07/26/88	11
North Carolina[b]	194 – 77	11/21/89	12
Pennsylvania	46 – 23	12/12/87	2
Rhode Island[c]	34 – 32	05/29/90	13
South Carolina	149 – 73	05/23/88	8
Virginia	89 – 79	06/25/88	10

[a]Second convention. First convention adjourned without a vote.
[b]Second convention. First convention voted 184 to 84 against ratification on August 1, 1788.
[c]Call for a convention defeated seven times. The Constitution was finally ratified after the federal government under the Constitution had been in effect 15 months and Providence had seceded from Rhode Island to protest the state's continued quixotic opposition to the Constitution.
Source: Main, *The Antifederalists*, p. 288; McDonald, *We the People*, pp. 113–346; and Elliot, *Elliot's Debates*, vol. I, pp. 318–337; vol. II, pp. 547–549 and 627–656.

by nine states are expected to have been less likely to vote no (see Table 12.2).[25]

Estimation Strategy

Voting behavior is estimated by means of logit analysis and a pooled sample of all thirteen ratifying assemblies. The advantage of pooling data across states is that it facilitates generalizations regarding the impact of personal and constituent interests on voting in the ratification process. Pooling, however, imposes restrictions on the nature of the voting patterns determined by the empirical analysis. In the pooled sample, for example, the estimated marginal effect of each independent variable on the probability of a vote for the Constitution is restricted to be the same across states. The impact on voting of institutional factors unique to each state is captured only through regional dummy variables and other dummy variables which reflect the approximate overall strength of the support for the Constitution across states. Likewise, the effect of timing considerations is assumed to be captured through one variable that measures the order of ratification and another variable that measures whether the issue was moot (the Constitution having already been ratified in nine states), with the marginal effects of personal and constituent interests restricted to be constant over time. Although the restrictions implied by pooling are potentially severe, data limitations necessitate the imposition of some restrictions on the nature of the specification of the empirical model.[26]

Estimates of Voting Behavior

The logit results for the pooled sample of all thirteen state assemblies for eight specifications are summarized in the first column of Table 12.3. The eight alternative specifications differ primarily in terms of the variables used to measure public security and slave interests. The marginal effects of the independent variables on the estimated probability of a vote for ratification are calculated at the means of the independent variables, with all other independent variables held constant. In the case of dummy independent variables, the incremental effect of a change in a dummy variable is calculated as the difference between the predicted probability of a yes vote when the variable has a value of 1 and the predicted probability when the variable has a value of 0, with all other variables at sample mean values.[27]

The estimated incremental effect of the dummy variable for merchant interests (DMERC) is positive and statistically significant at the .05 level or better in all specifications. The results indicate that delegates with merchant interests were more likely to have voted to ratify the Constitution than other delegates, other factors being constant. The estimated incremental effects of the dummy variables for western landowner (DWLAND) and private security interests (DPRIV) are positive and statistically significant at the .01 level or better in all specifications. The results suggest that delegates who owned western lands and delegates with banking interests also tended to have favored the Constitution. However, delegates who were in personal debt (DDEBT) were more likely to have opposed the Constitution. The incremental effect of the variable DDEBT is negative and statistically significant at the .01 level or better in all specifications. The incremental effect of the variable DFARM is not statistically significant in any of the specifications, contrary to expectations.

In terms of the magnitude of the effects, for a hypothetical delegate with average values of all other independent variables, owning private securities increases the predicted probability of a yes vote from about .59 to about .84. Being in personal debt, for a hypothetical

TABLE 12.3. Summary of Alternative Specifications of Logit Estimates of Voting Behavior at Ratifying Assemblies (Dependent Variable = VOTE)

Independent Variables	Sample[a]	
	Summary of All States Pooled[b]	Summary of All Subsamples[c]
Personal Economic		
Interests		
DMERC	YES	YES
DWLAND	YES	YES
DPRIV	YES	YES*
DDEBT	NO	NO
DFARM	0	?
DSLAVE	NO	NO
VSLAVE	0	0
DPCSLAVE	0	0
DPSECR	0	YES
DLPSECR	YES	YES
VPSECR	YES	YES
DPCSECR	YES	YES
Constituents' Economic		
Interests		
CSLAVE	0	?
NPSECRPC	NO	NO*
Constituents' Ideology		
POPW	NO	?
DISTN	NO	NO
ENGANS	0	YES*
Other		
ORDER	NO	NO
MOOT	YES	—
NEW ENGLAND	0	—
SOUTH	YES	—
PAPER	0	—
AMENDC	0	—
AMENDR	0	—

[a]YES and NO indicate that delegates with this characteristic were statistically more likely to have voted yes or no, respectively, on ratification in all alternative specifications that were significant, and that the majority of logit coefficients were significant; YES* and NO* indicate that delegates with this characteristic were statistically more likely to have voted yes or no, respectively, on ratification in most alternative specifications that were significant, and that less than a majority (but a nontrivial proportion) of the logit coefficients were significant; the symbol 0 indicates a consistently insignificant statistical relationship between voting and this characteristic; and the symbol ? indicates a large degree of inconsistency in the sign and significance of this characteristic.

[b]This column summarizes the sign and significance of the logit coefficients for each independent variable for eight alternative specifications for the 13 states pooled.

[c]This column summarizes the sign and significance of the logit coefficients for each independent variable used for a total of 73 specifications for 13 subsamples and seven individual states.

Source: See text.

delegate with average values of all other variables, decreases the predicted probability of a yes vote from about .62 to about .36. Merchant interests increase the predicted probability from about .59 to about .72, and western land interests increase the predicted probability from about .58 to .74, with all other independent variables held constant at the sample means. These effects are not trivial in magnitude, and they correspond to the predictions of our theoretical model.

With respect to the impact of personal slave holdings on the probability of voting for the Constitution, the results are somewhat mixed. The marginal effect of the dummy variable for slave owning (DSLAVE) is negative and statistically significant, but the coefficients of the variable for the value of the delegate's slave holdings (VSLAVE) or the variable for the difference between the delegate's slave holdings and average slave holdings in the area he represented (DPCSLAVE) are not statistically significant.[28] For a delegate who personally owned slaves and had average values of all other independent variables, the predicted probability of a yes vote is about .41; for a delegate who owned no slaves and had average values of all other independent variables, the predicted probability of a yes vote is about .75. A delegate who owned slaves was significantly less likely to have voted for the Constitution than one who owned no slaves, other things being equal. From the lack of statistical significance for the value of personal slave holdings (VSLAVE), however, we may infer that the amount of personal slave holdings did not significantly affect voting behavior.

To the extent that a pattern in voting related to slave owning per se (DSLAVE) is apparent from the pooled sample, as we expected, our results on personal slave holdings are at odds with those of McDonald (1958). The finding also contradicts Main (1961), Risjord (1974, 1978), and others who suggest that slave owners with large amounts of holdings tended to have supported the Constitution. Our results indicate that slave owners, all other factors being constant, were 40% less likely to have voted for the Constitution than delegates who did not own slaves.

With respect to constituents' slave holdings, the marginal effect on the vote is generally positive but not statistically significant. The lack of statistical significance is found whether constituents' slave interests are measured as slaves per 100 whites, as the percentage of families owning slaves, or as slaves per slave-owning household. Given the pooled results, Thomas's (1953) conclusion that constituents' slave interests did not affect the vote in the Virginia ratifying assembly appears to have a more general validity. Our results from the pooled sample contradict Main's (1961) and Risjord's (1974) findings that constituents' slave interests significantly increased support for the Constitution.

According to our pooled estimates, delegates who held relatively large amounts of public securities were more likely to have voted for the Constitution than delegates without public securities, *ceteris paribus.* The estimated incremental effect of the dummy variables for public security holdings (DPSECR) is positive, but only marginally significant statistically. The impact of public-security holdings, however, is stronger when the interests are measured either as the market value of the public securities held (VPSECR) or as a dummy variable for public security holdings with a market value in excess of $1,000 (DLPSECR). The estimated marginal effect of the value of public securities (VPSESR) is positive and statistically significant at the .01 level or better, as is the marginal effect of large public-security holdings (DLPSECR).

The results for public securities confirm to some degree the findings of Main (1961) and Schuyler (1961) but run counter to McDonald's (1958) assertion that no general voting patterns related to public-security holdings were present in the ratifying conventions. And the results contradict the treatment of the subject contained in the major economic history and political science textbooks (for examples, see Burnham, 1983; Hughes, 1983; Lineberry, 1980; Prewitt and Verba, 1983). The magnitude of the effects of incremental changes in the value of public-security holdings on voting was rather small, however. A 10% increase in the value of a delegate's public-security holdings from the sample mean of VPSECR increases the predicted probability of a yes vote by about .5%. But the predicted probability of a yes vote for a delegate with large public-security holdings (DLPSECR = 1) and average values of all other independent variables is .74, compared to a predicted probability of .58 for one without large public-security holdings (DLPSECR = 0). From the statistical result for the dummy variable, we can infer that substantial differences in public-security holdings apparently mattered. (A delegate with a value of public-security holdings in excess of $1,000 possessed assets in the range of at least 10 times the per capita income in the late 1780s.)

Delegates from coastal areas were more likely to have favored the Constitution than delegates from the back country, as indicated by the negative and significant marginal effect of the distance variable (DISTN) in all specifications. Estimates obtained by use of the distance from home to the Atlantic coast or the distance from home to the nearest major commercial city as substitutes for the variable DISTN are very similar to those summarized in Table 12.3 (see McGuire and Ohsfeldt, 1988). With the exception of McDonald (1958, 1963), the finding confirms the conclusions in the literature regarding the geographical distribution of the vote on the Constitution. There was no apparent pattern in the vote related to the ancestry of the delegates' constituents in the pooled sample, contrary to Main's (1961) suggestion.

Estimates of Less Restricted Models

The estimates of voting behavior drawn from the pooled sample rely on several potentially significant restrictive assumptions. To examine the robustness of the estimated voting patterns with respect to changes in these restrictive assumptions, we also estimated our model using data for thirteen subsamples of states and—where the data permit—for individual state ratifying assemblies. The subsamples of state assemblies are grouped by reasonable criteria: geographic region (the South, the Middle Atlantic, and New England—three subsamples), the nature of each state's ratification (whether or not the Constitution was ratified with suggested amendments or declarations of interpretation—four subsamples), the chronological order of ratification (four subsamples), and the nature of state paper-money issues (two subsamples). The seven individual states where the sample of delegates and the degree of variation in the vote on the Constitution and in the independent variables are sufficiently large to permit an estimation of the model are Connecticut, Massachusetts, New Hampshire, North Carolina, Pennsylvania, South Carolina, and Virginia. Among these seven states are most of the important contests in the ratification process. These subsample results are summarized in the second column of Table 12.3.

Many of our results from the pooled sample are confirmed by results from the various subsample estimates.[29] Even though some of our pooled results are altered significantly, the following general conclusions regarding the division of interests in the vote on the Constitution appear to be supported by our empirical analyses of the pooled sample and all subsamples (compare the two columns of Table 12.3): (1) delegates who had merchant interests, western lands, or private or public securities or who represented areas of English ancestry were more likely to have supported the Constitution than were other delegates; (2) delegates who were in personal debt, owned slaves, or represented back-country areas were more likely to have opposed the Constitution than were other delegates; and (3) no consistent patterns in the vote related to farmers, state population, or constituent slave interests are indicated. Most of these results are reasonably consistent with the expectations of our model.

Conclusions

Significant voting patterns related to several economic interests are found in the state ratifying assemblies which met over the period 1787–1790. To some degree, the nature of the impact of economic factors on voting behavior differs by region and among the states. Additional research using more complete data will be needed to resolve the issue of the source of differences in regional and other subsample estimates. But overall, the voting patterns as indicated by the statistical results are as expected in most cases. Merchants, western landowners, financiers, and large public-securities holders tended to have supported the Constitution, whereas debtors and slave owners tended to have opposed the Constitution. The voting patterns coincide approximately with Charles Beard's (1913) predictions, with the possible exception of slave owners. The results also confirm several conclusions of two of the most comprehensive but nonrigorous empirical studies of the ratification process: the works of Jackson Main (1961) and Forrest McDonald (1958). However, our results contradict many of their other conclusions, particularly several of McDonald's major conclusions.

Our results indicate that delegates to the ratifying assemblies responded at least in part to economic incentives when determining their vote on the Constitution, a finding suggesting that economic interests played an important role in this form of constitutional choice. The economic incentives are defined broadly to include the satisfaction of ideological interests and of constituents' economic interests, in addition to the advancement of personal economic interests. To some extent, shirking behavior was manifested in the pursuit of personal economic gain, not only in the satisfaction of ideological preferences. This knowledge of the influence of economic incentives on voting at the ratifying conventions, in addition to historical interest, may contribute to a more general understanding of the role of economic factors in the formation of political and economic institutions.

Acknowledgments. The authors have benefited from the comments and suggestions of many individuals at different stages of the study. We thank all who have commented. We especially thank Kathleen Kurz for her unending help and are deeply indebted to Peg McCray for her word processing. We also thank the editors for several helpful comments. Partial financial support for the research was provided to Robert McGuire by a George A. Ball Research Fellowship from the Ball Foundation, Muncie, Indiana.

Notes

1. For detailed surveys of most views about the Constitution, see Diggins (1981), Hutson (1981, 1984), and McCorkle (1984).
2. An exception is our earlier work on the Constitution. Preliminary results of an economic analysis of the making of the Constitution are contained in a brief progress report on a larger study (see McGuire and Ohsfeldt, 1984). Elsewhere, we examine in detail voting behavior at the Philadelphia Convention of 1787, which drafted the Constitution (see McGuire, 1988; McGuire and Ohsfeldt, 1985b, 1986).
3. Although we suggest this reflects Charles Beard's thesis, other scholars certainly will disagree because of the confusing nature of Beard's book. He uses terms imprecisely, continuously interchanging *economic interest* with *class interest*, *class* with *group*, and *economic interpretation* with *economic determinism*. As a result, his thesis is sufficiently broad and ambiguous to offer support for a variety of interpretations. One such interpretation, which many scholars consider Beard's fundamental contribution, is that his book is a "class analysis" of the delegates' behavior (see Buchanan and Tullock, 1962, pp. 25–27). Even if most scholars disagree when we argue that Beard's view may be consistent with an individualistic calculus (see Beard, 1912, pp. 80–81; 1913/1935, pp. 16–18, 73; 1922/1934, p. 67), we suggest that an important issue to analyze is whether the self-interest of the delegates affected their voting behavior. In this sense, our interpretation of Beard may more appropriately be said to reflect a "Beardian" view rather than "Beard's" view. Whether Beard's view of our Founding Fathers is an individual-interest or class-interest view is currently much debated (see McCorkle, 1984).
4. For several examples, see Deacon and Shapiro (1975), Fair (1978), Kau and Rubin (1979, 1982), and Peltzman (1984).
5. Elements of strategic voting behavior were, of course, present at the ratifying assemblies. Many delegates who opposed ratification were persuaded to vote for the Constitution under the condition that it would be amended by some form of bill of rights. In several states, both opponents and proponents of ratification sought to alter the timing of the vote on the Constitution until the outcomes at other ratifying assemblies were known. Political maneuvering also took place to enlarge the agenda considered by the state assemblies. But these examples of strategic voting behavior are minor relative to the strategic voting behavior at the Philadelphia convention which drafted the Constitution. For a model of the strategic behavior used to alter the structure of the rules under which ratification took place, see chapter 14. Our chapter analyzes the effects of different interests on each delegate's vote once the structure of rules was selected.
6. The quotes are from Gladstone (1878, p. 185) and Walker (1895, pp. 28–29), respectively. Also, see Bancroft (1882), Fiske (1888), Harding (1896), and Wilson (1902).

7. See McCormick (1950), Pool (1950), and Thomas (1953).

8. For an example of a major historical work that claims that Brown (1956) and McDonald (1958) are the definitive challenges to Beard (1913), see Wood (1969). Also, see chapter 13 by Cheryl Eavey and Gary Miller, neoinstitutionalists who understand the role of economic interests in the ratification of the Constitution, for a work that we believe still gives too much credit to Forrest McDonald for having completed "a meticulous analysis of the economic status of delegates" to the several conventions.

9. It is important to call to the reader's attention the fact that until now, no one involved in the debate (neither Charles Beard, his supporters, nor his critics) has ever completed the necessary statistical analyses to determine which factors significantly influenced the voting behavior of the numerous delegates to the several conventions. Yet, the dismissal of Beard and an economic interpretation of the Constitution (or for that matter support for alternative views) continues despite this complete absence of definitive empirical evaluations of the issues using modern statistical techniques. Our argument, simply put, is that qualitative case studies and anecdotal examples are not appropriate tests of the issues. For a recent use of such examples, see Riker (1979).

10. Schuyler (1961) notes, for example, that McDonald's (1958) data may support the hypothesis that public-security holders favored the Constitution if data from several states are pooled. Alternatively, Kaminski (1983) argues that the contest over ratification in each state was unique because of differences in local economic conditions, political institutions, and the timing of the ratifying assemblies. Pooling data across states is inappropriate, in his view.

11. While there is considerable disagreement in the literature, it is easy to overstate the lack of consensus. Many scholars agree that economic factors played an important role in the adoption of the Constitution, but disagree about the specific division of opinion. A typical example is Van Beck Hall (1972), who in his study of Massachusetts concludes that "the final vote on ratification, after all the speeches, pressure, compromises, and machinations, still reflected the basic socioeconomic divisions within the commonwealth" (p. 292). But different studies find different "basic socioeconomic divisions" in the vote on the Constitution, without any formal statistical analysis.

12. Through their textbook writings, economic historians and political scientists have most notably accepted the findings of Brown (1956) and McDonald (1958). For examples, see Brownlee (1979), Burnham (1983), Burns, Peltason, and Cronin (1981), Hughes (1983), Lebergott (1984), Lineberry (1980), Poulson (1981), Prewitt and Verba (1983), Ransom (1981), and Walton and Robertson (1983). It might be more accurate to state that the textbook authors have uncritically used McDonald's conclusion that Beard significantly overstated the role of public securities in the adoption of the Constitution to dismiss Beard's economic interpretation of the Constitution. This may, in part, reflect their desire to reject Beard's so-called Marxist analysis. But Beard's thesis bears a greater resemblance to modern public-choice theory than to a Marxist "class analysis" of the contest over the Constitution. As earlier noted, however, the true nature of Beard's thesis is not an issue for the present study. For a detailed discussion of the intellectual history of Beard's thesis, as well as of the common misinterpretations by both Beard's supporters and critics among historians, see McCorkle (1984).

13. The delegates were elected to represent particular counties at the state ratifying assemblies. It would have been costly for delegates to vote contrary to the

interests of their constituents because, as noted, many delegates hoped to continue political careers following the ratification assemblies. Many were legally bound to vote as they had pledged in the elections.

14. Buchanan and Tullock (1962, pp. 72–79) list six necessary conditions for a rational utility-maximizing individual to "support the adoption of rules designed specifically to further partisan interests" and additionally suggest that the first four conditions for partisan behavior may be satisfied frequently. They also state that their analysis at the constitutional level is not applicable to societies with widely divergent economic or social groups (p. 80). For evidence that the distribution of wealth in late eighteenth-century America was markedly unequal, see Alice Hanson Jones (1980, chaps. 6 and 7).

15. The U.S. Constitution, drafted in 1787, contained both general decision-making rules (voting rules) and numerous interest-specific provisions, for example, provisions concerning specific aspects of the use of import and export tariffs. Therefore, we would expect the ratifying assemblies to fall between the operational and the constitutional levels of collective choice. It follows that the delegates' voting behavior would be, at least partly, identified with the economic interests and ideologies of the delegates and their constituents, and statistical voting patterns may be expected to exist.

16. Chapter 14, by Evelyn Fink and William Riker, suggests that the amount of strategic behavior in the ratification process was significant. However, because we use a multivariate statistical technique that measures the partial effects of various interests on each delegate's actual vote on ratification after the structure of rules was determined, the strategy involved in determining that structure for the conventions should not affect our results significantly.

17. The quotes in this paragraph, while possibly more dramatic than found elsewhere, accurately summarize the conclusions of the standard works on economic conditions during the 1780s. The standard works include Nettels (1962), Bjork (1963, 1964), Ferguson (1961), Shepherd and Walton (1976), Walton and Shepherd (1979), and McCusker and Menard (1985).

18. The rhetoric on this issue by slave-owning delegates to the Constitutional Convention in 1787 is contained in Farrand (1911, vol. 2, pp. 95, 220–223, 364–374, 415–416). The rhetoric in the state ratifying conventions is contained in Elliot (1836, vol. 3, pp. 452–458, 589–590, 598–599, 621–623, and vol. 4, pp. 30–32, 100–102, 176–178, 271–274).

19. For the rhetoric on this issue by slave-owning delegates to the Constitutional Convention, see Farrand (1911, vol. 2, pp. 448–451, 631). For the rhetoric in the state ratifying conventions, see Elliot (1836, vol. 3, p. 621, and vol. 4, pp. 271–274, 298, 308–311). Also, because of the expected decrease in the costs of trade activities generally, it might be argued that the partial effect of slave owning, all other interests being constant, should be positive. That is, slave owners should be expected to have *favored* ratification of the Constitution. We believe that the rhetoric of the debates suggests that slave owners were well aware that the direct costs to them of potential restrictions on slavery and oppressive navigation acts would far outweigh the general benefits of the decreased costs of trade activities.

20. The reader will note that our theoretical voting model includes a delegate's ideology as an explanatory variable only to the extent that it is not determined by economic interests. Also, for a detailed discussion of quantitative measurement problems with the concept of ideology, see Higgs (1986, ch. 3).

21. The additional data are, with the exception of Pool (1950), limited to a few variables for relatively few delegates. All data for North Carolina, with the exception of McDonald's public-security figures, are from Pool (1950). We use only the data for the first North Carolina convention, which rejected the Constitution, in our empirical analysis. The second convention was held well after the Constitution was ratified by nine states. Votes from the second convention may be less likely to reflect true voting sentiments than votes from the first convention. Finally, the votes of the delegates were verified by use of Elliot (1836).

22. The availability of data severely limits our empirical measures of constituents' economic interests and ideologies. The 1790 Census appears to be the best source of contemporary data for all states for a number of variables at the aggregation level below the state level. The 1790 census data for each delegate's area of representation (township or county) are taken from U.S. Department of Commerce (1969).

23. Because no counties in New Hampshire or Georgia are included in Jones's estimates, we used her estimates of average wealth for the New England and southern regions as estimates of the average wealth in New Hampshire and Georgia, respectively. We used her 1774 estimates because contemporaneous measures of each state's wealth are not available. The estimates should be reasonable proxies for state wealth levels at the time of the ratifying assemblies to the extent that significant changes in price levels or real-wealth levels across states did not occur during the late 1770s and 1780s. However, we do not place much importance on the results for the wealth variable. Accordingly, the variable is omitted from all specifications reported here. For specifications including the wealth variable, see McGuire and Ohsfeldt (1985a).

24. A potential contradiction exists when it is claimed that delegates farther from the coast were more likely to have *opposed* the Constitution because their constituents were more "localist"-oriented. It might be argued that the same delegates were also representing constituents who *favored* the Constitution because of the increased protection it offered to those farther from coastal areas, particularly those on the frontier. If the distance variable appropriately proxies "localist" ideology, however, the delegates' frontier constituents probably would have preferred that the protection be provided with local control. Additionally, our western landowner variable should capture the effect of the pro-Constitution desire for increased protection on the frontier. The distance measures were calculated from the data contained in Lester Cappon (1976). In all cases, distance is measured by a straight-line method.

25. The standard historical argument is that the anti-Federalists (opponents of the Constitution) were not well organized and, thus, adopted delaying tactics. Their tactics worked best in the states where opposition to the Constitution was naturally strong. Ratifying assemblies later in the process, therefore, had more anti-Federalists. After the adoption by nine states, delaying tactics could no longer stop the Constitution. If delegates did not want to be left out of the union entirely, they would have been less likely to vote no after adoption than before. For a discussion of the tactics of the opponents, see Main (1961).

26. For three states (Maryland, New York, and Rhode Island), the sample size of delegates for whom data are available is too small to permit an analysis of voting patterns by state. The degree of multicollinearity associated with the extensive use of interaction terms between personal- or constituent-interest

variables and dummy variables (for state, region, or timing considerations) is too large. For three other states (Delaware, Georgia, and New Jersey), there is no variation in the dependent variable because all three voted unanimously in favor of ratification. Logit analysis is not possible when zero variance exists. Some form of pooling data across states, therefore, is necessary to estimate the voting patterns for the overall ratification process.

27. No coefficient estimates for any specifications are reported here. All estimates are contained in an appendix to the chapter which is available from the authors.

28. The lack of statistical significance for the variable (VSLAVE) may be explained in part by the large variance in the value of total assets among slave-owning delegates. By using all of the available data on the delegates' economic interests to compute the value of known assets, it is possible to construct a very rough measure of the delegates' total asset values by imputing the probable value of other assets owned by the delegates. The measure of the value of other (unknown) assets is based upon the average total assets of individuals within the state with a similar occupation and the proportion of the average total assets accounted for by the types of assets that each delegate was known to possess. From this information, we estimated each delegate's total assets using the value of known assets and our estimate of the proportion of total asset value accounted for by known assets. By use of the measure of total asset value, the delegate's slave holdings may be measured as the value of slaves as a share of total assets. The slave-asset-share variable yields negative and significant coefficients when used in the empirical model. Thus, delegates with a relatively large share of their assets in the form of slaves appear to have been less likely to have voted for the Constitution than delegates who owned no slaves. However, as the slave-asset-share variable rests on very rough estimates of the delegates' total asset values, the empirical results using the variable are tenuous and are not reported here. The results using the slave-asset-share variable, along with more details concerning the computation of the share variables, are provided in McGuire and Ohsfeldt (1985a).

29. For details concerning the results for the less restricted models, see McGuire and Ohsfeldt (1988).

CHAPTER THIRTEEN

Constitutional Conflict in State and Nation

Cheryl L. Eavey and Gary J. Miller

> Among the most formidable of the obstacles which the new Constitution will have to encounter may readily be distinguished the obvious interest of a certain class of men in every State to resist all changes which may hazard a diminution of the power, emolument, and consequence of the offices they hold under the State establishments.
>
> *Federalist* no. 1

Charles Beard (1913/1935), in his now classic analysis of economic interests and the ratification of the U.S. Constitution, argued that the patterns of support for and opposition to this new system of government could be identified on the basis of economic interests alone. Creditors, for example, would benefit from the ability of a strong national government to repay governmental securities and to control the inflationary policies of the state governments; merchants, too, would prosper, as the proposed federal system would both encourage and regulate interstate and international commerce.

McDonald (1958), in his much cited refutation of Beard, argues that one cannot reduce the complex patterns of conflict into simple dichotomies like debtors versus creditors. For example, according to McDonald, merchant interests were "effectively neutralized" in the ratification debates in Pennsylvania since merchants supported both factions (pp. 169–170). And in Maryland, Captain Charles Ridgely, a merchant and the "political boss" of Baltimore County, aligned himself with such noted anti-Federalists as Luther Martin and Samuel Chase (McDonald, 1958, p. 160; see also Renzulli, 1972, p. 39).

In chapter 12, McGuire and Ohsfeldt do an outstanding job of defending the role of economic interests in the ratification campaign. Using McDonald's (and others') data on the state ratifying conventions in aggregate form, they demonstrate that probabilistic voting patterns tend to support many of Beard's conclusions. For instance, McGuire and Ohsfeldt found that delegates who were merchants or who owned public or private securities were more likely to vote for the Constitution, while delegates from the back country or those in debt were more likely to oppose the Constitution. Thus, it appears that, in the aggregate, McDonald's conclusions are not supported by his own data. What emerges instead is a picture of a class-based economic struggle over the ratification of the Constitution.

We support McGuire and Ohsfeldt's contention that economic interests provided much of the fuel for the conflict over the Constitution. Yet, we fully recognize that interests were not homogeneous either across or within states. Although Beard has argued that it is rational, from an economic perspective, for merchants to support the Federalist stance, many merchants chose otherwise.

Why would some merchants and others with commercial interests presumably go against their economic preferences by failing to support the U.S. Constitution? Perhaps the answer to this question lies in understanding the role that political coalitions and institutions play in channeling conflicting interests.

On the Role of Preferences and Institutions

Recently, a number of studies have convincingly demonstrated the nonneutral character of structures. These studies, coming out of the rational choice literature, detail the critical role that institutions play in shaping preferences and determining outcomes (see, for example, Weingast and Marshall, 1984; Maser, 1985; Knott and Miller, 1987). Indeed, the public recognizes that constitutional and procedural rules can bias outcomes in favor of one set of policy preferences or another. That is why we see the kind of intense conflicts over constitutional rules of which the debate over the ratification of the U.S. Constitution is the foremost example. And the institutional setting for the ratification fights in the states was, first and foremost, the state constitutions themselves.

The Revolutionary period was more than a fight for independence against Britain; it was also a time of intense civil strife as different economic and political interests vied for dominance in many of the states (Hoffman, 1976, p. 276). Eleven different constitutions evolved out of this conflict, each reflecting the prevailing interests in that particular state.

Contrast the states of Pennsylvania and Maryland. In Pennsylvania, the economic interests supporting a radically democratic state constitution had been successful in 1776 and had fought back repeated attempts by Philadelphia merchants and others to replace it with a more conservative state constitution. In Maryland, a coalition of conservative Potomac planters and what has been called the new urban elite (O'Brien, 1979) fashioned a constitution which effectively squelched any democratic tendencies.

As a result, the shape of the economic and political conflict was very different in each of these states. We contend that in order to understand the struggles over the ratification of the Constitution, one must examine the patterns of conflict within the states, both during the time of the ratification debate and in the years immediately preceding the early state constitutions. Although our analysis in this chapter will focus exclusively on the states of Pennsylvania and Maryland, we believe that this line of reasoning could be extended to a number of other states.

Pennsylvania: Commercial Interests Against Rural Radicalism

Colonial Politics

The politics of the proprietary colony of Pennsylvania was dominated by conflicts between the Quaker party of the Assembly and the proprietary party of the governor. The Quakers were concentrated in the three eastern counties of Philadelphia, Chester, and Bucks. They retained control of the House by apportioning representation in such a way that these counties were overrepresented compared to the western counties of the frontier (Hindle, 1946, p. 462). The frontiersmen, a potentially destabilizing third group, were thus little more than a pawn in the Quakers' struggle for power. For example, by the mid-1750s, the government recognized, albeit reluctantly, the need for an army to defend the frontier from Indian attacks. However, the governor's efforts were blocked by the Assembly, which would pass defense bills only if the governor would agree to specific concessions like the taxation of proprietary lands (Hindle, 1946, p. 464).

In this supercharged atmosphere, frontiersmen resorted to violence. In December 1763, a group of farmers known as the Paxton

Boys massacred twenty peaceful Indians living in Lancaster County. This lawless violence united the proprietary and Quaker parties in efforts to capture the Paxton Boys. However, the discontented on the frontier saw these massacres as only the beginning and began to put into motion plans to march on the city of Philadelphia. In response, the governor passed a riot act and called upon Benjamin Franklin, one of the leaders of the Quaker party, to serve as his spokesman. Franklin met the rioters at Germantown and persuaded them to return home, with the exception of a small delegation that proceeded to Philadelphia with grievances.

The grievances of the frontiersmen in 1764 amounted to little more than a call for fair representation of the western counties. However, it would take another twelve years before anyone would honor their request. The event which would serve as the catalyst for change was the Revolutionary War.

Revolutionary Politics

The conservatives who had always controlled Pennsylvania were reluctant to follow the fiery New Englanders toward independence. As a result, the New Englanders maneuvered in the Continental Congress to give "the still submerged radicals in Pennsylvania an opportunity to sieze power" (Jensen, 1940, p. 98). On May 10, 1776, John Adams offered a famous resolution urging those colonies which had not yet abandoned their colonial governments to do so now and to establish in their place governments more conducive to the revolutionary cause. The motion was successful, in spite of attempts by Pennsylvania conservatives like James Wilson, a lawyer with mercantile interests, to stop the resolution.

The Assembly must have anticipated some sort of action because just prior to the announcement, in an attempt to appease the frontier, the Assembly gave the western counties an additional thirteen seats in the House; by May, representation in the Assembly was nearly equally divided between the western and the eastern counties (Nevins, 1924, p. 132). Yet, the margin of victory was still in the hands of the conservatives. So when the resolution passed in Congress, the already politicized western frontiersmen joined with the radical supporters of independence to displace the conservatives. In June of that year, the conservatives lost power, leaving to the radicals the task of writing a new state constitution (Jensen, 1940, p. 19).

The provincial conference assumed the responsibilities of the dissolved assembly (Brunhouse, 1942, p. 13). The conference, dominated by frontier radicals, established the terms for the election of representatives to the constitutional convention. Although property requirements for suffrage were removed, new restrictions were added, like an oath denying allegiance to the king. The net effect of these changes in election procedures was to place the radicals firmly in control of the convention; and in fact, only one man of note, Benjamin Franklin, was elected to the convention. The product of its labors, the Pennsylvania Constitution of 1776, was perhaps the most democratic of the constitutions to emerge from the Independence period.

Institutional features which might check or constrain majority rule were eliminated. Instead of a bicameral legislature, a unicameral legislature was established which was to be checked not by an upper house, but by the public, who were to consider bills prior to their passage. Representatives were elected annually by the people and were rotated out of office after four consecutive terms; the latter feature was unique to the state of Pennsylvania (Wood, 1969, p. 231). Property qualifications were eliminated for representatives, and restrictions on suffrage were minimal: every taxpayer twenty-one or over was allowed to vote. In terms of regional apportionment, an initial six legislative seats were assigned to each county and the city of Philadelphia; however, provisions were established in the constitution (Section 17) for a later switch to representation based upon the taxable population.

Finally, Pennsylvania created an executive with few powers. The Supreme Executive Council replaced a single governor as the executive body. The council, containing a representative from each county plus the city of Philadelphia, was a council divided in terms of responsibilities. Further, the council lacked effective measures to counteract the actions of the assembly.

With every check on majority rule eliminated, the new constitution handed power over to the frontier radical forces and their eastern allies. Realizing that their power derived from the document they had created, the radicals took extraordinary measures to protect their constitution. The document was never presented to the public at large for their approval. Further, the radicals irritated conservatives by insisting that voters and officeholders alike swear an oath of allegiance to the new government. The oath served a useful purpose, in that the means for revising the new constitution was embedded in the document. The radicals established the Council of Censors as the only legal channel through which a convention could be called to amend the constitution. The council was to meet every seven years, beginning in 1783, to review the actions of government and to amend the constitution, if necessary. Members of the council were to be elected by freemen, two from each county. Thus, representation in the council favored the back counties (Nevins, pp. 152–153; Brunhouse, p. 15).

Confederation Politics

The unveiling of the 1776 radical constitution generated immediate opposition and led to the formation of two distinct parties: the radicals, or Constitutionalists, and the conservatives, or Anti-Constitutionalists (also called Republicans). Even before the new government was in place, the conservatives expressed their objections to the document.

The conservatives' reaction was well founded. In short order, the policy shifts that the conservatives feared from such a democratic document were, in fact, realized. The government took a very hard line toward the Quakers, the colonial opponents of the frontiersmen. When the Quakers declared themselves neutral in the war, the radicals had them arrested and required extra taxes of them (Nevins, 1924, pp. 254–256). The radicals legalized the greatly depreciated continental paper money, requiring that all accept the worthless currency (Brunhouse, p. 26). Further, the government refused to raise sufficient taxes to support the military effort. The Pennsylvania Line was the worst-paid and worst-supported outfit in the army. As one general wrote, the Pennsylvania legislature urged its troops to fight, but "are forges, tents, wagons, etc., ever thought of? No." (Nevins, 1924, p. 267).

This is not to imply that the Constitutionalists were always in complete control of the government; in fact, power in the assembly fluctuated between the Constitutionalists and the Republicans throughout the Confederation period. What endured, however, was the state constitution of 1776. The Republicans attempted, unsuccessfully, to alter the constitution in 1777, 1778, and 1783–1784 (Brunhouse, 1942, p. 221). It was, in part, their lack of success in changing the foundation of the radical components of their state government which caused the Republicans to focus their attention on strengthening the national government, as a check on the irresponsible actions of their radical counterparts.

The federal Constitution that came out of the Constitutional Convention was very attractive to Pennsylvania's conservatives; in fact, it embodied many of the principles they had espoused over the

TABLE 13.1. Vote by Assemblymen in Pennsylvania on Call for Ratifying Convention[a]

Vote	Republicans	Radicals	Total
For	33	7	40
Against	0	13	13
Total	33	20	53

[a]Corrected X^2 = 25.06; phi = −0.73. Excludes votes (nine in all) from the counties of Bedford, Dauphin, and Westmoreland. *Source:* Data compiled from Brunhouse (1942, p. 207).

years. The Republican platform on government reorganization issued in 1783 included, among other things, a bicameral legislature, a single executive with veto power, and the elimination of the provision for rotation in office (Brunhouse, p. 157; Wood, 1969, p. 441). Further, the conservatives had done well in the Fall 1786 elections and thus were in a position to ensure consideration of the Constitution, provided, of course, that the ratifying convention was called while the conservatives were still in power.

The Constitution arrived in the state legislature just one day before the legislature was to adjourn. The conservatives were as determined to call a ratifying convention prior to adjournment as the radicals were to delay the vote. So when the conservatives refused to delay action, the radicals resorted to a technique they had used on other occasions, which was to absent themselves to prevent a quorum. The conservatives, now familiar with radical tactics, sent the sergeant-at-arms to find the absentee members. Although the sergeant-at-arms was unsuccessful, a federalist mob was not: the mob dragged two Constitutionalist legislators to the assembly to procure a quorum. The necessary votes for calling the state convention were thereby procured.

Pennsylvania's convention ratified the Constitution by a 2-to-1 majority. The process of ratification by state conventions was part of the Federalists' strategy to dilute the influence of state legislatures (Boyd, 1979a, p. 15; also see chapter 14). Yet, voting patterns appear to follow partisan lines. Notice that a moderately high correlation (.73) exists between the partisan affiliation of the assemblymen elected in September of 1786 and the vote to call a ratifying convention (Table 13.1). Interestingly, all seven Constitutionalists who defected from the party line by voting for the ratifying convention were from counties bordering the Susquehanna River, specifically, Berks, Northampton, and Northumberland (Ireland, 1978, p. 328; Brunhouse, 1942, p. 207). As for the ratifying convention itself, we

TABLE 13.2. Partisan Characteristics of Counties and Delegate Vote on the Ratification of the Constitution[a]

Vote	Republicans	Radicals	Total
For	33	12	45
Against	1	19	20
Total	34	31	65

[a]Corrected X^2 = 23.45; phi = −0.63. Affiliation of four members unknown. *Source:* Data compiled from Brunhouse (1942, p. 207).

were unable to determine the partisan affiliation of its delegates. However, it does appear that the partisan characteristics of the counties (as determined by the October 1787 election of assemblymen) correlate well (.63) with the delegates' vote (by county) on the ratification question (Table 13.2).

Pennsylvania's ratification of the Constitution, combined with the Constitution's success in other states, threw the Constitutionalist party into disarray. Divided on such basic issues as whether or not to participate in the new government, and not knowing whether opposition to the new government would be equated with disloyalty, the Constitutionalists won only two of the eight House seats in the Fall 1788 federal elections (Boyd, 1979b, pp. 132–135).

Within two years, the "counterrevolution" in Pennsylvania was complete, and the radical democratic constitution of the frontiersmen was replaced by a more moderate document. The conservatives encountered little opposition from the demoralized radicals, although a few of the frontier counties like Cumberland and Franklin were vocal in their opposition to the convention (Brunhouse, 1942, p. 223). In the end, radicals and conservatives alike worked together in the convention to draft the new state constitution, using the 1776 constitution as the starting point. The final document bore a marked similarity to the recently approved federal Constitution. Gone were the more unusual features of the earlier document, including rotation in office and the much-despised Council of Censors. The unicameral assembly gave way to a bicameral legislature, and the plural executive was replaced by a single governor. In short, those features which had worked to the advantage of the frontier forces were excluded from the new document.

Analysis

It is true that there is no simple way to classify the economic interests of those supporting or opposing the federal Constitution in

Pennsylvania; not all frontiersmen were Constitutionalists, just as not all merchants were Republicans. However, there do appear to be some general trends. It seems reasonable to argue that commercial interests, in general, supported the federal Constitution. Geographically, the Republican party was strongest in the east, particularly in the city of Philadelphia (Boyd, 1979b, p. 125). The Republicans included a number of wealthy and powerful Philadelphia merchants, most notably Robert Morris, as well as farmers, lawyers, and others with commercial interests (Main, 1961, p. 193; Boyd, 1979b, p. 125).

McDonald's (1958, pp. 169–170) contention that merchant interests were "effectively neutralized" in the Pennsylvania campaign is difficult to understand. Although some Constitutionalists were merchants or others with commercial interests, evidence at the county level suggests that the Philadelphia Constitutionalists defected from the party line on the issue of the federal Constitution (Main, 1961, p. 190). At the individual level, one such defector was Thomas McKean, a Philadelphia lawyer who obtained the position of chief justice as a Constitutionalist (McDonald, 1958, p. 175; Brunhouse, 1942, p. 35).

Further, if "effectively neutralized" implies equal and opposite political influence by merchants on both sides, then that is certainly not the case in Pennsylvania. To begin with, urban Constitutionalists formed an easy alliance with their Republican counterparts; for example, on the question of repeal of the tender laws in 1780, urban radicals, including merchant John Bayard, voted for repeal and thus against the interests of the frontier counties (Brunhouse, 1942, p. 83). In terms of relative strength, one has only to look at the Philadelphia-based clique supporting Republican Robert Morris and the Bank of North America to recognize the influence of commercial interests not only in Pennsylvania, but in the nation as a whole.

On the other hand, the evidence is overwhelming that the back counties generally opposed any action which would endanger the 1776 state constitution, including the ratification of the federal Constitution. These small farmers to the west of the Susquehanna River formed the core of the Constitutionalist party (Boyd, 1979b, p. 124).

Thus, it appears that a neo-Beardian stance is defensible: economic interests played a major role in determining who would or would not support the ratification of the federal Constitution. More important, Pennsylvania's 1776 state constitution reified these positions by guaranteeing the frontier radicals a prominent position in government, from which they could frustrate select economic ventures like the charter for the Bank of North America.

In Maryland, a different situation prevailed, one in which urban commercial interests found themselves on both sides of the ratification question. The reason? Maryland's constitution of 1777.

Maryland: The Planter Aristocracy Versus the New Urban Elite

Colonial Politics

Like Pennsylvania, the proprietary colony of Maryland was characterized by a two-party style of colonial politics. There was the party of the proprietor (the "court party") and an opposing faction (the "country party") centered in the lower house of the Assembly; however, unlike Pennsylvania, there was little history of frontier rebellion and politicization to destabilize the bipolar elite pattern of conflict. In Maryland, the struggle for power took place between the large planters, merchants, and lawyers of the country party against the friends of the proprietors.

This soon-to-be-ruling coalition had its beginnings in an alliance which formed in opposition to the Stamp Act of 1765. The Annapolis–Baltimore alliance, consisting of the Baltimore Sons of Liberty and the lawyer-politician Samuel Chase, successfully pressured the government into doing business without stamped paper (Hoffman, 1973, p. 55). Later, the alliance would form again, this time in response to one of the many forms of patronage that existed in the proprietary system—specifically, the charging of fees by proprietary officials for the performance of public services. In the past, this coalition had proved to be unstable, but with the addition of Charles Carroll of Carrollton, a merchant and a planter who had gained popularity for his public opposition to the governor's fee schedules, the alliance solidified in 1773 and became the foundation for the popular party of the revolutionary era (Hoffman, 1973, pp. 92–124).

Revolutionary Politics

The movement for independence was accompanied by violence and social disorder. Loyalists were organizing along the Eastern Shore, the militia was insubordinate, and black slaves were becoming "insolent" (Hoffman, 1976, pp. 281–284). The leaders of the popular party were conservatives at heart. Once they realized that a reconciliation with Britain was impossible, they sought to establish a frame of government which would provide the stability and social order lost to the Revolution.

Opposing them in that effort was a coalition of former adversaries from their days in the lower house of the Assembly. The Hammond–Hall faction capitalized on the democratic sentiment of the population. They, with the support of the Anne Arundel County militia, argued for a decentralized government with a powerful state legislature elected directly by the people on an annual basis. The governor, chosen by the legislature, was to preside without the power of veto. In addition, the militia called for a reform of the tax system and the postponement of all suits against debtors until a later date (Hoffman, 1973, p. 173).

As a result of their actions, and in spite of the enforcement of property restrictions on voting, a majority of the elected delegates to the state constitutional convention had never participated in a convention before. Further, the Hall–Hammond faction persuaded Anne Arundel County to instruct its delegates (including Chase) to support the above program (plus an additional demand for the elimination of property restrictions on suffrage). The latter victory precipitated Chase's resignation from the convention; however, he was reinstated in a later election (Hoffman, 1973, pp. 172–176).

In the end, the radical voices accomplished little indeed. Samuel Chase, Carroll of Carrollton, and other prominent, popular party members were elected as delegates to the convention. It was these men, as in earlier times, who controlled the course of the convention and the writing of the state constitution. Their fear and distrust of democracy, especially simple democracy, resulted in the "most conservative of all of the state constitutions framed in 1776–1777" (Crowl, 1943, p. 32).

Maryland's aristocracy was indeed successful in preserving the old order in the new state constitution. Suffrage requirements were set at fifty acres valued at over thirty pounds in current money. Assembly members were elected by *viva voce* voting, a procedure criticized by Crowl (1943) as one which allowed the aristocracy to exert an undue influence over the voters.

The bicameral assembly was divided into a House of Delegates and a Senate. Unlike the Pennsylvania constitution, which placed no property requirements on its delegates, the Maryland constitution required House members to be worth 500 pounds in real or personal property and Senate members to be worth even more (1000 pounds, real or personal). One feature of the new constitution especially admired by Madison was the indirect election of Senate members by an electoral college. In *Federalist* no. 63, Madison applauded the Maryland constitution, saying that it gave Maryland "a reputation in which it will probably not be rivaled by that of any state in the Union."

Confederation Politics

Constitutional authority was lodged in the Senate, and thus in the hands of the planter elite. It was this group of men, under the leadership of Charles Carroll of Carrollton, who would eventually dominate state politics. The Senate became the "symbol of upper-class rule." Its member's actions were guided by their desire to preserve the status quo and thus the influence of the state's aristocracy (O'Brien, 1979, pp. 2–3).

Control over the House was exercised by Samuel Chase and his supporters. In the beginning, Chase and Carroll worked closely together in an effort to return a semblance of order to the state. At times, this meant passing legislation that many of the elite found personally distasteful (specifically, the 1777 paper-money act), but nevertheless necessary for the maintenance of control (O'Brien, 1979, pp. 4–8; Hoffman, 1973, pp. 206–222).

By 1778, the democratic protest movement had been effectively controlled, and the unanimity of the "popular party" was crumbling. The Baltimore merchants were divided and were no longer a support for the party; thus, the Senate did not hesitate in passing legislation which prohibited merchants from representing Maryland in Congress (O'Brien, 1979, p. 10; Hoffman, 1973, pp. 242–243).

The alliance was permanently severed by Chase's attempts to improve, at any cost, his own social and financial position. Carroll was outraged by the self-interested actions of Chase in particular and the lower house in general. In response to Chase's (and others') speculations in confiscated property, Carroll issued the following statement:

> Merchants are useful members of the community, and as such ought to be countenanced and encouraged by the legislature; but the spirit of the times and circumstance may justify a temporary exclusion of that order of men from the public councils. If all merchants were men of known propriety, and tried integrity, the exclusion would be improper; however as past occurrences have discovered that all are not to be trusted, it is prudent to exclude the latter which cannot be done, but by a general law; for certainly in times, when an insatiable thirst of accumulating wealth and of rising into opulence instantaneously, and not by the gradual progress of unremitting industry has taken the place of a sober and well regulated spirit of trade, when occasions present themselves of making thousands by one bold though publicly injurious stroke of speculation, mercantile men can more readily turn such occasions to their own emolument, than others not engaged in trade.
>
> (Hoffman, 1973, pp. 249–250)

This cleavage between Tidewater planters and Upper Bay merchants widened in the fight over paper money, which was to consume much of the decade before ratification. Chase led the fight for paper money in the House and was joined by a number of other speculators, including Charles Ridgely, Luther Martin, and William Paca (Renzulli, 1972, p. 29). In terms of statewide support, it was the Upper Bay counties that generally favored paper-money bills (O'Brien, 1979, p. 195). It was also the Upper Bay counties that had been the most attractive in terms of investment opportunities, particularly the counties of Baltimore and Harford (O'Brien, 1979, p. 15; Renzulli, 1972, p. 29).

Thus, in the years immediately preceding the ratification debates, the House was involved in a bitter struggle to wrench control away from the Senate (Renzulli, 1972, p. 10). The stakes were high, for the winner of this battle would dictate the direction of Maryland's economy (O'Brien, 1979). The House employed a familiar tactic: they attempted to expand their influence by broadening the scope of conflict. Speculators desiring relief cloaked their remarks in terms of paper money for the masses, and House members attempted to undermine the constitutional authority of the Senate by proposing such democratic measures as public review of Senate actions (O'Brien, 1979, p. 198).

With the internal stability of the state at stake, planter elites sought the means to curtail this threat to the old order. In the ratification of the federal Constitution, they saw an alternative to the destruction of the existing society (O'Brien, 1979, p. 240). Since the fate of the federal Constitution rested in their hands, Maryland's ratification was an easy victory for the Federalists. Out of the 74 delegates elected to the state ratifying convention, 57 were planters. The 54 planters that voted for the Constitution constituted a solid majority all by themselves; they were, however, joined by 9 other delegates, and the document was approved by a vote of 63 to 11.

Analysis

With few exceptions, the merchants in Pennsylvania supported the ratification of the federal Constitution. Yet, in Maryland, commercial interests were clearly split on the question of ratification. Although the cities of Annapolis and Baltimore voted for ratification and merchants paraded down the streets of Baltimore in celebration of their victory, three urban counties—Baltimore, Anne Arundel and Harford—voted against ratification (McDonald, 1958, pp. 152–161; Renzulli, 1972, p. 94).

In order to understand this apparent anomaly, one must remember the political context in Maryland at the time of ratification. Maryland's leaders were preoccupied with internal affairs (O'Brien, 1979, pp. 210, 223). Chase and other speculators in the Upper Bay region were concerned with their immediate economic situation; their economic solvency could be achieved only by gaining control of the state government (O'Brien, 1979, pp. 33–34). The planter aristocracy was determined to retain political control; the federal Constitution was one means of achieving that goal. Under a strong national government, the state would no longer be responsible for such matters as coining money; thus, those forces working to undermine the state government would have to take their battle elsewhere (O'Brien, 1979, p. 240).

Perhaps, then, it's not so surprising that commercial interests were on both sides of the ratification question. Those merchants and lawyers in debt because of their speculations generally cared less about the benefits of free trade than about debt relief. Conversely, those merchants and other commercial interests who were not involved in such trades tended to place a greater value on the benefits to commerce under the federal Constitution.

Conclusion

Why did the frontiersmen in Pennsylvania and Maryland's new urban elite both oppose the ratification of the federal Constitution? In each case, opposition to the Constitution stemmed from the recognition that the new order was a threat to their economic and political position within the state. In the case of the Pennsylvania anti-Federalists, the fear was that the Constitution would undermine the authority of the existing state constitution, while in Maryland, the urban elites feared just the opposite; their concern was that the federal Constitution would reinforce the state constitution and concomitantly the dominant position of the planter aristocracy.

These state constitutions were the product of the internal revolution in each state; as such, they reflected the unique preferences of the dominant group in that state at the end of the revolutionary period. In Pennsylvania, where the internal revolution was most dramatically successful in shaping the state constitution, radical majoritarian elements were full partners in often dominant state-level coalitions. The radicals supported the state constitution so vigorously because it gave them the means—minimal suffrage restrictions and a unicameral legislature—to enforce their distinct policy positions on such issues as land settlement, taxation, and Indians.

In Maryland, where the internal revolution had been thwarted by traditional planter and merchant elites, state politics tended to be a matter of competition between elite factions, with the old ruling class heavily favored by such state constitutional features as high property requirements for Senate members and the election of Senators by electoral college. Thus, the state constitution reinforced a degree of inequality between the planter class and the new urban elite.

Although we have confined our analysis to only two states, we believe it is possible to generalize beyond these states to the ratification campaigns in other states. Our explanation follows from a basically neoinstitutionalist rational-choice perspective: individuals have preferences over outcomes, they anticipate the effects of institutional rules on policy choice-making and then they support those institutional rules (at both the state and the national level) that they perceive will advance their policy preferences.

Thus, our focus is on the role of internal conflicts in the ratification campaigns. This is not to say that external threats were unimportant. We recognize that in states such as Georgia, the external threat was overwhelming, and that in several other key states (Virginia, New York, and New Hampshire), the external threat changed enough votes at the margin to make the difference in the state's ratification (Riker, 1979). Yet, an explanation based on external threats alone leaves unexplained the role of internal issues in the ratification debate. We would argue that the federal Constitution was often viewed as a vehicle for resolving intrastate conflicts, and it was these internal disputes that determined the patterns of support and opposition to that Constitution.

Acknowledgments. We would like to thank Anne Khademian for her research assistance and Evelyn Fink, William Galston, Michael Gillespie, Tom Hammond, and William Riker for their useful comments on earlier drafts of this chapter.

CHAPTER FOURTEEN

The Strategy of Ratification

Evelyn C. Fink and William H. Riker

Many interpreters of the framing of the American Constitution see a puzzle in the events of ratification in 1787–88. Believing that the anti-Federalists were the numerically stronger party, they have struggled to answer the negative question: Why did the anti-Federalists lose? As a consequence, these interpreters often underappreciate the strength of the Federalists' strategy relative to the anti-Federalists'. By doing so, they ignore the interplay of strategy between the two sides during the nine-month ratification campaign. Indeed, the outcome is often depersonalized and attributed to numerous nameless events (e.g., the mails were delayed, a momentum for ratification developed, and the institutional rules for ratification favored the Federalists; Main, 1974, pp. 252–255; Boyd, 1979a, pp. 15–22) without appreciating how many of these nameless events were, indeed, the product of Federalist strategy. Explanations of this sort fail to recognize how, given a significant opposition, the Federalists were able to garner a majority of the votes in the ratification conventions and to win ratification in eleven out of thirteen states. In order to avoid these oddities, we will pose the question positively: Why did the Federalists win? Our formulation produces, we hope, a somewhat more believable interpretation of the whole campaign over ratification and thus shows that the earlier and unsatisfactory interpretation resulted, in part at least, from posing a convoluted question.

If ratification had been a two-sided dispute in which the interests were strictly opposed, then the negative formulation would make no difference. It would simply be the converse of the more obvious (i.e., positive) formulation. But, in fact, ratification was neither two-person nor zero-sum.

There were degrees of Federalism and anti-Federalism, some of which admitted compromise. A chief merit of a game-theoretic approach is that the stark anti-Federalist–Federalist dichotomy is removed when we take into account the variety and dynamic of opinions held in the electorate during the ratification campaign. One main feature of the ratification campaign was the invention of new alternatives besides simple ratification and rejection. Some were quite feasible (e.g., ratification with amendments subsequently to be adopted). Others, though strongly supported, were probably less feasible (e.g., ratification conditional on previous adoption of amendments).

Still, there were at least three or four main feasible or possible additional alternatives, as well as various combinations, one of which was, in fact, the ultimate social choice. Nesting among these specific alternatives was simple indifference. Some New England towns thought sending a delegate too expensive, which means, if the outcome was in doubt, that they placed a low valuation on it, whatever it might turn out to be. In most states, some delegates simply did not attend, and many of these may have valued the outcome at nearly zero. Finally, perhaps one third to two fifths of the eligible voters actually voted. While this is a larger proportion than had hitherto turned out in state elections, it still indicates a pretty high degree of indifference.

The simple bifurcation into Federalists and anti-Federalists is thus clearly erroneous for a society with many moderates. Such bifurcation is, unfortunately, a common error—with respect to all kinds of elections—by highly politicized interpreters who naively imagine that everybody is as concerned and extreme as themselves.

Nor was the dispute zero-sum, which is the property that winners win exactly what losers lose. Where the possibility of compromise or cooperation exists, both sides can end up doing better than they might have originally forecast. Except for, perhaps, duels, total wars, or two-candidate elections, politics is comprised of non-zero-sum events. The very process of building winning and losing coalitions for the formal decision involves a realignment of many participants and a reformulation of many issues. This is what happened here. There were two dominant themes: the Federalists emphasized the need for centralization and energy; the anti-Federalists emphasized the danger

TABLE 14.1. Ratification in 1787–1788

State	Date		Federalist	anti-Federalist
Delaware	7 December	1787	30	0
Pennsylvania	12 December	1787	46	23
New Jersey	18 December	1787	38	0
Georgia	31 December	1787	26	0
Connecticut	9 January	1788	128	40
Massachusetts	6 February	1788	186	168
Rhode Island[a]	24 March	1788	(239)	(2,711)
Maryland	26 April	1788	63	11
South Carolina	23 May	1788	149	73
New Hampshire	21 June	1788	57	47
Virginia	25 June	1788	89	79
New York	26 July	1788	30	27
North Carolina	2 August	1788	84	184

[a]Rhode Island held a referendum by towns, which was boycotted by Federalists. Figures given are of the popular vote.

to liberty in a strong government. A natural compromise was strong government with guarantees of liberties, which is excatly what resulted.

If we abandon the zero-sum, two-sided viewpoint, the formulation of the question makes a big difference. To explain why the losers ultimately lost, while interesting, tells us only that the game was stacked against them or that they played badly. It does not explain the outcome, which depends on the ultimate winners' successful strategy. The campaign strategy of both sides, anti-Federalist and Federalist, is necessary to understand the ratification. Hence we pose the question positively: Why did the Federalists win?

The Federalist Plurality

That the Federalists won is perfectly straightforward. Eleven states ratified between September 1787, when the Constitution was submitted to the states, and July 1788, when the first round of ratification concluded. Since only nine states (70%) were required and eleven (85%) ratified initially, the Constitution won by considerably more than a minimally winning coalition. Furthermore, the number of delegates voting for the Constitution was much larger than the number voting against (see Table 14.1). So it is clear that the Federalists won. The explanation of their victory varies with the assumptions made about their support. If one assumes that they represented a plurality of adult white males, then the appropriate explanation is a description of how they persuaded a plurality in eleven states to accept a radical reordering of government. If, however, one assumes that the anti-Federalists were a plurality, then the appropriate explanation is a description of how, by bad management or on account of constitutional obstacles, they lost their plurality.

Unfortunately, the evidence about pluralities is very weak. Jackson Main (1974), whose judgment is often cited, estimates that the two sides were nearly equal, with the anti-Federalists having the slight advantage, and guesses that they comprised about 52% of the population at the time of the elections to the ratification conventions (p. 249). The true party balance is ambiguous, since the election returns for the delegates are generally not reported, and since the size of the winning majorities varied tremendously from town to town (cf. Main, 1974, pp. 285–286).

We have attempted to work backward from the actual representation at the ratifying conventions to an estimate of the factional division. While Main estimated the division of public opinion from the election of delegates to the state conventions, we estimate it from the final vote in each state's ratifying convention, which shows the ambiguity of the estimates. Our technique avoids the issue of identifying all delegates to the ratification conventions by their initial party predispositions. Since many delegates were either persuaded to switch sides by the debates in their conventions or joined together because of an advantageous compromise, it is easier to identify the delegates by their final vote. Further, it is not clear whether, in their switching, those delegates initially elected to oppose the Constitution unamended did not represent their constituency. Main's use of election returns presumes that they did not. We believe that it is plausible that in many cases they did. With our method of identifying party supporters, we find that the final level of support for the Constitution may just as easily have been a small plurality in favor of it as against it.

From the data in Table 14.2, we have calculated the following ratios:

F_R = number of free persons residing in 1790 in districts represented in the conventions of 1787–1788 by delegates who voted *for* the Constitution

---

total free population

TABLE 14.2. Representation in State Ratifying Conventions[a]

State	Population	− Slaves	= Free Persons	= Federalist	+ Anti-Federalist	+ Unrepresented
				Represented by		
NH	141,885	158	141,727	69,458	58,818	13,451
MA	475,376	0	475,376	220,884	188,344	66,148
RI	68,825	948	67,877	15,686[b]	52,191	—
CT	237,946	2,764	235,182	184,643	50,539	—
NY	340,120	21,324	318,796	118,018	198,117	2,661
NJ	184,139	11,423	172,716	172,716	—	—
PA	434,373	3,737	430,636	286,947	133,539	10,150
DE	59,094	8,887	50,207	50,207	—	—
MD	319,728	103,036	216,692	180,154	36,538	—
VA	821,282	305,059	516,233	253,928	250,436	11,869
NC	429,442	103,984	325,458	81,291	234,500	9,667
SC	249,073	107,094	141,979	58,149	69,199	14,631
GA	82,548	29,264	53,284	53,284	—	—
Total	3,843,841	697,678	3,146,163	1,745,365	1,272,221	128,577

Sources: For the enumeration, *Return of the Whole Number Persons within the Several Districts of the United States, First Census, U.S. Census Office* (reprinted 1976, Arno Press, from edition printed by William Duane, 1802). For the election results, Turner (1983, New Hampshire), Elliot (1836, Vol. 2, Massachusetts; Vol. 4, North Carolina and South Carolina); Labaree (1945, Connecticut); Staples (1971, Rhode Island); DePauw (1966, New York); McMaster and Stone (1888, Pennsylvania); Renzulli (1972, Maryland); Grigsby (1969, Virginia).

[a]The census of 1790 was conducted for the same units as the elections were held in 1787–88 for New Hampshire (towns), Massachusetts (towns), Rhode Island (towns), Pennsylvania (counties), Maryland (counties), Virginia (counties), North Carolina (counties),and South Carolina (counties and parishes). In Connecticut, the election was by towns, but the enumeration was by counties. Hence, some unrepresented towns are counted as part of the representation of counties. In New York, the election was by counties, and the enumeration was by towns, so no difficulty arises. Since the conventions in New Jersey, Delaware, and Georgia were unanimous, the entire population is placed in the Federalist column.

[b]In Rhode Island, a referendum was held by towns, which the Federalists boycotted where they had the overwhelming majority. I have assigned Providence and Newport to the Federalist column, as well as the towns they actually carried (Bristol and Little Compton).

AF_R = number of free persons residing in 1790 in districts represented in the conventions of 1787–1788 by delegates who voted *against* the Constitution

––

total free population

U_R = number of free persons residing in 1790 in districts unrepresented in the conventions of 1787–1788 or represented
by delegates who did not vote

$$\text{total free population}$$

and find them to be:

$$F_R = .56;\ AF_R = .40;\ U_R = .04$$

Our calculation would indicate that the Federalists had, in the end, a majority, and that the story of the ratification campaign is how the Federalists were able to gain their majority in time for the final vote. It does not, however, reveal the relative strength of the two factions because it more frequently ignores anti-Federalist sentiment in districts that they lost than it similarly ignores Federalist sentiment in districts that they lost. Nor does it account for the variation between districts in the degree of factional opinion.

To compensate for the bias from the numerical strength of the Federalist voting districts, one must also estimate an index of factional sentiment, F or AF. Lacking information, we estimate that, on the average, the winning candidate won each district with the support of 60%; then the indices would be

$$F = (.60F_R + .40AF_R)$$

$$AF = (.40F_R + .60AF_R)$$

and, in this case, $F = .50$ and $AF = .46$. Incidentally, varying the assumption to splits of, say, 55-45 or 65-35 makes little difference here.

While our estimate of anti-Federalist "strength" differs by only 6 percentage points from Main's, the difference is nevertheless significant because it reverses the plurality—and this reversal is fundamental to the entire interpretation of ratification. Our estimate is derived from simplifying assumptions. We assume that all delegates who voted for Federalist proposals of ratification were representing their districts when they did so. Main's calculation, based on election returns, counts those who switched their vote at the convention to the Federalist side as still representing anti-Federalist-dominated districts. Although it is well known that a few delegates who switched did, indeed, face electoral trouble on their return home, many others reported no such difficulties. Instead, the difference in our estimate from Main's highlights the approach that we have taken not to force the ratification contest into a zero-sum game. The key to the ratification contest was that the Federalists were able to turn a few key states whose elections sent an anti-Federalist majority to their convention into Federalist victories. For the most part, these victories were the result of persuasion or alterations in the proposed form of ratification. It seems reasonable to suggest that these delegates may have been representing their district when they switched their vote either on the basis of new information or new alternatives. Whether these delegates who were elected as anti-Federalists but who then switched either to abstention or to the Federalist side did, indeed, fairly represent their districts is difficult to know. Instead, it is probably safer to avoid a two-sided interpretation of the ratification and simply to label them as moderates: men who although elected under the anti-Federal label chose the side that, on further information and negotiation, best represented their more moderate preferences.[1]

There is a bit of evidence on this point. In New York State, Federalist strength centered in New York City, Brooklyn, Staten Island and Westchester. Anti-Federalists were strong upstate (i.e., upriver—Ulster, Columbia, and Albany counties). The switchers came from the borders of the Federalist center, and for the most part, the closer to the city, the larger the shift. Thus, the delegates were all the delegates from Queens, three fourths of the delegates from Suffolk (eastern Long Island), two thirds of the delegates from Dutchess (adjacent to Westchester on the north), and one fourth of the delegates from Orange (across the river from Westchester and Dutchess). Main (1974) characterizes the switchers as coming from the more commercially oriented farming areas than the region of "isolated upstate farmers" (p. 240). Presumably, those delegates represented moderates who were more influenced by the need for a strong union government than were the anti-Federalist diehards up the Hudson and the Mohawk. Thus, when the moderates were persuaded to switch their allegiance and vote for ratification with recommendatory amendments, a position many of them had explicitly run against in the elections, they may have been representing their constituents' preferences as altered by the new information learned in the convention. While this neat geographical shading from the core of initial Federalists in Manhattan, through the switchers bordering the city, and finally to the core anti-Federalists upstate is not visible on the maps of the other states, switchers elsewhere very likely made similar calculations about their constituents' commitment to steering a moderate course.

The point is that, just as Main counts the switchers in his determination of an anti-Federalist plurality and we count them as Federalists in our evaluation of the final votes, the truer course is to recognize the swing districts and to model in their influence. The anti-Federalists had won them prior to the convention, and the Federalists won them afterward. If one allows for representation to occur legitimately at the convention, as we argue, it is plausible that the Federalists were able to win a plurality of support in the general public by the final vote.

The question then becomes: How did the Federalists win? This leads to an examination of the dynamic of the ratification campaign. Estimates of the final level of support say little, by themselves, as to who was ahead at the start of the campaign, and in the convention. What counted was, as Main also points out (p. 249), why the Constitution was ratified in eleven state ratification conventions even in states that had, at the start of their conventions, anti-Federalist majorities (i.e., Massachusetts, New Hampshire, and New York). These three states, added to the anti-Federal outcomes in Rhode Island and North Carolina and the presumed anti-Federal leanings in Virginia, should have been enough to prevent ratification. Yet it occurred.

The Federalist Advantage

That the Federalists ended up with a plurality or majority is a credit to their ability to structure the ratification process to their advantage and to rhetorically hold delegates in compliance with their chosen agenda. Initially, the framers at Philadelphia offered a simple choice of ratification or rejection. But the anti-Federalists (and some Federalists) wanted to expand the range of choice. Early in the campaign, the anti-Federalists introduced a plan for a second convention. Later, they also considered various degrees of ratification. These may have been merely delaying tactics, but they nevertheless expanded the agenda. Similarly, the Federalists introduced the alternative of ratification with the promise of proposing specified amendments after ratification. This was a hurrying tactic and was, of course, also agenda-expanding. As a result, at least the following positions, complicated with various proposals for temporary adjournment, existed on the dimension of possible ratification:

1. Unconditional ratification.
2. Ratification with the Federalists' promise that specified amendments would be proposed and adopted (recommendatory amendments).
3. Indifference.
4. Ratification with the condition of withdrawal if specified amendments

were not adopted or a second convention was not held by a specified time (conditions subsequent).

5. Ratification conditional upon the prior adoption of specified amendments or a second convention (conditions precedent).
6. Rejection with the call for a second convention.
7. Rejection.

Initially, the Federalists held the first position, while anti-Federalists held the seventh, which gradually expanded to the fourth, fifth, sixth, and seventh. By a number of remarkable heresthetical maneuvers, the Federalists created the second position as a compromise to which some anti-Federalists could adhere. At the same time, the Federalists managed to convince both themselves and enough anti-Federalists that the fourth, fifth, and sixth positions were identical with the seventh. Consequently, the Federalists forced the anti-Federalists in these positions to choose between the second (or third) and the seventh. From this maneuver, as well as from the creation of the second position, the Federalists were able to transform a significant number of initially anti-Federalist delegates into Federalists, at least in Massachusetts, New Hampshire, and New York.

These two maneuvers were surely one of the main reasons that the Federalists won. As for the persons represented by the switchers, they had presumably voted for an opponent of the Constitution who turned out to support it. Were they thus misrepresented? Probably not. Delegates had been elected during campaigns that bifurcated the issue: ratification or rejection. But during the conventions, the Federalists presented the motion to ratify in an amended form (i.e., with suggested amendments). Anti-Federalist delegates were thus forced to reinterpret the sense of their constituents: Did their constituents really want rejection once a milder form of ratification was available? Given that the delegates were experienced politicians, some of them who switched must have judged correctly that their constituents would be pleased with a weaker ratification. That is, the constituents, as well as the delegates, must have been arranged on the 7-point scale previously described, and the switching delegates probably represented constituents who were comfortable with the second position.

The Anti-Federalist Disadvantage

The Federalists obtained eleven ratifications, even with only a small majority of citizen supporters, mainly because they brought forward an alternative method of ratification—in effect, an alternative Constitution. Nevertheless, a puzzle remains. Given that the supporters of the Constitution were not evenly dispersed (i.e., the Federalists had very large majorities in Connecticut, New Jersey, Pennsylvania, Delaware, Maryland, and Georgia), how did the Federalists manage to carry eleven of thirteen states? For the most part, the solution to this puzzle is that they won in several difficult states by inventing some local tactic. In New Hampshire, they recessed the convention in order to persuade some towns to rescind their instructions to their delegates to vote against the Constitution. In New York, they persuaded some delegates to switch by pointing out that New York, the eleventh ratifier, might be left out of a ten-state union if it ratified with conditions. Leaving aside these unique circumstances, the Federalists benefited from the anti-Federalists' constitutional disadvantages. One of these was factionally unfair districting, which undoubtedly existed in several states. Another may have been the property qualifications for voting, although it is doubtful that the anti-Federalists were hurt by it.

Districting did, in fact, turn out to be dramatically unfair in South Carolina and, in a lesser degree, in North Carolina, Maryland, New York, and possibly Virginia and New Hampshire (Roll, 1969). Note, however, that the Federalists failed in North Carolina; they carried Maryland by so large a majority that districting was irrelevant; and they carried New York and New Hampshire in the end by a maneuver that worked even though they had initially had fewer delegates. Furthermore, they carried Pennsylvania, Connecticut, and Massachusetts even though the anti-Federalists had the advantage of rotten boroughs. So only in South Carolina and Virginia was unfair districting conceivably relevant to the Federalist victory. (See Table 14.3.)

The Constitution was written, however, with the system of representation of these two states in the back of the delegates' minds. Had districting been different, so, we believe, would the Constitution itself have been different. The framers may have exploited the knowledge of unfair districting to ensure support for the Constitution. Hence, no one can really tell what the marginal effect of districting was.

The main feature of the Constitution that guaranteed the support of the greatly overrepresented planters on the Carolina coasts was the vote trade between Massachusetts and South Carolina on the slave trade and navigation acts. It was precisely this trade that endangered Virginian ratification—or so George Mason, the leader of the Virginia opposition, later told Jefferson (Farrand, 1966, III, 367). At the

TABLE 14.3. Free Persons per Delegate to Nonunanimous Ratifying
Conventions

State	Vote		Delegates		Free Persons Delegate	
	Fed.	Anti-Fed.	Fed.	Anti-Fed.	Fed.	Anti-Fed.
NH	69,458	58,818	57	47	1,219	1,251
MA	220,884	188,344	186	168	1,188	1,121
CT	184,643	50,539	128	40	1,442	1,263
NY	118,018	198,117	30	27	3,934	7,338
PA	286,947	133,539	46	23	6,237	5,806
MD	180,154	36,538	63	11	2,859	3,321
VA	253,928	250,436	89	79	2,853	3,170
NC	81,291	234,500	83	184	979	1,272
SC	58,149	69,199	149	73	390	948

Constitutional Convention, South Carolinians convincingly argued that, without some guarantee of continuation of the slave trade, their state would never ratify. Virginians, on the other hand, wanted to close down the foreign trade in slaves (presumably because, with a large natural increase of slaves, they were domestic suppliers). At the same time, Virginians wanted to make navigation acts (i.e., domestic monopolies of the carrying trade) difficult in order to prevent New England carriers from obtaining monopoly profits out of carrying Virginian tobacco. Massachusetts delegates chose to support South Carolina, which conceded on the navigation acts, and to run the risk on ratification in Virginia. As it turned out, this was a wise choice, because both Virginia and South Carolina ratified. But suppose South Carolina had been districted so that the back country was as heavily represented as the planters on the seacoast. Then, it is likely that South Carolina would have voted similarly to North Carolina and the back-country farmers in southern Virginia. In that case, the vote trade would have been senseless because South Carolina would have refused to ratify. So Massachusetts would instead have been constrained to come to some accommodation with Virginia. Thus, the particular content of the Constitution took account of the districting in South Carolina, and the outcome in one state, at most, was influenced by the districting. That is, while the districting helped carry both South Carolina and Virginia for the Constitution, under exactly fair districting in both states the Constitution would doubtless have been written to carry at least one of them. Unfair districting is thus not a general feature of Federalist success but simply another unique local circumstance in, especially, South Carolina.

A second constitutional advantage that the Federalists are said to have possessed is that in many states, there were still property qualifications for voting. Early economic interpretations have assumed that the "rich" favored the Constitution and the "poor" opposed. While it is an odd notion of rich and poor that assigns about half the population to each category, these writers have compounded the confusion by arguing further that property qualifications rendered impoverished opponents ineligible to vote. Such an argument misconstrues the nature of property qualifications in the eighteenth century. If they had any significant effect at all, it was to favor, not harm, the anti-Federalists, as indicated by the fact that in New York, the Federalists·were the ones who insisted on eliminating property qualifications for the election of the ratifying convention. While the anti-Federalists were opposed to Federalist attempts to vote their manor lessees, they did not protest the measure lest they be characterized as antidemocratic. One must surmise that they did not see property qualifications as significant.

The reason is that the usual property qualification was the ownership of a small amount of land—often, the 40-shilling freehold derived from the medieval English electoral law, and then diminished by inflation to a trivial requirement. In an economy consisting very largely of subsistence farming on small holdings, nearly every farmer, especially in the back country, held enough property to vote. Those disfranchised by the qualifications were urban mechanics, merchants with small capital, sailors, fishermen, foresters, and, generally, workers in occupations other than family farming. Farmers were generally disenfranchised if they were tenant farmers or if they owed back taxes. How rigorously the qualifications were imposed against such people is impossible to say, and perhaps the qualifications were ignored when potential ineligibles had a settled place of residence.

In any case, the presumed pattern of ineligibility is all wrong to advantage the Federalists. They carried the urban areas, where disfranchisement was most likely. Every major city was strongly Federal: Portsmouth, Salem, Boston, Plymouth, Newport, Providence, Hartford, New Haven, New York, Philadelphia, Baltimore, Norfolk, New Bern, Charleston, Beaufort, and Savannah. And it was not just the rich who were enthusiastic Federalists. Enthusiasm obliterated class lines.[2] In Philadelphia, the "mob" compelled the anti-Federalists to make a quorum for the Constitution. In Boston, the mechanics' enthusiasm compelled Sam Adams, who was personally disinclined, to vote for the Constitution, and in Baltimore the enthusiasm silenced Samuel Chase, who was even more strongly disinclined. In New York, the mechanics' enthusiasm was so great that they carried through moblike celebrations of each step in the ratifying process. So if the urban poor were disfranchised—which is doubtful—they would, as voters, have simply swelled the Federalist total.

Conversely, the few disfranchised rural laborers would, in the conventional interpretation, have voted anti-Federalist, and thus, their votes would simply have swelled the anti-Federalist majorities in the back country. Hence, in both the city and countryside, the putatively disfranchised would, as voters, simply have confirmed the results that actually occurred. This supposed disadvantage of the anti-Federalists is no more than a contemporary misinterpretation of eighteenth-century politics.

The Federalists' Problem

The Federalists did not win because of statutory advantages like districting and electoral qualifications. They won because they achieved at least a plurality and parlayed it into a majority in eleven states. To understand their victory, then, it is necessary to investigate the actual campaign.

The Federalists did indeed have a problem. Initially, they constituted, probably, a plurality of the society. But their support was soft since the Constitution itself had yet to withstand close scrutiny. To win, the Federalists had to solidify their early lead and convince a majority (or something close to it) in 9/13 of the states that a truly radical reorganization of government was desirable. Had the Constitution consisted merely of minor revisions of the Articles of Confederation, they might have had an easier time; but the revisions were major and astonishing. In place of a loose league, the Constitution provided for a real government, rather like the governments of the states, but piled on top of them. A sizable majority had to be encouraged to support this radical change.

The Federalists' strategy consisted of:

1. Initially changing the method of ratification in order to make their campaign easier.
2. Ratifying state-by-state as quickly as possible.
3. Changing the alternative offered in order to accommodate anti-Federal objections.

4. Maneuvering with *ad hoc* adjustments and arguments (especially in New Hampshire and New York) to carry individual states.
5. And, through it all, arguing for the necessity and desirability of the Constitution and refuting anti-Federal criticisms.

We will describe elements 1–3 in turn, leaving the local adjustments (4) and the element of rhetoric (5) for another occasion.

The Method of Ratification

If the amendment procedure prescribed in the Articles of Confederation had been followed, it is certain that the Constitution would have failed of adoption. Any one state could veto. By hindsight, we know that Rhode Island, New York, and North Carolina would certainly have done so. During the Constitutional Convention, Wilson (Pa.) predicted that Rhode Island, New York, and Maryland would veto (Farrand, 1966, Vol. II, 562; hereinafter cited as *Records*). Remembering the fate of the impost (i.e., a proposal to allow Congress to collect a tariff), which was vetoed the first time by Rhode Island and the second by New York, the Federalists recognized the need for an alternative procedure. So in the Virginia Plan, state conventions were to ratify; thus the state legislatures would be bypassed entirely. This was quite in tune with the rest of the plan, which, as one of us has shown elsewhere (Riker, 1987), consistently isolated state governments and subordinated them to the national government.

Even though this procedure for amendment ratification strikingly departed from the procedures of the Articles, the delegates easily accepted it. Probably, most of them agreed with G. Morris, who urged them to ignore the Articles, saying "This Convention is unknown to the Confederation" (*Records*, I, 92). Initially, several delegates did indeed advocate the procedure of the Articles as shown in *Records:* I, 122 (Sherman, Ct.); I, 123 (King, Ma.); II, 88 (Ellsworth, Ct.); II, 88 (Paterson, N.J.); II, 476–77 (Martin, McHenry, Carroll, Md.); and especially I, 124 (Gerry, Ma., the leading anti-Federalist, who feared popular ratification because in Massachusetts, the people "have the wildest ideas of government in the world"). But with the endorsement of Madison and Wilson, the provision of the Virginia Plan was adopted 6-3, with two states divided (*Records*, I, 123). It was confirmed by the defeat, 3-7, of Ellsworth's proposal for ratification by state legislatures (*Records*, II, 93). By the end of the Convention, Sherman and King were enthusiastic proponents of the Virginia procedure (*Records*, II, 468, 476).

The reasons given for bypassing the state legislatures ranged from the philosophical to the strategic. Madison thought ratification by "the supreme authority of the people" to be "essential" and "indispensable" for the Constitution to prevail over the states (*Records*, I, 122). Mason (Va.) also thought it "most important" to refer the Constitution to "the authority of the people," both because they were "the basis of free government" and, more practically, because he wished to forestall the legislatures from subsequently revoking what they had once ratified (*Records*, II, 88).

Descending from the high ground of principle, Randolph, who introduced the Virginia Plan, bluntly defended it on the most practical basis:

> Whose opposition will most likely to be excited agst. the System (i.e., the Constitution)? That of the local demagogues who will be degraded by it from the importance they now hold . . . It is of great importance therefore that the consideration of this subject (i.e., ratification) should be transferred from the Legislatures where this class of men, have their full influence to a field in which their efforts can be less mischievous. (*Records*, II, 89).

The most definitive statement, however, was made by Gorham (Ma.), who urged ratification by state conventions rather than legislatures because:

1. Men chosen by the people for the particular purpose, will discuss the subject more candidly than members of the Legislature who are to lose power which is to be given up the Genl. Govt.
2. Some of the Legislatures are composed of several branches. It will consequently be more difficult in these cases to get the plan through the Legislatures, than thru' a Convention.
3. In The States many of the ablest men are excluded from the Legislatures, but may be elected into a Convention. Among these may be ranked many of the Clergy who are generally friends to good government . . .
4. The Legislatures will be interrupted with a variety of little business. [B]y artfully pressing which, designing men will find means to delay from year to year.
5. If the last art: of the Confederation is to be pursued the unanimous concurrence of the States will be necessary. But will any one say. That all the States are to suffer themselves to be ruined, if Rho. Island should persist in her opposition to general measure. . . . The present advantage which N. York seems to be so much attached to, of taxing her neighbours ⟨by the regulation of her trade⟩, makes it very probable, that she will be of the number. It would therefore deserve serious consideration whether provision ought not to be made for giving effect

to the System without waiting for the unanimous concurrence of the States (*Records,* II, 90).

One cannot say which was most influential in the Convention, the strategic rationale or the philosophical rationale. Probably they reinforced each other: Madison's and Mason's appeal to first principles referred to the survival of the proposed Constitution, once it was ratified, while Randolph's and Gorham's strategic rationale referred immediately to ratification. Doubtless most delegates thought both kinds of considerations were important.

In the decision, however, on the number of state ratifications necessary for the Constitution to operate, only strategic considerations were mentioned. The framers sought a balance between what was easiest and what was probably acceptable. Various numbers were proposed: seven, eight, nine, ten, and thirteen. Wilson moved boldly for seven and was supported by Washington (*Records,* II, 468, 482). Madison proposed seven states with at least 33 representatives. Randolph and Mason thought nine a customary number, rather like Schelling's "prominent solution," and nine it became by a vote of 8-3, where the dissenters presumably wished for eight or seven (*Records,* II, 477).

Thus, the proto-Federalists, who were the vast majority of the Convention (probably 48 out of 55), arranged for a procedure greatly to their advantage. This accounts in part, we believe, for the passionate resentment that the anti-Federalists displayed throughout the campaign for ratification. Many anti-Federalist leaders had ignored the Convention. Patrick Henry refused to be a delegate, later saying "I smelt a rat." But we think he and others were unwilling also because they knew that, under the procedure of the Articles, they could defeat any reform they disapproved. It must have then infuriated them that the Convention's procedure bypassed both Congress and the state legislatures.

Despite anticipation of this fury, the proto-Federalists at the Constitutional Convention were grimly determined to stick with their advantageous procedure. The one thing that might have derailed their plan was an anti-Federalist Congress that insisted on following the procedures of the Articles. But the Congress, which was chosen in the same political climate as the Convention itself, was ideologically similar to the Convention. The only difficulty was inspired by Richard Henry Lee, an outspoken anti-Federalist. Lee wanted to transmit the Constitution with language that identified the revolutionary nature of the Constitution. He also proposed that "the [state]

conventions had best have the liberty to alter [the Constitution]"
(Jensen, 1976, p. 333) and, to that end, proposed attaching a set of
amendments to Congress's transmittal. Lee's first motion of neutral,
if not hostile, transmittal was outvoted. On this crucial vote in
Congress, the Constitution was favored ten states to one, and 30 out
of 35 Congressmen voted for the procedure proposed by the Convention. This is not surprising, given that three of the eleven
congressional delegations had a majority consisting of delegates to
the Convention, and four more congressional delegations contained
one framer.[3] Congress submitted the Constitution to the states
unanimously but, in a concession to Lee, said nothing about its
merits. Still, unanimous transmittal, even if neutral, is a remarkable
achievement.

The Setting for the Campaign: A Closed Rule

Advantageous as the procedure of ratification was to the Federalists
in comparison with what would have been required under the
Articles, there were still many pitfalls in their way to victory. By
reason of the procedure implicit in calling the Constitutional Convention, the framers were constrained to play a game that had many
opportunities for error in choosing strategy.

When the American states first adopted constitutions (in 1776–
1777), typically the legislatures wrote and adopted them as if they
were simply legislating (Adams, 1980), just as in some contemporary
constitution-writing (e.g., in India and the Fourth French Republic).
The Articles of Confederation were a hybrid: Congress wrote them
but sought ratification from the states. In 1777–1778, the states began
to use special conventions rather than legislatures to write constitutions and then to seek popular ratification in one way or another. This
stylistic change (from legislature to convention) was completed by the
time of the Constitutional Convention. So the framers, themselves a
convention, were more or less constrained to seek ratification by
constituents.[4]

Serial ratification by popularily chosen conventions of a completed
document is as close as the men of the eighteenth century could come
to the modern procedure of referendum, that is, an up-or-down vote
by the citizenry. Serial conventions, however, come close to the
referendum and display many of its advantages and disadvantages.
Conventions also avoided some further disadvantages in that this
procedure restricted participation to what was hoped to be a select
few and placed them in an arena devised for debate. So the method

of serial conventions provided a nice blend of the advantage of a referendum (a controlled offer) with the advantage of a legislative setting (a selective arena for persuasion and leadership).

Thinking of the country as a whole as a legislature, then a referendum, which cannot be amended once it is on the ballot, is equivalent to a motion offered by a legislative committee (here, the Convention) under a closed rule (that is, a rule prohibiting amendment of the committee motion on the floor of the whole house). On the other hand, the legislative method of writing and adopting constitutions, as used in 1776–1777, is equivalent to an open rule, which permits floor amendments. We can thus look at the framers' situation by comparing strategic considerations under open and closed rules.

A committee with a closed rule has one great advantage: It can pick its members' most preferred motion from the set, W_q, of all motions that can win against the status quo (Krehbiel, 1986). Even though many different potential majorities might each prefer many other motions in the win set of the status quo, W_q, still most of these majorities will not have a chance to vote on their preferred motions because the committee alone chooses the motion to vote on. By definition, this motion passes, but only the majority of committee members—or people exactly like them—are fully satisfied. All others who prefer the committee motion to the status quo, however slightly, and however lowly they rate the committee motion itself, are nevertheless constrained to give up their more preferred alternatives in order to avoid something even worse than the committee motion. If, as often happens and as almost certainly happened here, the set W_q is very large, then the committee members (or the framers) have considerable freedom of action.

As against this advantage from the closed rule, there is one major disadvantage, namely, that the committee members may not be able discover, *a priori*, what alternative motions are in W_q. If they choose a motion not in W_q and their closed rule is sustained on the floor, they lose everything in an up-or-down vote. This potential disadvantage may not matter in a small legislative body with personal interaction among all members. Still, in a very large body, the chance seems high that a committee may misunderstand other members' tastes. The way, then, to protect against the choice of a motion that is subsequently revealed to be outside of W_q is an open rule which permits revision of the committee motion on the basis of information gathered during debate. But for the nation as a whole, the referendum procedure precludes an open rule.

The Framers' Choice of Strategy

This, then, was the situation faced by Federalists at the end of the Convention. The committee (i.e., the framers) gave them a closed rule (i.e., the serial ratifying conventions) on a motion (i.e., the Constitution) located close to the boundary of—and perhaps outside—the win set of the status quo, W_q. A difficult situation. In order to analyze the Federalists' achievement, let us treat ratification as a game where the possible strategies are all known to the players at the beginning. (In actual fact, of course, the alternative strategies were worked out as the campaign progressed.)

Let us begin with the voters, who, we assume, compare the Constitution with what they will be left with if it is not ratified. This pits the motion (the Constitution) against the status quo (the Articles). Although the referendum procedure admits only this one comparison, still the voters themselves can imagine a range of alternatives in between these two extremes. (We know from the debates and from the method of ratification ultimately adopted that, in fact, many voters were quite aware of such a range.) So we place the motion and the status quo on the same dimension, which we label, arbitrarily but not unhistorically, as *consolidation*. And we assume that the voters have preferences over this dimension.

In Figure 14.1, we depict the tastes of typical Federalists and anti-Federalists on the consolidation dimension, where $U_i(x_k)$ is the ordinal utility, U, of voter or group i for the degree of consolidation represented at point x_k on the consolidation axis (i.e., the x axis). The curve $U_i(x)$, which measures a height above the x axis, is the utility of voter i for all points on the axis.[5] Since the offering of the pair of alternatives (Articles and Constitution) bifurcates the voters into a bimodal distribution, these typical voters may be interpreted as examples of persons whose ideal points are near the two modes. To express the bifurcation, we assume that the typical Federalist prefers the Constitution and its neighboring modifications to the Articles, and also that he prefers the Articles to minor reforms (e.g., greater congressional authority over interstate commerce) which give the appearance of reform without the reality of it. Conversely, the typical anti-Federalist prefers the Articles to the Constitution and also prefers small changes (e.g., again, more extensive congressional authority over interstate commerce) to the Articles themselves.

These tastes are, we believe, historically accurate: The anti-Federalists were forced to acknowledge the need for, at least, modest reform by the almost unanimous support in the spring of 1787 for the

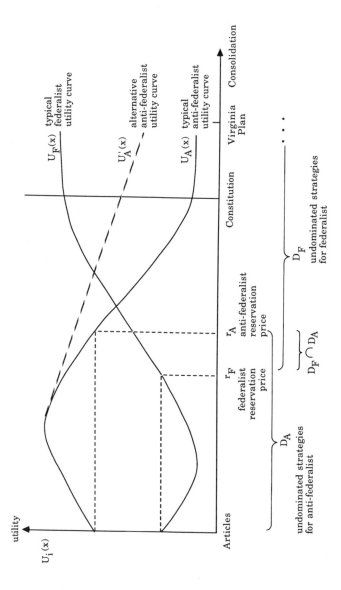

FIG. 14.1. **Estimate of utility functions for typical Federalist and anti-Federalist over alternatives to the Articles of Confederation.**

Constitutional Convention. The Federalists, on the other hand, having rejected modest reform at Philadelphia, were thus committed to believing it nothing more than false reassurance on the way to collapse.

These considerations lead to a smooth, single-peaked curve for the anti-Federalists and a smooth, single-troughed one for the Federalists. Note, however, that Figure 14.1 is not a frequency distribution, and we intend no suggestion of a set of cyclical preferences.

If we use Figure 14.1 to illustrate the framers' problem, they must choose some alternative (i.e., write a constitution) on the horizontal axis that yields them at least as much utility as the status quo, namely, the Articles. We call this minimally satisfying constitution the reservation price, r_F, of the proto-Federalists at the Convention and write $U_F(Articles) = U_F(r_F)$. Presumably, the framers, anticipating the future Federalists' reaction, reject all potential constitutions lying in the range $[Articles, r_F]$ and adopt some constitution, x_k, where $U_F(x_k) \geq U_F(r_F)$. Similarly, the anti-Federalists also have a reservation price, $U_A(r_A) = U_A(Articles)$, and can be expected to support any constitution in the range $[Articles, r_A]$ and to reject any constitution, x_k, where $U_A(x_k) < U_A(r_A)$.

These features set the terms of the framers' problem. They could not know, of course, how many people had utility curves of these two classes of shapes. Nor could they know exactly what shapes the proto-anti-Federalist utility curves might take. For example, the typical shape might be the dotted line $U_A(x)$, rather than the solid line $U_A(x)$. Hence, the framers' problem is one of constrained maximization. That is, they want to pick some x_k so that it maximizes their own preferences subject to the constraint that, for some voters, i, $U_i(k_k) > U_i(Articles)$, and that voters with this utility constitute a majority in each of nine states.

If the framers believed that proto-Federalists with curves like $U_F(x)$ were an absolute majority of the society, then, they might reasonably choose x_k, so that $U_F(x_k)$ is maximum—something, perhaps, like the Virginia Plan. But one frequent refrain at the Convention was that the people or the states would not accept extreme consolidation. In order to preserve some functions for the states, the framers modified the Virginia Plan into the Constitution as submitted for ratification.

On what basis was the Constitution selected out of the whole range $[r_F, max\ (x_k)]$? If the framers had known exactly what would turn out to be r_A, then the calculation would have been fairly simple: Let the alternatives in the range $[r_F, max\ (x_k)]$ be the set of proto-Federalists' undominated strategies, $\mathcal{D}_F$, which are each better than the status quo of the Articles. Similarly, for the proto-anti-Federalists, the set $\mathcal{D}_A$ is the set of alternatives in the range [*Articles*, r_A]. Then, the framers would know that the intersection, $\mathcal{D}_F \cap \mathcal{D}_A$, contained constitutions with near unanimous support. This intersection is, however, probably much smaller than W_q, which is the set of alternatives that some majority favors against the status quo. That is, some atypical anti-Federalists might well support constitutions to the right of r_A. The task of the framers was to estimate the probable numbers of anti-Federalists located at each point right of r_A in order then to determine which of these points lay in W_q.

Having identified W_q, the framers would then have a choice that would vary according to whether they prescribed procedures comparable to a closed or open rule. Facing an open-rule type of procedure, it is permissible, even appropriate, for the framers to select some x_k fairly far to the right. If they err, in the sense that x_k is not in W_q, they can attempt to rectify their error by floor amendments. With an open rule, however, the initial proposal is just as subject to amendments from the anti-Federalists, and the final outcome is dependent on the counteroffers from the opponents of the Constitution and the sequencing of the votes used in the separate state conventions. In a word, the outcome is more uncertain. On the other hand, facing a closed-rule type, the framers ought to strive mightily to select initially an x_k in W_q. If they err, they cannot recover unless they open up the procedure to the legislative open-rule setting, with all of its uncertainties. Hence, the advantages of the referendum procedure should make the framers somewhat more cautious and moderate than they might otherwise be.

The Federalists' Advantage of Speed

The framers were, in fact, quite cautious. True, they did propose a striking, perhaps extreme, reform; but they compromised on many peripheral features of the Virginia Plan, insisting only on its central feature of a national government somewhat independent of the states. An example of one of many more-or-less cosmetic alterations is the word *national*, which the extreme centralizers (e.g., Hamilton and G. Morris) initially persuaded the Convention to adopt as its description of the goal of the Virginia Plan. Once the nationalizing core of the Virginia Plan had been accepted, however, the framers unanimously dropped the word *national*, presumably in order to avoid giving offense (*Records*, I, 34–35, 335).

Still, as it turned out, they were not cautious enough. Since a motion under a closed rule cannot be altered, its supporters should choose an alternative x_k that can survive throughout the possibly changing circumstances of the referendum campaign. This the framers failed to do. Hence, when the anti-Federalists dragged out the campaign, the Constitution looked much less attractive than it had initially. One main anti-Federalist, therefore, strategy was delay, as, for prospective losers, it should be. (An almost universal strategic norm for prospective winners is to try to bring issues to decision as soon as propriety permits, lest, by time and debate, their chance of winning decline, while the converse norm for prospective losers is to delay in the hope that, because of time and debate, their chance of winning will improve. Both sides in this campaign followed the strategy appropriate to their status.)

As discussed, when the Constitution was before Congress, Richard Henry Lee proposed alterations with the understanding that they would be taken up by a second convention, and this remained a frequent theme right up to the ratification, in the summer of 1788, by Virginia and New York, both of which recommended another convention. The doubtless genuine desire to improve the Constitution was coupled with the heresthetical intent to delay. A second convention, which would have taken a year to call and convene, was an excellent temporizing device.

Even without a convention call, however, the anti-Federalists emphasized delay. As the opponents of an initially popular proposal, they needed time to develop their arguments and their alternatives. The anti-Federalists, in October and November 1787, responded with appeals for going slow. Here, for example, is Federal Framer:

> The first principal question that occurs is, Whether, considering our situation, we ought to precipitate the adoption of the proposed constitution? If we remain cool and temperate, we are in no danger of any commotions; we are in a state of perfect peace, and in no danger of invasions; the state governments are in the full exercise of their powers; and our governments answer all present exigencies, except the regulation of trade, securing credit, in some cases, and providing for the interest, in some instances, of the public debts; and whether we adopt a change, three or nine months hence, can make but little odds with the private circumstances of individuals; their happiness and prosperity, after all, depend principally on their own exertions. (Kaminski and Saladino, 1983, vol. 2, p. 20)

So when they were able to do so, the anti-Federalists put off state conventions as long as possible: in New York, until June 17, 1788; in Virginia, until June 2, 1788; in North Carolina, until July 21, 1788; and so on. The hope was that, by delay, the anti-Federalists in the several states could coalesce behind a single list of proposed amendments and the procedure for instituting the amendments (positions 4–7 from above). They also needed time to persuade the public of the necessity of amending the Constitution.

The Federalists, on the other hand, countered with a strategy of haste. Of the seven states that ratified by majorities of two thirds or more, five did so in 1787 or early 1788: Delaware, December 7, 1787; Pennsylvania, December 12, 1787; New Jersey, December 18, 1787; Georgia, December 31, 1787; and Connecticut, January 3, 1788. This is indeed swift, given the communications of the era. In no more than about three months, the Federalists in these states had arranged, if necessary, a legislative session to call a convention, had campaigned for delegates, and then had convened and ratified.

The Anti-Federalists' Delay as a Threat to Open Conventions

In a contest between haste and delay, haste could win only with overwhelming support in nine states, but the Federalists had, at most, seven. So a strategy of haste was doomed to failure. On the other hand, the anti-Federalists' successful delay allowed them to rally their supporters. They found the Constitution's defects and highlighted them in debate, in turn weakening the Federalists at the polls. In most of the later conventions, the anti-Federalists either initially held the majority (New Hampshire, Massachusetts, New York, and North Carolina) or were about even in numbers (Virginia). In these conventions, the majority position of the anti-Federalists threatened the control of the Federalists in keeping the conventions operating under a closed rule. The anti-Federalists had been developing packages of proposed amendments in a national print campaign. It was expected that, as soon as a convention occurred where they had the votes, they would open up the convention proceedings to consider amendments. This strategy made sense, since the anti-Federalists, through their national campaign, had been searching for an alternative, x_k, that was in the set W_q, that maximized *their* preferences subject to the constraint of gaining a majority in the five conventions needed to block the ratification of the Constitution unamended. The campaign shows that the anti-Federalists had been developing proposals presuming that they could bring in enough moderates and weak Federalists who preferred the change of the Constitution, but with added securities such as a Bill of Rights or an express delegation of powers. Like the framers at the Constitutional Convention, the anti-Federalists aimed strategically for the set of undominated alternatives held by a majority. The Federalists' rhetorical requirement that the conventions operate under a referendum procedure was doomed in the changed political climate.

The Federalists' Allowance for Error

But the Federalists found a response. They abandoned their insistence on a closed rule and themselves proposed modifications, which, however, did not interfere with the momentum for ratification. These proposals, that states ratify and simultaneously append recommendations of amendments to be adopted by the new government, in effect opened up the closed rule. Seeing that the chance of insisting on a closed rule was low, the Federalists used the opportunity to reposition their alternative to accommodate the new information about public opinion and preferences.

This proposal was first made in Massachusetts and was used thereafter in South Carolina, New Hampshire, Virginia, and New York, that is, in all subsequent ratifications in 1788 except Maryland (where the Federalists had a five-sixths majority). Most historians believe that this modification was the marginal influence on the final ratification of the Constitution.

To summarize, let us revert to the program begun at the beginning of the section "The Framers' Choice of Strategy." We will state the framers' and Federalists' strategy as if it had all been planned in September 1787. (And, indeed, it may well have been loosely planned from the beginning. The tradition in Massachusetts, at least, allowed for it. A convention there in 1778 had written a constitution, a majority of the towns had rejected it or asked for revisions, and a new convention then produced a constitution that was ratified. In that case, the framers had adopted a closed-rule strategy which failed and forced a new convention, in effect forcing an open rule. There is every reason to suppose that the framers of 1787 knew and understood this event and, perhaps, incorporated it in their planning.) Whether or not the strategy was fully planned in September, the statement of it as it would appear if they had done so reveals, we believe, the quality and magnitude of the Federalists' achievement. The Federalists chose a Constitution which, presumably, they believed was the most advantageous one for them in W_q. They gave it a closed rule (i.e., the ratifying conventions), so that the voters, forced to choose between only the Articles and the Constitution, preferred the Constitution. The Federalists' strategy can be stated thus:

- If the Constitution remains in W_q, ratify as quickly as possible; but
- If the Constitution is forced out of W_q, transform the closed rule into an open one by promising to adopt recommended modifications as soon as the new Constitution is ratified and its government is in operation.

This was an unbeatable strategy because it confused the opposition. It replaced what appeared to be a fixed target with a moving target whose exact content was not only uncertain but could not even be identified until after the issue was decided.

The Massachusetts Convention

Of course, this remarkable strategy was manifest only *a posteriori*. Still, we are entitled to think of it as a strategy because it was the procedure actually followed, whether chosen *a priori* or worked out in the process of the event.

Perhaps the most remarkable feature of the whole period of constitution-making in 1787–1788 was the adoption of this strategy. It was revealed at the Massachusetts convention as the Federalists there sought to alter the closed rule (under which they expected to lose) to an open rule (under which they hoped to, and did indeed, win). In order to appreciate the Federalists' achievements fully, it is worthwhile, therefore, to review the events of that convention and to inquire into the reason for the Federalists' success.

Despite the Federalists' initial haste, by the time of the Massachusetts elections (November 19, 1787–January 7, 1788), the anti-Federalists had put their arguments together. Substantively, they had mounted an impressive attack on national consolidation and the absence of a bill of rights, tying these together as evidence that the Constitution was a conspiracy of the rich and well-born to deprive ordinary people of their liberties. Procedurally, they had utilized the Federalists' haste—especially in Pennsylvania, where it had indeed been unseemly—as additional evidence of conspiracy.

Furthermore, Massachusetts was the most difficult state the Federalists had yet attempted. Delaware, the first to ratify, had been enthusiastic for the Constitution, presumably as a makeweight against Pennsylvania. Similarly, New Jersey and Connecticut had been enthusiastic about a national government that would suspend New York's tariffs. (The Upstate New York farmers of the Clinton party operated the state government at minimal expense to themselves by imposing tariffs on New York City trade, much of the burden of which fell on the city itself and on New York's neighbors.

Naturally, both groups resented the imposition and were enthusiastic Federalists.) Georgia was enthusiastic about a national government that would help in their war with the Creeks (and indirectly, Spain). Only in Pennsylvania, the second state to ratify, had the Federalists faced significant opposition. (While anti-Federalists were only about one-third of the ratifying convention, they were able to magnify their position by claiming that they were few only because of the Federalists' unfair haste.)

But when the Federalists faced the electorate of Massachusetts, their path was rougher. In Massachusetts, the fear of losing personal liberty, if through nothing else than oppressive taxation, was an anti-Federalist theme that struck deep into a state that had recently experienced an armed debtor revolt. The Massachusetts government, which sent mainly proto-Federalist delegates to Philadelphia, was the very government whose initial reaction to Shays' rebellion was to put it down by force. In the spring of 1787, the voters threw out of office the governor (Bowdoin) who had levied the taxes and consented to the use of force, and they replaced him with a moderate (Hancock) who promised to repeal the taxes. The anti-Federalists exploited these themes of loss of liberty and excessive use of uncontrolled force to turn opinion away from the Constitution. Thus, the elections for the ratifying conventions took place under a quite different regime from the elections of the delegates to Philadelphia. Not unaccountably for us, but apparently unexpectedly for the Federalists, the elections resulted in an anti-Federalist majority of at least 45 and perhaps as high as 84 in a convention of 360 seats (Fink, 1987, p. 118).

Consequently, the Massachusetts Federalists chose a strategy that Federalists elsewhere had not used. In Pennsylvania, the Federalists had gladly followed the strategy of the closed rule, insisting on a vote only on the whole Constitution, prohibiting ratification conditional on amendments, and denying temporary adjournment for the public discussion of proposed amendments. By contrast, in Massachusetts the Federalists required debate (but not votes) by paragraphs. This debate created an arena both for persuasion and for information gathering. Expecting that their rhetorical efforts would be insufficient, they also used the debate to reveal what conciliatory amendments might be appropriate. The strategy of the Federalists coincided with that of the anti-Federalists, who also wanted an extended debate to build support for a platform of conditional amendments.

The Federalist leaders anticipated that the anti-Federalists would propose a ratification conditional on emasculating amendments, roughly position $max_A(x)$ in Figure 14.2, which has the same structure

as Figure 14.1. (Typical "switchers" are described by $U_S(x)$, which combines features of $U_A(x)$ and $U_F(x)$.) The Federalists therefore persuaded Governor Hancock to offer their compromise, making it credible by his neutrality. Up to that point, Hancock, unwilling to jeopardize his extraordinary popularity, had stayed away, ostensibly because of gout, from the convention, to which he had been elected president. The Hancock compromise, devised by the Federalist leaders, King, Gorham, and Parsons, consisted of a proposal to vote, immediately after the paragraph-by-paragraph debate, on a motion to ratify with recommended amendments. By virtue of his status as governor and president of the convention Hancock was able to propose his form of ratification (ratification with recommendatory amendments) first, following the conclusion of the debate and prior to the expected anti-Federalist offer of conditional amendments. This proposal was intended, of course, to attract delegates who, though elected to oppose ratification, were willing to change sides if the Constitution were modified. Thinking of these potential switchers as having a reservation price, r_S, and undominated strategies, D_S, consisting of the Articles and the range $[r_S, r_S']$, then the Hancock proposal lies in the intersection $\mathscr{D}_S \cap \mathscr{D}_F \cap \sim\mathscr{D}_A$, where "$\sim\mathscr{D}_A$" is the complement on the horizontal dimension of $\mathscr{D}_A$.

This move stunned the anti-Federalists. Instead of moving to $max_A(x)$, ratification conditional on amendments made precedent to Massachusetts's entry into the new government (Point 5 in the second section of this chapter), they retreated to the status quo by arguing for rejection of the Constitution in an up-or-down vote. They attacked the Hancock proposal as illegal. It is not quite clear why they did this. They had already lost many supporters in debate, and perhaps they feared, as happened, further erosion from the Hancock proposal. The other explanation for their action may have been that they did not wish to engage with the Federalists in a bargaining game over the median modification. Some historical evidence exists that they mistakenly believed that they still had a majority of ten to twelve votes. We are inclined to believe the latter explanation because a preference for an up-or-down vote is characteristic of those who believe themselves winners.

One main feature of the Massachusetts convention was that the Federalists were able to behead the anti-Federal party in the elections by defeating or otherwise constraining the voices of the party's most experienced leaders. These anti-Federal leaders, excluded from the convention, took more notice of the danger of the Hancock proposals than did the anti-Federalists inside the convention. (Those outside included the Speaker of the House, James Warren.) These men contradicted the anti-Federal strategy inside and printed various forms of conditional ratification in the local Boston newspapers. Speaker Warren, a declared advocate of conditions precedent, on hearing of the Hancock proposal, suggested that the convention adjourn until spring, when the New York and Virginia conventions would meet.[6] Another anti-Federalist, James Sullivan, printed a variation on conditions subsequent (position number 4 from the second section of this chapter.[7] Even the most extreme anti-Federalist leader, James Winthrop, who wrote under the pseudonym "Agrippa," came finally to support conditional ratification rather than the outright rejection he had hitherto supported. "Agrippa's" offer was a clear example of a concession as a sophisticated strategy to ensure an anti-Federal outcome. In his essay of February 5 (the day before the final vote), "Agrippa" argued that amendments

> be made as conditions of our accepting the constitution . . . not to retract anything with regard to the expediency of amending the old confederation, and rejecting the new one totally; but only to make a proposition which comprehends the general idea of all parties.
> Another reason which I had in stating the amendments to be made, was to shew how nearly those who are for admitting the system with necessary alterations agree with those who are for rejecting this system and amending the old confederation.[8]

Clearly, the experienced political leaders outside the convention had their own head counts and accordingly offered strategies in response to their information. Yet, within the convention, the anti-Federalist leadership undertook no concerted effort to unite their party behind either an early decision to adjourn or conditional amendments. They insisted on their tactic (asserted after the Hancock proposal) to return the convention to a closed rule and the up-or-down vote.

Still, as the time for the vote approached, the anti-Federalists modified their position by proposing temporary adjournment for a popular discussion of Hancock's amendments. In Figure 14.2 this is described as point x_A, which is in $\mathcal{D}_A$, but perhaps not in $\mathcal{D}_S$ and $\mathcal{D}_F$. This motion lost badly (115-214), with a lack of support from all three groups. Many anti-Federalists did not support the motion, presumably because they believed themselves a majority. Nor did the Federalists vote for it, even though adjournment might have been preferable to an anti-Federalist outcome (in a similar situation, in the New Hampshire convention, the Federalists supported a motion to adjourn). Presumably, they voted against adjournment on a sophisticated bet that their preferred alternative of recommendatory amendments would win. Since this motion failed, one of the switchers, Samuel Adams, proposed to use Hancock's device with fifteen more amendments especially attractive, so he believed, to the anti-Federalists. We show this as a movement left toward $\mathfrak{D}_A$. But, "they not meeting the approbation of those gentlemen whose minds they were intended to ease, after they were debated a considerable time, the honorable gentleman withdrew them."[9]

The Effect of the Open Rule

In the end, Massachusetts ratified by a small majority, 187-168. The Federalists, through a combination of persuasion and then concession, turned an anti-Federalist convention into a Federalist victory. One of us has estimated the number of switchers at sixteen, although the distinction between who switched for reasons of conviction and who switched because of the amendments is difficult to ascertain precisely. What we do know is that the final anti-Federalist head count predicted a majority in their favor of ten to twelve. In any case, this indefinite, but certainly small, number is crucial to an understanding of the Federalists' success. Many have wondered why the switchers apparently believed the Federalists' promise of adopting the recommended amendments. This was also contemporaneously debated. One excluded anti-Federalist leader made precisely that point when he labeled the Hancock proposal as a "gilded trap" of promises that were sure to be broken:

> And when the thin vizard that has been cast before your injured optics shall fall from your lids, you may find that the men, who have lured you into the snare, are the least disposed to meliorate your sufferings.[10]

The primary reason is that the moderate anti-Federalists who had switched had nowhere else to go once the extreme anti-Federalist leaders in the convention insisted on rejection (point 7). The Hancock proposals were nearer to their preferred form of ratification than outright rejection. That they believed that the recommendations might have some force other than mere words on paper is the issue. One key change in the Constitution, from the Articles, was the loss of the institution of instruction and recall, a sure way to enforce compliance with the promise of future legislative action. Without instruction and recall, the Federalist promises to work for the recommendatory amendments were, as "Helvidicus Priscus" pointed out, unenforceable. The explanation is, we believe, the expectation of reciprocity among the people involved and their appreciation of the necessity of keeping promises in order to profit from future interactions (Axelrod, 1984).

Here and in other states, reciprocity depended crucially on the fact that only a few people were involved in face-to-face agreements among the active politicians. One can see the importance of the small number by comparing the promise in conventions with the omission of the promise in Rhode Island. One might expect Federalists, having won by the modification in Massachusetts, to use the same device in Rhode Island, the next and neighboring state. But Rhode Island did not call a convention as required by the framers' procedure and instead submitted the Constitution directly to town meetings. With large numbers of people involved, most of whom would never again interact with the Federalist leaders, promises would mean very little. So the Federalists did not even try to modify the Constitution; they simply boycotted the town meetings as irregular.

Whatever the reason for the success of the open rule in Massachusetts, Federalists elsewhere were delighted to copy it. Ignoring Maryland, where the Federalists did not need to compromise, they used the strategy of the open rule wherever they were weak, although, of course, each use was complicated by locally idiosyncratic factors. In North Carolina, the open rule was their only hope, but even with it, they lost by 2 to 1. In South Carolina, they had two thirds of the delegates but probably half or less of the voters, so the recommended amendments were a reconciling compromise in the society at large. In New Hampshire, while probably over half the delegates were initially anti-Federalist, debate and news of the Hancock compromise worked to the Federalists' benefit to create a Federalist majority. Yet, some of this majority had been instructed by town meetings to vote against ratification. So the Federalist leaders adjourned the convention to give these new Federalists an opportunity to persuade their towns to rescind their instructions— and doubtless the modifications implicit in the idea of the recommended amendments were helpful in persuasion. In Virginia, the margin between the parties was very close, though apparently the Federalists had a slight majority throughout. While the recommended amendments were unnecessary in the convention, they may well have rendered the Federalists more acceptable in the campaign. Finally, in New York, where initially the anti-Federalists had been a majority, marginal anti-Federalists switched even though they had run for election explicitly opposed to recommendatory amendments. Here, the Federalist outcome was dependent on the rhetorical capabilities of the Federalist leadership, John Jay and Alexander Hamilton, in exploiting the fact that ten states had ratified and had thus changed the frame of decision. No longer, they argued, was it a question of the degree to which amendments should be made conditional; rather, it was now simply the decision of New York to join the new union unencumbered by a unique form of ratification.[11] However opportunistic the switch may have been, the modification by recommendations, with a local addition of a circular letter, allowed the switchers to justify their actions as still being anti-Federalist in tone.

To conclude, we outline the strategy of ratification as set forth in Figure 14.3. At node I, the framers had a choice between the lower branch to a payoff (in outcome 4) which was better than their worst (namely, the Articles in outcome 1), but which was evidently not as good as the expected value of the three outcomes reached by the upper branch that they actually chose. At node II, the anti-Federalists necessarily chose the upper branch (delay and the offering of alternatives) because the lower branch (acquiescence) would lead to their worst outcome. Finally, at node III, the Federalists chose the open rule of the lower branch because it produced, at outcome 2, a better payoff than outcome 1 (whether the Articles were amended in the future or not). Thus, outcome 2 is a subgame perfect equilibrium in which each player has a dominant strategy and, historically, chose it.

In thinking of this diagram another way, assume that the Federalists reach node III between the Articles and the Constitution with recommended amendments. Naturally they will choose the latter, which means the lower branch leading to outcome 2. We can therefore substitute outcome 2 for node III. Moving backward on the tree, this gives the anti-Federalists at node II a choice between an upper branch (now outcome 2) and a lower branch with outcome 3. Since the anti-Federalists preferred the Constitution with recommended amendments (outcome 2) to the Constitution as initially proposed (outcome 3), we may substitute outcome 2 for node II. Again moving backward, this gives the Federalists at node I a choice between an upper branch leading to outcome 2 (the Constitution with recommended amendments) and a lower branch leading to outcome 4 (a weak Constitution, in the set of undominated anti-Federalist strategies). Of course, the Federalists would choose the upper branch. So what happened in nature coincided with what rational players ought to choose.

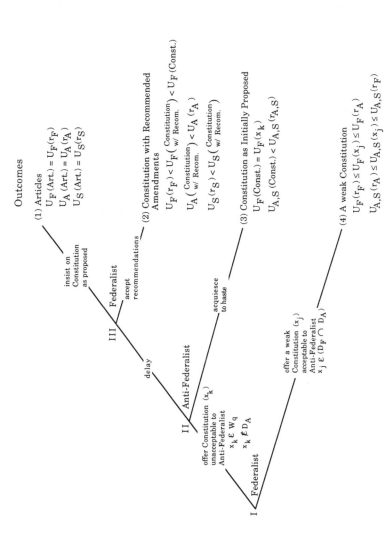

FIG. 14.3. Extensive game form of the strategy of ratification.

Conclusion

Initially, the Federalists were very strong in five states and very weak in two. In the remaining six states, with 65% of the free population, the Federalist strength was probably about evenly divided on average, but was fairly strong in some states and fairly weak in others. To win, the Federalists had to carry four, at least, of the six states. Given the anti-Federalist strategy of delay, given the success of anti-Federalist rhetoric, and given the acknowledged anti-Federalist lead in New York, it seemed likely that the Federalists could, at most, hope to carry three: Pennsylvania, Virginia, and South Carolina. Had they stuck with the closed rule, this is probably exactly what they would have achieved, although Virginia was too close to call. But in the end, they also carried Massachusetts, New Hampshire, and New York, mainly, we believe, because they changed the form of ratification to a kind of open rule. The serial nature of the convention process and the fact that the rules for procedure were, like the rules in a legislature, subject to approval from the floor allowed them the time and the chance to recover from the error in their strategy. That is, they either proposed or accepted recommended amendments. That they devised this strategy, the cleverest kind of heresthetical maneuver, is the explanation of their success in the face of the more-or-less equal, if not disadvantageous, division in the six marginal states.

Acknowledgments. We wish to thank Brian Humes, Jane Mather, Michael Munger, and participants at the Irvine conference, "The Federalist Papers and the New Institutionalism," particularly Donald Wittman, for their helpful comments. This chapter was prepared with the assistance of NSF grant SES 8410092 to William H. Riker.

Notes

1. The exact level of public support is, as seen, difficult to estimate. Some anti-Federalists known to be rather extreme in their preferences also switched to the Federalist side. In many conventions, rumors existed that anti-Federalist delegates were being influenced for pecuniary reasons. And still a few others, in the early unanimous conventions, were convinced to vote in favor to create an appearance of unanimity.
2. Main (1974) similarly argues that support for the Constitution did not follow class lines, distinguishing between the "commercial-cosmopolitan segment of society and the non-commercial-self subsistence sector" (pp. 69–70).
3. The dominance of Congress by delegates elected in an earlier political climate can be seen in this vote to postpone Richard Henry Lee's motion of transmittal of the report of the Philadelphia convention. New Hampshire, Massachusetts, Virginia (except for Lee), and North Carolina all voted against Lee, yet these

states all developed strong anti-Federalist contingents and, with the exception of Virginia, elected clear anti-Federalist majorities to their conventions.

4. Ellsworth of Delaware commented on the change in standards: "a new sett of ideas seemed to have crept in since the articles of Confederation were established. Conventions of the people, or with the power expressly derived from the people, were not then thought of. The Legislatures were considered competent" (*Records*, II, 91).

5. We thank Brian Humes and Jane Mather for advice on these diagrams.

6. Cf. "A Republican Federalist," Letter 6, 30 January 1788, *Massachusetts Centinel*, reprinted in Storing (1981b) 4:181.

7. Cf. "Hampden" (James Sullivan), 26 January and 2 February, 1788, *Massachusetts Centinel*, reprinted in Storing (1981b) 4:198–201.

8. "Agrippa," Letter XVI, 5 February 1788, *Massachusetts Gazette*, reprinted in Storing (1981b) 4:111, 114.

9. Report from the convention, reprinted in Elliot (1836), vol. 2, p. 162. These same fifteen amendments were reintroduced by the anti-Federalists in the final hours of the convention. They were apparently ignored as too little, too late, and the decision that followed stood.

10. "Helvidicus Priscus" (either General Warren or Samuel Adams), 5 February 1788, *Massachusetts Centinel*, reprinted in Storing (1981b) 4:160.

11. See Fink (1987) for a study of the rhetorical attack used to accomplish this change in dimensions.

References List/Author Index

Numbers in parentheses following each reference indicate the page or pages on which the work is cited. Below is an alphabetical listing of coauthors cited in references, followed by the name of the senior author under whose name a complete entry will be found. Many of these coauthors' names will also be found listed as senior authors for other works.

Affuso, P. J., See Brams, S.
Bibby, J. See Ornstein, N. J.
Buchanan, J. M. See Brennan, G.
Cronin, T. E. See Burns, J. M.
Davidson, R. See Parker, G.
Dempsey, G. See Page, B. I.
Demsetz, H. See Alchian, A.
Edwards, D. V. See Bell, R.
Eubanks, C. L. See Jillson, C. C.
Feld, S. L. See Schofield, N.
Ferejohn, J. See Cain, B.
———. See Coleman, J.
Fiorina, M. See Cain, B.
Franklin, G. R. See Ripley, R.
Grofman, B. See Feld, S.
———. See Lijphart, A.
———. See Owen, G.
———. See Schofield, N.
Handlin, M. See Handlin, O.
Hinich, M. J. See Enelow, J. M.
———. See Davis, O.
Jackson, J. See Hanushek, J.
Jones, W. T. See Cain, B. E.
Kaminski, J. See Jensen, M.
Keech, W. See Chappell, H.
Kiewiet, D. R. See Cain, B. E.
Kilgour, D. M. See Brams, S.
Lerner, R. See Kurland, P. B.
Lijphart, A. See Grofman, B. N.
Malbin, M. See Ornstein, N. J.
Mann, T. E. See Ornstein, N. J.

Marshall, W. See Weingast, B.
McCubbins, M. D. See Calvert, R.
McKay, R. See Grofman, B.
Mernard, R. See McCusker, J.
Miles, R. See Dyer, J.
Miller, G. J. See Hammond, T. H.
———. See Knott, J.
Muris, T. J. See Clarkson, K.
Noll, R. See Fiorina, M.
———. See McCubbins, M. D.
North, D. C. See Davis, L.
Ohsfeldt, R. See McGuire, R.
Oppenheimer, B. See Dodd, L.
Ordeshook, P. C. See Davis, O.
———. See McKelvey, R.
Page, B. I. See McCubbins, M. D.
Peltason, J. W. See Burns, J. M.
Peters, J. G. See Welch, S.
Petracca, M. P. See Page, B. I.
Raiffa, H. See Luce, R. D.
Rivers, D. See Kiewiet, D. R.
Rubin, P. H. See Kau, J. B.
Saladino, G. See Jensen, M.
———. See Kaminski, J. P.
Scarrow, H. See Grofman, B.
Schick, A. See Ornstein, N. J.
Schott, R. See Dodd, L.
Schwartz, T. See McCubbins, M.
Sen, A. See Runciman, W.
Shapiro, P. See Deacon, R.
Shapiro, R. Y. See Page, B. I.

Shapley, L. S. See Dubey, P.
———. See Riker, W.
Shepherd, J. See Walton, G.
Shepsle, K. See Greenberg, J.
Shubik, M. See Shapley, L. S.
Stone, F. D. See McMaster, J. B.
Thomas, P. See Hammond, T.
Tullock, G. See Buchanan, J.
Uhlaner, C. See Grofman, B.

Verba, S. See Prewitt, K.
Wagner, R. H. See Bell, R.
Walton, G. W. See Robertson, R. M.
———. See Shepherd, J.
Weingast, B. See Shepsle, K.
———. See Calvert, R.
———. See McCubbins, M. D.
Zupan, M. A. See Kalt, J. P.

References

Abraham, Henry J. (1980). *The Judicial Process* (4th ed.). New York: Oxford University Press. (165)

Adams, John (1954). *The Political Writings of John Adams.* Edited with an Introduction by George A. Peek, Jr. New York: Liberal Arts Press.

Adams, Willi Paul (1980). *The First American Constitutions: Republican Ideology and the Making of the State Constitutions in the Revolutionary Era* (transl. by Rita and Robert Kimber). Chapel Hill: University of North Carolina Press. (236)

Alchian, Armen, and Harold Demsetz (1972). Production, information costs, and economic organization. *American Economic Review* 62: 777–795. (182)

Arrow, Kenneth J. (1963). *Social Choice and Individual Values* (2nd ed.). New Haven: Yale University Press. (First ed., Wiley, 1951.) (1, 2, 36, 58)

Axelrod, Robert (1984). *The Evolution of Cooperation.* New York: Basic Books.

Bancroft, George (1882). *History of the Formation of the Constitution of the United States.* Boston: Little, Brown. (200)

Banzhaf, John F., III (1965). Weighted voting doesn't work: A mathematical analysis. *Rutgers Law Review* 19(Winter): 317–343. (121, 129)

Barro, Robert J. (1973). The control of politicians: An economic model. *Public Choice* 14: 19–42. (182)

Barry, Brian (1973). *The Liberal Theory of Justice.* Oxford: Clarendon. (58)

Barry, Brian (1980a). Is it better to be powerful or lucky? Part I. *Political Studies* 28: 183–194. (5)

Barry, Brian (1980b). Is it better to be powerful or lucky? Part II. *Political Studies* 28: 338–352. (5)

Beard, Charles A. (1912). *The Supreme Court and the Constitution.* New York: Macmillan. (186)

Beard, Charles A. (1913/1935). *An Economic Interpretation of the Constitution of the United States.* New York: Macmillan. (84, 175, 178, 199, 200, 201, 205)

Beard, Charles A. (1922/1934). *The Economic Basis of Politics.* New York: Alfred A. Knopf.

Becker, Carl L. (1960). *The History of Political Parties in the Province of New York, 1760-1776.* Madison: The University of Wisconsin Press.

Bell, Roderick, David V. Edwards, and R. Harrison Wagner, eds. (1969). *Political Power: A Reader in Research and Theory.* New York: Free Press. (140)

Benson, Lee (1960). *Turner and Beard: American Historical Writing Reconsidered.* Glencoe, IL: Free Press. (179)

Bessette, Joseph M. (1980). Deliberative democracy: The majority principle in republican government. In Robert A. Goldwin and William A. Schambra (eds.), *How Democratic is the Constitution?*, pp. 102–116. Washington: American Enterprise Institute. (56)

Bibby, John (1966). Committee characteristics and legislative oversight of administration. *Midwest Journal of Political Science* 10: 78–98. (151)

Bibby, John (1968). Congress' neglected function. In Melvin Laird (ed.), *Republican Papers*. New York: Praeger. (151)

Bishop, Hillman M. (1949). Why Rhode Island opposed the Federal Constitution: Paper money and the Constitution. *Rhode Island History* 8: 85–95.

Bjork, Gordon Carl (1963). Stagnation and growth in the American economy, 1784-1792. Ph.D. dissertation, University of Washington. (202)

Bjork, Gordon Carl (1964). The weaning of the American economy: Independence, market changes, and economic development. *Journal of Economic History* 24: 541–560. (202)

Black, Duncan (1958). *The Theory of Committees and Elections*. Cambridge: Cambridge University Press. (2)

Boyd, Steven R. (1979a). *The Politics of Opposition: Antifederalists and the Acceptance of the Constitution*. Millwood, NY: KTO Press. (211, 213, 220)

Boyd, Steven R. (1979b). Antifederalists and the acceptance of the Constitution: Pennsylvania, 1787-1792. *Publius* 9: 123–137. (212, 213)

Brams, Steven J. (1975). *Game Theory and Politics*. New York: Free Press. (5, 139)

Brams, Steven J. (1976). *Paradoxes in Politics*. New York: Free Press. (38, 165)

Brams, Steven J., Paul J. Affuso, and D. Marc Kilgour (1989). Presidential power: A game-theoretic analysis. In Paul Brace, Christine Harrington, and Gary King (eds.), *The Presidency in American Politics*. New York: New York University Press, forthcoming. (140)

Brennan, Geoffrey, and James M. Buchanan (1985). *The Reason of Rules: Constitutional Political Economy*. Cambridge: Cambridge University Press. (109, 111, 120)

Brown, Richard D. (1976). The Founding Fathers of 1776 and 1787: A collective view. *William and Mary Quarterly* 33: 465–480.

Brown, Robert E. (1956). *Charles Beard and the Constitution: A Critical Analysis of An Economic Interpretation of the Constitution*. Princeton, NJ: Princeton University Press. (179, 201)

Brownlee, W. Elliot (1979). *Dynamics of Ascent: A History of the American Economy* (2nd ed.). New York: Knopf. (201)

Brunhouse, Robert L. (1942). *The Counter-Revolution in Pennsylvania: 1776-1790*. Harrisburg, PA: The Pennsylvania Historical Commission. (180, 208, 211, 212, 213)

Bryce, James (1889). *The American Commonwealth*. London: Macmillan.

Buchanan, James, and Gordon Tullock (1962). *The Calculus of Consent*. Ann Arbor: University of Michigan Press. (2, 36, 176, 184, 185, 200, 201)

Burnham, Walter Dean (1983). *Democracy in the Making: American Government and Politics*. Englewood Cliffs, NJ: Prentice-Hall. (197, 201)

Burns, James MacGregor, J. W. Peltason, and Thomas E. Cronin (1981). *Government by the People* (11th ed.). Englewood Cliffs, NJ: Prentice-Hall. (201)

Butler, Nicholas Murray (1939). *Building the American Nation*. New York: Scribner's. (178)

Cain, Bruce, John Ferejohn, and Morris Fiorina (1979a). The roots of legislator popularity in Great Britain and the United States. Social Science Working Paper No. 288. California Institute of Technology. (156)

Cain, Bruce, John Ferejohn, and Morris Fiorina (1979b). Casework Services in Great Britain and the United States. Unpublished manuscript, California Institute of Technology. (156)

Cain, Bruce, and W. T. Jones (1986). Implementing representation: A framework and two applications. In Robert M. Stewart (ed.), *Readings in Social and Political Philosophy*. Oxford: Oxford University Press. (17)

Cain, Bruce, and D. Roderick Kiewiet (1987). Latinos and the 1984 elections: A comparative perspective. In Rudy O. de la Garza (ed.), *Ignored Voices: Public Opinion Polls and the Latino Community*. Austin, TX: University of Texas Press. (24)

Calendars of the United States House of Representatives and History of Legislation (1949-1986). 80th-99th (1st Session) Congresses, Washington, DC: U.S. Government Printing Office. (140)

Calvert, Randall, Mathew D. McCubbins, and Barry R. Weingast (1986). Political control and agency discretion: The fallacy of execution. Unpublished manuscript, University of Texas, Austin. (157)

Cappon, Lester, ed., (1976). *Atlas of Early American History: The Revolutionary Era, 1770-1790*. Princeton, NJ: Princeton University Press. (203)

Casper, Jonathan D. (1976). The Supreme Court and national policy making. *American Political Science Review* 70: 50–63. (168)

Ceasar, James (1979). *Presidential Selection: Theory and Development*. Princeton, NJ: Princeton University Press. (57)

Chappell, Henry W., Jr., and William R. Keech (1983). Welfare consequences of the six-year presidential term evaluated in the context of a model of the U.S. economy. *American Political Science Review* 79: 10–27. (49)

Clarkson, Kenneth M., and T. J. Muris (1981). *The Federal Trade Commission*. Cambridge: Cambridge University Press. (151)

Clausen, Aage R. (1973). *How Congressmen Decide*. New York: St. Martin's Press. (171)

Coase, Ronald (1960). The problem of social cost. *Journal of Law and Economics* 3: 1–44. (2, 75)

Cohen, Linda (1979). Cyclic sets in multidimensional voting models. *Journal of Economic Theory* 20: 1–12. (89)

Coleman, James S. (1971). Control of collectivities and the power of a collectivity to act. In B. Lieberman (ed.), *Social Choice*. New York: Gordon and Breach. (121)

Coleman, Jules, and John Ferejohn (1986). Democracy and social choice. *Ethics* 97: 6–25. (43)

Coleman, Kenneth (1958). *The American Revolution in Georgia, 1763-1789*, Athens, GA: University of Georgia Press.

Commager, Henry Steele (1958). The Constitution: Was it an economic document? *American Heritage* 10: 58–61, 100–103. (179)

Condorcet, Nicolas (1785). *Caritat de essai sur l'application de l'analyse á la probabilité des décisions rendues à la pluralité des voix*. Paris. (2, 71, 88)

Connolly, William E. (1983). *The Terms of Political Discourse* (2nd ed.). Princeton, NJ: Princeton University Press. (42)

Corwin, Edward S. (1920). *The Constitution and What it Means Today*. Princeton, NJ: Princeton University Press. (178)

Crowl, Philip A. (1943). *Maryland During and After the Revolution: A Political and Economic Study*. Baltimore: The Johns Hopkins Press. (181)

Crowl, Philip A. (1947). Anti-federalism in Maryland, 1787-1788. *William and Mary Quarterly* 4: 446–469. (181, 215)

Dahl, Robert A. (1956). *A Preface to Democratic Theory*. Chicago, IL: University of Chicago Press. (11, 54, 58)

Dahl, Robert A. (1957). Decision-making in a democracy: The role of the Supreme Court as a national policy maker. *Journal of Public Law* 6: 279–295. (168)

Dahl, Robert A. (1961). *Who Governs*. New Haven: Yale University Press. (11)

Daniell, Jere R. (1970). *Experiment in Republicanism: New Hampshire Politics and the American Revolution, 1741-1794*. Cambridge, MA: Harvard University Press. (180)

Davis, Lance and Douglass C. North (1971). *Institutional Change and American Economic Growth*. New York: Cambridge University Press. (176)

Davis, Otto A., and Melvin J. Hinich (1966). A mathematical model of policy formation in a democratic society. In Joseph L. Bernd (ed.), *Mathematical Applications in Political Science* II, pp. 175–205. Dallas: Southern Methodist University Press. (54)

Davis, Otto A., Melvin J. Hinich, and Peter C. Ordeshook (1970). An expository development of a mathematical model of the electoral process. *American Political Science Review* 64: 426–448. (54)

De Pauw, Linda (1966). *The Eleventh Pillar: New York State and the Federal Constitution*. Ithaca: Cornell University Press. (224)

Deacon, Robert, and Perry Shapiro (1975). Private preference for collective goods revealed through voting and referenda. *American Economic Review* 65: 943–955. (200)

Diggins, John P. (1981). Power and authority in American history: The case of Charles A. Beard and His Critics. *American Historical Review* 86: 701–730. (200)

Dodd, Lawrence and Bruce Oppenheimer, eds. (1977). *Congress Reconsidered*. New York: Praeger. (155)

Dodd, Lawrence and Richard Schott (1979). *Congress and the Administrative State*. New York: Wiley. (151)

Dodd, William E. (1913). Review of Beard's *An Economic Interpretation of the Constitution*. *American Historical Review* 19: 162–163. (178)

Dodd, William E. (1916). Economic interpretation of American History. *Journal of Political Economy* 24: 489–495. (178)

Douglass, Elisha P. (1955). *Rebels and Democrats*. Chapel Hill: The University of North Carolina Press.

Downs, Anthony (1957). *An Economic Theory of Democracy*. New York: Harper and Row. (3, 32, 36, 54)

Dubey, Pradeep, and Lloyd S. Shapley (1979). Mathematical properties of the Banzhaf power index. *Mathematics of Operations Research* 4(May): 99–131. (133, 139)

Dyer, James, and Ralph Miles (1976). An actual application of collective choice theory to the selection of trajectories for the Mariner Jupiter/Saturn 1777 Project. *Operations Research* 24: 220–244.

Elliot, Jonathan, ed. (1836). *The Debates in the Several State Conventions on the Adoption of the Federal Constitution*. Philadelphia: J. B. Lippincott, (Second ed., 5 vols). (192, 193, 202, 203, 224, 255)

Elster, Jon (1983). *Sour Grapes: Studies in the Subversion of Rationality*. Cambridge: Cambridge University Press. (7, 45, 51, 52)

Enelow, James M., and Melvin J. Hinich (1984). *The Spatial Theory of Voting: An Introduction*. New York: Cambridge University Press. (54)

Epstein, David F. (1984). *The Political Theory of the Federalists*. Chicago: University of Chicago Press. (41, 43, 55, 56)

Fair, Ray C. (1978). The effect of economic events on votes for president. *Review of Economics and Statistics* 60: 159–173. (200)

Farrand, Max (1913). *The Framing of the Constitution of the United States*. New Haven: Yale University Press. (163)

Farrand, Max, ed. (1966). *The Records of the Federal Convention of 1787*. (Revised ed., 4 vols.). New Haven: Yale University Press. (Originally published in 1911.) (161, 227, 233)

Faulkner, Harold Underwood (1924). *American Economic History*. New York, NY: Harper and Row. (178)

Federalist, The (Alexander Hamilton, James Madison, and John Jay). Edition of *The Federalist Papers*. New York: The Heritage Press, 1945.

Federalist Papers, The (Alexander Hamilton, James Madison, and John Jay), edited by Clinton Rossiter (1961). New York: New American Library.

Feld, Scott L., and Bernard Grofman (1986). On the possibility of faithfully representative committees. *American Political Science Review* 80(3): 863–879. (3)

Feld, Scott L., and Bernard Grofman (1987). Necessary and sufficient conditions for a majority winner in n-dimensional spatial voting games: An intuitive geometric approach. *American Journal of Political Science* 31(4): 709–728. (5)

Fenno, Richard, Jr. (1966). *The Power of the Purse*. Boston: Little, Brown & Co. (155)

Fenno, Richard, Jr. (1973a). *Congressmen in Committees*. Boston: Little, Brown. (155)

Fenno, Richard, Jr. (1973b). The internal distribution of influence: The House. In David Truman (ed.). *The Congress and America's Future* (2nd ed.), pp. 52–76. Englewood Cliffs, NJ: Prentice- Hall. (155)

Fenno, Richard, Jr. (1978). *Home Style: House Members and Their Districts*. Boston: Little, Brown. (21, 156)

Ferejohn, John A. (1986). On a structuring principle for administrative agencies. In Mathew D. McCubbins and Terry Sullivan (eds.), *Congress: Structure and Policy*. Cambridge: Cambridge University Press. (156)

Ferguson, E. James (1961). *The Power of the Purse: A History of American Public Finance, 1776-1790*. Chapel Hill: University of North Carolina Press. (180, 191, 202)

Fink, Evelyn C. (1987). Political rhetoric and strategic choice in the ratification conventions on the federal constitution. University of Rochester. (246, 255)

Fiorina, Morris (1977a). *Congress: Keystone of the Washington Establishment*. New Haven: Yale University Press. (21, 151, 156)

Fiorina, Morris (1977b). Control of the bureaucracy: A mismatch of incentives and capabilities. Social science working paper no. 182. California Institute of Technology. (151)

Fiorina, Morris (1982). Group concentration and the delegation of legislative authority. Unpublished manuscript, California Institute of Technology. (151)

Fiorina, Morris, and Roger Noll (1978). Voters, bureaucrats and legislators: A rational choice perspective on the growth of bureaucracy. *Journal of Public Economics* 9: 239–254. (156)

Fiorina, Morris, and Roger Noll (1979a). Voters, legislators and bureaucracy: Institutional design in the public sector. In *Problemi di administrazione publica, Centro di formazione e studi per il Messogiorno*. *Formes* 4(2): 69–89. (Naples.) (156)

Fiorina, Morris, and Roger Noll (1979b). Majority rule models and legislative election. *Journal of Politics* 41: 1081–1104. (156)

Fishkin, James S. (1979). *Tyranny and Legitimacy: A Critique of Political Theories*. Baltimore: Johns Hopkins University Press. (58)

Fiske, John (1888). *The Critical Period of American History: 1783-1789*. Boston: Houghton, Mifflin and Sons. (200)

Fuller, Lon L. (1969). *The Morality of Law*. New Haven: Yale University Press. (First published 1964.) (112)

Funston, Richard (1975). The Supreme Court and critical elections. *American Political Science Review* 69: 795–811. (168)

Gauthier, David (1986). *Morals by Agreement*. Oxford: Clarendon Press. (119)

Gillespie, Michael A. (1987). The ratification of the Constitution in Massachusetts. Mimeo.

Gladstone, William Ewart (1878). Kin beyond the sea. *North American Review* 127: 179–212. (200)

Goodwin, George, Jr. (1970). *The Little Legislatures*. Amherst: University of Massachusetts Press. (155)

Gramlich, Edward M. (1984). How bad are the large deficits? In Gregory B. Mills and John L. Palmer (eds.), *Federal Budget Policy in the 1980s*, pp. 43–68. Washington, DC: Urban Institute Press. (48)

Greenberg, Joseph, and Kenneth Shepsle (1987). The effect of electoral rewards in multiparty competition with entry. *American Political Science Review* 81(2): 525–537. (3)

Grigsby, Hugh (1969). *The History of the Virginia Federal Convention of 1788*. New York: DeCapo Press. (Reprinted from Richmond, Va., Collections of the Virginia Historical Society New Series, Vol. 9). (224)

Grofman, Bernard N. (1975). A review of macro-election systems. In Rudolph Wildenmann (ed.), *German Political Yearbook (Sozialwissenschaftliches Jahrbuch fur Politik)*, Vol. 4, pp. 303–352. Munich: Günter Olzog Verlag. (3)

Grofman, Bernard N. (1987). Will the real new institutionalism stand up and take a bow. Unpublished manuscript. School of Social Sciences, University of California, Irvine (August). (4)

Grofman, Bernard N., and Arend Lijphart, eds. (1986). *Electoral Laws and Their Political Consequences*. New York: Agathon Press. (3, 4)

Grofman, Bernard N., Arend Lijphart, Robert McKay and Howard Scarrow, eds. (1982). *Representation and Redistricting Issues*. Lexington, MA: Lexington Books. (3, 4)

Grofman, Bernard N., and Carole Uhlaner (1985). Metapreferences and reasons for stability in social choice: Thoughts on broadening and clarifying the debate. *Theory and Decision* 19: 31–50. (5)

Hall, Arnold B. (1913). Review of Beard's *An Economic Interpretation of the Constitution, American Journal of Sociology* 19: 405–408. (178)

Hall, Van Beck (1972). *Politics without Parties: Massachusetts, 1780-1791*. Pittsburgh: University of Pittsburgh Press. (180, 201)

Hammond, Thomas H., and Gary J. Miller (1987). The core of the Constitution. *American Political Science Review* 81(Dec.): 1155- 1174. (86)

Hammond, Thomas, and Paul Thomas (1982). The impossibility of a neutral hierarchy. Prepared for delivery at the Annual Meeting of the American Political Science Association, Denver.

Handlin, Oscar, and Mary Handlin (1944). Radicals and conservatives in Massachusetts after independence. *New England Quarterly* 17: 343–355. (180)

Hanushek, Eric, and John E. Jackson (1977). *Statistical Methods for Social Scientists*. New York: Academic Press. (188)

Hardin, Russell (1982a). Exchange theory on strategic bases. *Social Science Information* 21: 251–272. (2, 102)

Hardin, Russell (1982b). *Collective Action*, chaps. 10–14. Baltimore: Hopkins University Press. (114)

Hardin, Russell (1985). Sanction and obligation. *Monist* 68(July): 403–418. (117)

Hardin, Russell (1987). Does might make right? In J. Roland Pennock and John W. Chapman (eds.), *NOMOS 29: Authority Revisited*. New York: New York University Press. (119)

Hardin, Russell (1988). Bargaining for Justice. *Social Philosophy and Policy* 5(Spring): 65–74. (107)

Harding, Samuel (1896). *The Contest over the Ratification of the Federal Constitution in the State of Massachusetts.* New York: DaCapo Press, reprinted 1970. (200)

Hartz, Louis (1955). *The Liberal Tradition in America.* New York: Harcourt, Brace. (168)

Hess, Stephen (1976). *Organizing the Presidency.* Washington, DC: The Brookings Institution. (151)

Higgs, Robert (1986). *Crisis and Leviathan: Critical Episodes in the Growth of American Government.* San Francisco: Pacific Institute. (183, 203)

Hinckley, Barbara (1978). *Stability and Change in Congress* (2nd ed.). New York: Harper and Row. (171)

Hindle, Brooke (1946). The march of the Paxton Boys. *William and Mary Quarterly* 3: 461–486. (207)

Hirschman, Albert O. (1977). *The Passions and the Interests: Political Arguments for Capitalism before Its Triumph.* Princeton, NJ: Princeton University Press. (44, 45)

Hoffman, Ronald (1973). *A Spirit of Dissension: Economics, Politics, and the Revolution in Maryland.* Baltimore: John Hopkins University Press. (214, 215, 216)

Hoffman, Ronald. (1976). The 'disaffected' in the revolutionary South. In A. Young (ed.), *The American Revolution: Explorations in the History of American Radicalism.* DeKalb, IL: Northern Illinois University Press. (207, 214)

Holler, Manfred, ed. (1981). *Power, Voting and Voting Power.* Wuerzburg: Physica-Verlag. (5)

Hughes, Jonathan (1983). *American Economic History.* Glenview, IL: Scott, Foresman. (187, 197, 201)

Huitt, Ralph (1973). The internal distribution of influence: The Senate. In D. Truman, *The Congress in America's Future,* pp. 77–101. (155)

Huntington, Samuel (1973). Congressional responses to the twentieth century. In D. Truman, *The Congress in America's Future,* pp. 5–31. (151)

Hutson, James H. (1981). Country, Court and Constitution: Anti-federalism and the historian. *William and Mary Quarterly* 38: 337–368. (171, 200)

Hutson, James H. (1984). The creation of the Constitution: Scholarship at a standstill. *Reviews in American History* 12: 463–477. (177, 200)

Ireland, Owen. (1978). Partisanship and the Constitution: Pennsylvania 1787. *Pennsylvania History* 45: 315–332. (211)

Jackson, Carlton (1967). *Presidential Vetoes: 1792-1945.* Athens, GA: University of Georgia Press. (140)

Jensen, Merrill (1940). *The Articles of Confederation: An Interpretation of the Social-Constitutional History of the American Revolution, 1774-1781.* Madison: University of Wisconsin Press. (208)

Jensen, Merrill (ed.) (1976). *Constitutional Documents and Records, 1776-1787.* Volume 1 of Jensen et al., eds., *The Documentary History of the Ratification of the Constitution.*

Jensen, Merrill, John Kaminski, and Gaspare Saladino, eds. (1976). *The Documentary History of the Ratification of the Constitution,* 11 vols. Madison: State Historical Society of Wisconsin.

Jillson, Calvin C. (1981). Constitution making: Alignment and realignment in the Federal Convention of 1787. *American Political Science Review* 75: 598–612. (191)

Jillson, Calvin C., and Cecil L. Eubanks (1984). The political structure of Constitution making: The Federal Convention of 1787. *American Journal of Political Science* 28: 435–458. (191)

Jones, Alice Hanson (1980). *Wealth of a Nation to Be: The American Colonies on the Eve of the Revolution.* New York: Columbia University Press. (191, 202)

Kalt, Joseph P., and Mark A. Zupan (1984). Capture and ideology in the economic theory of politics. *American Economic Review* 74: 279–300. (182)

Kaminski, John P. (1983). Antifederalism and the perils of homogenized history: A review essay. *Rhode Island History* 42: 30–37. (201)

Kaminski, John P., and Gaspare J. Saladino (eds.) (1983). *Commentaries on the Constitution: Public and Private*, Volume 2 of Jensen et al., eds., *The Documentary History of the Ratification of the Constitution*. (242)

Kammen, Michael (1986). *The Origins of the American Constitution: A Documentary History*. New York: Penguin. (120, 162, 163, 171)

Katznelson, Ira (1986). The silence of policy. *Political Science Quarterly* 101 (Summer): 307–325. (168)

Kau, James B., and Paul H. Rubin (1979). Self-interest, ideology, and logrolling in congressional voting. *Journal of Law and Economics* 22: 365–384. (182, 200)

Kau, James B., and Paul H. Rubin (1982). *Congressmen, Constituents, and Contributors: Determinants of Roll Call Voting in the House of Representatives*. Boston: Nijhoff. (182, 200)

Kenyon, Cecelia (1955). Men of little faith: The Anti-federalists on the nature of representative government. *William and Mary Quarterly* 12: 3–43. (179)

Ketchum, Ralph (ed.) (1986). *The Anti-Federalist Papers and the Constitutional Convention Debates*. New York: New American Library. (149)

Kiewiet, D. Roderick, and Douglas Rivers (1985). The economic basis of Reagan's appeal. In John E. Chubb and Paul E. Peterson (eds.), *The New Direction in American Politics*, pp. 69–90. Washington, DC: The Brookings Institution. (46)

Kingdon, John (1981). *Congressmen's Voting Decisions* (2nd ed.). New York: Harper and Row. (171)

Knott, Jack, and Gary Miller (1987). *Reforming Bureaucracy: The Politics of the Institutional Choice*. Englewood Cliffs, NJ: Prentice-Hall. (206)

Kramer, G. H. (1977). Dynamical model of political equilibrium. *Journal of Economic Theory* 16(2): 310–334. (2, 206)

Krehbiel, Keith (1986). Sophisticated and myopic behavior in legislative committees. *American Journal of Political Science* 30: 5542-5561.

Kurland, Philip B., and Ralph Lerner, eds. (1987). *The Founders' Constitution*, 5 vols. Chicago: University of Chicago Press. (84, 108, 119, 120)

Labaree, Leonard Woods, ed. (1945). The Public Records of the State of Connecticut from May 1785 through January 1789 compiled in accordance with an act of the General Assembly, Hartford. Published by the State of Connecticut. (224)

Langlois, Richard N. (1986). *Economics as a Process: Essays in the New Institutional Economics*. London: Cambridge University Press. (4)

Latané, John H. (1913). Review of Beard's *An Economic Interpretation of the Constitution*, *American Political Science Review* 19: 697–700. (178)

Lebergott, Stanley (1984). *The Americans, An Economic Record*. New York: Norton. (186, 201)

Lengle, James (1981). *Representation and Presidential Primaries: The Democratic Party in the Post Reform Era*. Westport, CT: Greenwood Press. (3)

Levermore, Charles H. (1914). Review of Beard's *An Economic Interpretation of the Constitution*. *American Economic Review* 4: 117–119. (178)

Levi-Strauss, Claude (1979). Science: Forever incomplete. *Society* (July/August): 16–18. (170)

Libby, Orin G. (1894). *The Geographical Distribution of the Vote of the Thirteen States on the Federal Constitution*. Madison: University of Wisconsin Press. (191)

Lijphart, Arend (1981). Political parties: Ideologies and programs. In David Butler, Howard R. Penniman, and Austin Ranney (eds.). *Democracy at the Polls: A Comparative Study of Competitive National Elections*. Washington, DC: American Enterprise Institute for Public Policy Research. (3)

Lijphart, Arend, (1982). Comparative perspectives on fair representation: The plurality-majority rule, geographical districting, and alternative electoral arrangements. *Policy Studies Journal* Special Issue on Reapportionment, Vol.9, No.6 (April 1981): 899–915. Reprinted in B. Grofman, A. Lijphart, R. McKay, and H. Scarrow (eds.). *Representation and Redistricting Issues*, 143–159. Lexington, MA: Lexington Books.

Lijphart, Arend, (1984). Advances in the comparative study of electoral systems. *World Politics* 36(3) (April): 424–436.

Lijphart, Arend, and Bernard Grofman, eds. (1984). *Choosing an Electoral System*. New York: Praeger. (3, 4)

Lindblom, Charles E. (1982). The market as prison. *Journal of Politics* 44: 324–336. (168)

Lineberry, Robert L. (1980). *Government in America: People, Politics, and Policy*. Boston: Little, Brown. (197, 201)

Lowi, Theodore (1969). *The End of Liberalism*. New York: Norton. (151)

Luce, R. Duncan, and Howard Raiffa (1957). *Games and Decisions*. New York: Wiley. (36)

Lynd, Staughton (1962). *Anti-Federalism in Dutchess County, New York: A Study of Democracy and Class Conflict in the Revolutionary Era*. Chicago: Loyola University Press. (190)

Lynd, Staughton (1967). *Class Conflict, Slavery, and the United States Constitution*. New York: Bobbs-Merrill.

Main, Jackson T. (1960). Charles A. Beard and the Constitution: A critical review of Forrest McDonald's *We the People. William and Mary Quarterly* 17: 86–110. (179, 197)

Main, Jackson T. (1961). *The Antifederalists: Critics of the Constitution, 1781-1788*. Chapel Hill: University of North Carolina Press. (Reprinted, 1974, W.W. Norton.) (180, 181, 191, 193, 196, 197, 198, 199, 203, 213, 220, 223, 226, 227, 254)

Main, Jackson T. (1973). *Political Parties Before the Constitution*. Chapel Hill: University of North Carolina Press. (190)

Mansfield, Harvey C. Jr. (1987) Social science and the Constitution. Unpublished manuscript, Harvard University. (8)

Marshall, Geoffrey (1984). *Constitutional Conventions: The Rules and Forms of Political Accountability*. Oxford: Clarendon Press. (120)

Matthews, Donald (1960). *U.S. Senators and Their World*. Chapel Hill: University of North Carolina Press. (155)

May, Kenneth O. (1952). A set of independent, necessary, and sufficient conditions for simple majority decision. *Econometrica* 20: 680–684. (58)

Mayhew, David (1974a). *Congress: The Electoral Connection*. New Haven: Yale University Press. (21, 156)

Mayhew, David R. (1974b). Congressional elections: The case of the vanishing marginals. *Polity* 6(Spring): 295–317.

Mazer, Steven (1985). Demographic factors affecting constitutional decisions: The case of municipal charters. *Public Choice* 47: 121–162. (206)

McConnell, Grant (1966). *Private Power and American Democracy*. New York: Vintage Books.

McCorkle, Pope (1984). The historian as intellectual: Charles Beard and the Constitution reconsidered. *American Journal of Legal History* 28: 314–363. (200, 201)

McCormick, Richard (1950). *Experiment in Independence: New Jersey in the Critical Period.* Brunswick, NJ: Rutgers University Press. (181, 201)

McCubbins, Mathew (1982). On the form of regulatory intervention. Paper presented at the 1983 Annual Meeting of the Public Choice Society, Savannah, March 24-26, 1983. (156)

McCubbins, Mathew, Roger G. Noll, and Barry R. Weingast (1986). The political implications of administrative procedures. Unpublished manuscript, University of Texas. (156)

McCubbins, Mathew, and Benjamin I. Page (1984). Rational public opinion and its measurement. Paper delivered at the Annual Meeting of the Midwest Political Science Association, Chicago. (59)

McCubbins, Mathew, and Talbot Page (1982). On the failure of environmental, health and safety regulation. Paper presented at the 1983 Annual Meeting of the Midwest Political Science Association, Chicago, April 20-23, 1983.

McCubbins, Mathew, and Thomas Schwartz (1984). Congressional oversight overlooked: Police patrols *versus* fire alarms. *American Journal of Political Science* 28: 165–179. (3, 123, 157)

McCusker, John J., and Russell R. Menard (1985). *The Economy of British America, 1607-1789.* Chapel Hill: University of North Carolina Press. (202)

McDonald, Forrest (1958). *We the People: The Economic Origins of the Constitution.* Chicago: University of Chicago Press. (179, 180, 181, 188, 190, 192, 193, 196, 197, 198, 199, 201, 205, 206, 213, 217)

McDonald, Forrest (1963). The Anti-Federalists, 1781-1789. *Wisconsin Magazine of History* 46: 206–214. (179, 180, 198)

McDonald, Forrest (1965). *E Pluribus Unum: The Formation of the American Republic, 1776-1790.* Boston: Houghton-Mifflin. (187)

McFadden, Daniel (1974). Conditional logit analysis of qualitative variables. In Paul Zarembka (ed.). *Frontiers in Econometrics.* New York: Academic Press. (188)

McGrath, Dennis R. (1983). James Madison and Social Choice Theory: The possibility of republicanism. Unpublished dissertation, Department of Political Science, University of Maryland, College Park. (88)

McGuire, Robert A. (1988). Constitution-making: A rational choice model of the Federal Convention of 1787. *American Journal of Political Science* 32: 483–522. (200)

McGuire, Robert A., and Robert L. Ohsfeldt (1984). Economic interests and the American Constitution: A quantitative rehabilitation of Charles A. Beard. *Journal of Economic History* 44: 509–519. (200)

McGuire, Robert A., and Robert L. Ohsfeldt (1985a). Self-interest, voting behavior, and the ratification of the United States Constitution. Presented at the First World Congress of the Cliometrics Society, Evanston, Illinois. (200, 203, 204)

McGuire, Robert A., and Robert L. Ohsfeldt (1985b). A new economic interpretation of the formation of the United States Constitution. Mimeo.

McGuire, Robert A., and Robert L. Ohsfeldt (1986). An economic model of voting behavior over specific issues at the Constitutional Convention of 1787. *Journal of Economic History* 46: 79–111. (200)

McGuire, Robert A., and Robert L. Ohsfeldt (1988). Self-interest, agency theory, and political voting behavior: The ratification of the Constitution, *American Economic Review* 78: in press. (198, 204)

McKelvey, Richard D. (1976). Intransitivities in multidimensional voting models: Some implications for agenda control. *Journal of Economic Theory* 12: 131, 472–482. (2, 89)

McKelvey, Richard D. (1979). General conditions for global intransitivities in formal voting models. *Econometrica* 47: 1085–1111.(2, 89)

McKelvey, Richard D., and Peter C. Ordeshook (1986). Information, electoral equilibria, and the democratic ideal. *Journal of Politics* 38: 909–937. (54)

McMaster, John Bach, and Frederick D. Stone (1888). *Pennsylvania and the Federal Constitution.* Lancaster: Pennsylvania Historical Society. (224)

Mill, John Stuart (1962). *Considerations on Representative Government.* Chicago: Henry Regnery Co. (originally published in 1862.) (169)

Miller, Gary J. (1985). Progressive reform as induced institutional preferences. *Public Choice* 47: 163–181.

Mitnick, Barry (1980). *The Political Economy of Regulation.* New York: Columbia University Press. (151)

Moynihan, Daniel Patrick (1987). The 'new science of politics' and the old art of government. *Public Interest* (Winter) No. 86: 22–35. (4)

Mueller, Dennis (1979). *Public Choice.* Cambridge: Cambridge University Press. (36, 41)

Nadelhaft, Jerome J. (1981). *The Disorders of War: The Revolution in South Carolina.* Orono, ME: University of Maine at Orono Press. (180)

Nettels, Curtis P. (1962). *The Emergence of a National Economy, 1775-1815.* New York: Holt, Rinehart and Winston. (202)

Neustadt, Richard (1976). *Presidential Power* (revised ed.). New York: Wiley. (164)

Nevins, Allan (1924). *The American States During and After the Revolution: 1775-1789.* New York: Macmillan. (208, 210)

North, Douglass C. (1981). *Structure and Change in Economic History.* New York: Norton.

O'Brien, William (1979). Challenge to consensus: Social, political and economic implications of Maryland sectionalism, 1776-1789. Ph.D. dissertation, University of Wisconsin, Madison. (207, 216, 217, 218)

Ogul, Morris (1976). *Congress Oversees the Bureaucracy.* Pittsburgh: University of Pittsburgh Press. (151)

Ogul, Morris (1977). Congressional oversight: Structure and incentives. In Dodd and Oppenheimer, *Congress Reconsidered,* 207–221. (151)

Olson, Mancur (1965). *The Logic of Collective Action.* Cambridge, MA: Harvard University Press. (Reprinted, 1968, by Schocken Books, NY). (2, 36)

Ordeshook, Peter C. (1986). *Game Theory and Political Theory.* Cambridge, UK: Cambridge University Press. (36)

Ornstein, Norman, ed. (1975). *Congress in Change.* New York: Praeger. (155)

Ornstein, Norman, Thomas E. Mann, Michael J. Malbin, Allen Schick, and John F. Bibby (1984). *Vital Statistics on Congress, 1984-1985 Edition.* Washington, DC: American Enterprise Institute. (171)

Owen, Guillermo, and Bernard N. Grofman (1984). Coalitions and power in political situations. In Manfred Holler (ed.), *Coalitions and Collective Action.* Wuerzburg: Physica-Verlag. (123)

Page, Benjamin I., and Mark P. Petracca (1983). *The American Presidency.* New York: McGraw-Hill. (169)

Page, Benjamin I., and Robert Y. Shapiro (1982). Changes in Americans' policy preferences, 1935-1979. *Public Opinion Quarterly* 46: 24–42. (61, 62, 65)

Page, Benjamin I., and Robert Y. Shapiro (1984). Presidents as opinion leaders: Some new evidence. *Policy Studies Journal* (June): 649–661. (65, 67)

Page, Benjamin I., and Robert Y. Shapiro (1987a). Educating and manipulating the public. Paper delivered at the Annual Meeting of the Midwest Political Science Association, Chicago. (67)

Page, Benjamin I., and Robert Y. Shapiro (1987b). The rational public: Fifty years of opinion trends (in draft). (61, 65, 67)

Page, Benjamin I., Robert Y. Shapiro, and Glenn R. Dempsey (1987). What moves public opinion. *American Political Science Review* 81: 23–43. (65)

Parenti, Michael (1986). *Inventing Reality: The Politics of the Mass Media.* New York: St. Martin's. (67)

Parker, Glenn, and Roger Davidson (1979). Why do Americans love their Congressmen so much more than their Congress? *Legislative Studies Quarterly* 4: 53–62. (156)

Pearson, James (1975). Oversight: A vital yet neglected congressional function. *Kansas Law Review* 23: 277–288. (151)

Peek, George A., Jr. (1954). Introduction. In *The Political Writings of John Adams.* New York: Liberal Arts Press. (170)

Peltzman, Sam (1984). Constituent interest and congressional voting. *Journal of Law and Economics* 27: 181–210. (182, 200)

Peltzman, Sam (1985). An economic interpretation of the history of the Congressional voting in the twentieth century. *American Economic Review* 75: 656–675. (182)

Petracca, Mark P. (1986). Having Your way: Taking liberties with the concept of political power. Chapter in 'Agenda-Building and National Policy Formation.' Unpublished Ph.D. dissertation, Department of Political Science, University of Chicago. (171)

Plott, Charles R. (1967). A notion of equilibrium and its possibility under majority rule. *American Economic Review* 57: 787–806. (2)

Plott, Charles R. (1976). Axiomatic social choice theory: An overview and interpretation. *American Journal of Political Science* 20: 511–596.(1)

Polishook, Irwin H. (1969). *Rhode Island and the Union 1774-1795.* Evanston, IL: Northwestern University Press.

Polsby, Nelson (1963). *Community Power and Political Theory.* New Haven, CT: Yale University Press. (11)

Polsby, Nelson (1983). *Consequences of Party Reform.* New York: Oxford University Press. (3)

Pool, William C. (1950). An economic interpretation of the ratification of the Federal Constitution in North Carolina. *North Carolina Historical Review* 27: 119–141 (Part I). 289–313 (Part II). 437–461 (Part III). (181, 190, 201, 203)

Posner, Richard (1981). *The Economics of Justice.* Cambridge: Harvard University Press. (2)

Poulson, Barry W. (1981). *Economic History of the United States.* New York: Macmillan. (201)

Prewitt, Kenneth, and Sidney Verba (1983). *An Introduction to American Government* (4th ed.). New York: Harper and Row. (197, 201)

Provine, Doris Marie (1980). *Case Selection in the United States Supreme Court.* Chicago: University of Chicago Press. (165)

Ranney, Austin (1976). The divine science: Political engineering in American culture. *American Political Science Review* 70: 140–148. (4, 9)

Ransom, Roger (1981). *Coping with Capitalism: The Transformation of the United States, 1776-1980.* Englewood Cliffs, NJ: Prentice- Hall. (201)

Rawls, John (1972). *A Theory of Justice.* Cambridge, MA: Harvard University Press. (43)

Renzulli, L. Marx (1972). *Maryland: The Federalist Years.* Rutherford, NJ: Fairleigh-Dickinson University Press. (206, 217, 224)

Rhoads, Steven E. (1985). *The Economist's View of the World: Government, Markets, and Public Policy.* New York: Cambridge University Press. (5, 51)

Riker, William H. (1979). The verification of scientific generalizations by historical case studies: The genesis of the American Constitution. Presented at the Annual Meeting of the Social Science History Association, Cambridge, MA. (201, 219)

Riker, William H. (1980). Implications from the disequilibrium of majority rule for the study of institutions. *American Political Science Review* 74: 432–458.

Riker, William H. (1982). *Liberalism against Populism: A Confrontation between the Theory of Democracy and the Theory of Social Choice*. San Francisco: W. H. Freeman. (39, 40, 50)

Riker, William H. (1984). The heresthetics of constitution-making: The presidency in 1787, with comments on determinism and rational choice. *American Political Science Review* 78: 1–16.

Riker, William H. (1987). The invention of centralized federalism. In William H. Riker (ed.), *The Development of American Federalism*. Boston: Kluwer-Nijhoff. (233)

Riker, William H., and Lloyd S. Shapley (1968). Weighted voting: A mathematical analysis for instrumental judgments. In J. Roland Pennock and John W. Chapman (eds.), *Representation: Nomos X*. New York: Atherton. (139)

Ripley, Randall (1969). *Power in the Senate*. New York: St. Martin's. (155)

Ripley, Randall (1971). *The Politics of Economic and Human Resource Development*. Indianapolis: Bobbs-Merrill.

Ripley, Randall (1978). *Congress: Process and Policy* (2nd ed.). New York: Norton. (151)

Ripley, Randall, and Grace Franklin (1976). *Congress, the Bureaucracy and Public Policy*. Homewood, Il: Dorsey. (155)

Risjord, Norman K. (1974). Virginians and the Constitution: A multivariant analysis. *William and Mary Quarterly* 31: 613–632. (181, 196, 197)

Risjord, Norman K. (1978). *Chesapeake Politics 1781-1800*. New York: Columbia University Press. (196)

Robert, Henry M. (1951). *Robert's Rules of Order Revised*. Chicago: Scott, Foresman (inside back cover). (109, 115)

Roberts, Steven V. (1986). Key to strategy: The pocket veto. *New York Times* (September 18): B10. (137)

Roll, Charles W., Jr. (1969). We, some of the people: Apportionment in the thirteen state conventions ratifying the Constitution. *Journal of American History* 9: 21–40. (229)

Rossiter, Clinton (1965). *1787: The Grand Convention*. New York: Macmillan. (110, 111, 120)

Runciman, W. G. and Amartya K. Sen (1965). Games, justice and the general will. *Mind* n.s. 74: 554–562. (42)

Rutland, Robert Allen (1966). *The Ordeal of the Constitution: The Antifederalists and the Ratification Struggle of 1787-1788*. Norman, OK: University of Oklahoma Press. (180)

Schelling, Thomas (1960). *The Strategy of Conflict*. Cambridge, MA: Harvard University Press. (120)

Schelling, Thomas (1984). *Choice and Consequence*. Cambridge, MA: Harvard University Press. (45)

Scher, Seymour (1963). Conditions for legislative control. *Journal of Politics* 25: 526–551. (151)

Schofield, Norman (1978). Instability of simple dynamic games. *Review of Economic Studies*. XLV(3): 575–594. (2, 89)

Schofield, Norman, Bernard Grofman, and Scott L. Feld (1988). The core and the stability of group choice in spatial voting games. *American Political Science Review.* (5)

Schuyler, Robert L. (1961). Forrest McDonald's critique of the Beard thesis. *Journal of Southern History* 27: 73–80. (179, 180, 197, 201)

Schwartz, Thomas (1986). *The Logic of Collective Choice.* New York: Columbia University Press. (1, 36, 58)

Schwartz, Thomas (1987). Votes, strategics, and institutions: An introduction to the theory of collective choice. In Mathew D. McCubbins and Terry Sullivan (eds.), *Congress: Structure and Policy.* Cambridge, UK: Cambridge University Press. (36, 38)

Seidman, Harold (1975). *Politics, Position, and Power: The Dynamics of Federal Organization.* New York: Oxford University Press. (151)

Sen, Amartya K. (1970). *Collective Choice and Social Welfare.* San Francisco: Holden-Day. (1, 36, 58)

Shapley, L. S., and Martin Shubik (1954). A method of evaluating the distribution of power in a committee system. *American Political Science Review* 48: 787–792. (121, 139, 149)

Shepherd, James F., and Gary M. Walton (1976). Economic change after the American Revolution: Pre- and post-war comparisons of maritime shipping and trade. *Explorations in Economic History* 13: 397–422. (186, 202)

Shepsle, Kenneth A. (1979). Institutional arrangements and equilibrium in multidimensional voting models. *American Journal of Political Science* 23: 27–59. (2)

Shepsle, Kenneth A., and Barry R. Weingast (1981). Structure-induced equilibrium and legislative choice. *Public Choice* 37: 503–519.

Shepsle, Kenneth A., and Barry R. Weingast (1984). Uncovered sets and sophisticated voting outcomes with implications for agenda institutions. *American Journal of Political Science* 28(1): 49–74. (2)

Smyth, Albert Henry (1907). *The Writings of Benjamin Franklin,* Vol. 10. New York: Macmillan. (120)

Spaulding, E. Wilder (1932). *New York in the Critical Period: 1783-1789.* New York: Columbia University Press.

Staples, William R. (1971). *Rhode Island in the Continental Congress, 1765-1790,* edited by Reuben A. Guild, 1870. (Reprinted, New York: Da Capo Press.) (224)

Storing, Herbert J. (1981a). *What the Anti-Federalists Were For.* Chicago: University of Chicago Press. (160, 164)

Storing, Herbert J., ed. (1981b). *The Complete Anti-Federalist,* 7 vols. Chicago: University of Chicago Press. (255)

Storing, Herbert J. ed. (1985). *The Anti-Federalist.* Chicago: University of Chicago Press. (160, 162, 170)

Straffin, Philip D. Jr. (1977). Homogeneity, independence and power indices. *Public Choice* 30(Summer): 107–118. (123)

Sugden, Robert (1984). Free association and the theory of proportional representation. *American Political Science Review* 78(1): 31–43. (3)

Thomas, Robert E. (1953). The Virginia Convention of 1788. *Journal of Southern History* 19: 63–72. (181, 196, 201)

Thorpe, Francis N. (1909). *The Federal and State Constitutions of the United States of America.* Washington, DC: U.S. Government Printing Office.

Tideman, Nicholas, ed. (1977). Special issue on demand revelation. *Public Choice* 29(2; suppl.). (4)

Tollison, Robert (1982). Rent Seeking: A survey. *Kyklos* 35: 575–602. (182)

Truman, David, ed. (1973). *The Congress in America's Future* (2nd ed.). Englewood Cliffs, NJ: Prentice Hall.

Tulis, Jeffrey Kent (1987). *The Rhetorical Presidency*. Princeton, NJ: Princeton University Press. (58, 66)

Tullock, Gordon (1967). *Toward a Mathematics of Politics*. Ann Arbor: University of Michigan Press. (36)

Turner, Lynn (1983). *The Ninth State*. Chapel Hill: University of North Carolina Press. (224)

U.S. Department of Commerce, Bureau of Census (1969). *A Century of Population Growth*. New York: Reprinted by Genealogical Publishing Company. (203)

U.S. Senate (1963). *Proposed Amendments to the Constitution of the United States of America*. Washington, DC: U.S. Government Printing Office.

U.S. Senate (1978). *Presidential Vetoes, 1789-1976*. Washington, DC: U.S. Government Printing Office.

U.S. Senate (1985). *Presidential Vetoes, 1977-1984*. Washington, DC: U.S. Government Printing Office.

Walker, Francis A. (1895). *The Making of the Nation, 1783-1817*. New York: Scribner's. (200)

Walton, Gary M., and Ross W. Robertson (1983). *History of the American Economy*, 5th Ed.. New York: Harcourt Brace Jovanovich. (183, 201)

Walton, Gary M., and James Shepherd (1979). *The Economic Rise of Early America*. New York: Cambridge University Press. (186, 202)

Weingast, Barry (1984). A principal-agent perspective on congressional-bureaucratic relations. *Public Choice* 44: 147–191.

Weingast, Barry, and William Marshall (1984). A reconsideration of the railroad problem: The economics and politics of the Interstate Commerce Act. Prepared for delivery at Annual Meeting of American Political Science Association, Washington, DC. (206)

Welch, Susan, and John G. Peters (1983). Private interests and public interests: An analysis of the impact of personal finance on congressional voting on agriculture issues. *Journal of Politics* 45: 378–396. (182)

Wilson, James Q. (1980). *The Politics of Regulation*. New York: Basic Books. (151)

Wilson, Woodrow (1902). *A History of the American People*, Vols. 1–5. New York: Harper and Brothers. (200)

Wise, David (1973). *The Politics of Lying*. New York: Vintage. (66)

Wittman, Donald (1973). Parties as utility maximizers. *American Political Science Review* 67: 490–498. (182)

Wittman, Donald (1976). Various concepts of power: Equivalence among ostensibly unrelated approaches. *British Journal of Political Science* 6: 449–462. (123)

Wittman, Donald (1982). Efficient rules in highway safety and sports activity. *American Economic Review* 72: 78–90. (2)

Wittman, Donald (1983). Candidate motivation: A synthesis of alternative theories. *American Political Science Review* 77: 142–157. (182)

Woll, Peter (1977). *American Bureaucracy*. New York: Norton. (151)

Wood, Gordon S. (1969). *The Creation of the American Republic, 1776-1787*. Chapel Hill: University of North Carolina Press. (201, 209, 211)

Wood, Gordon S. (1980). Democracy and the Constitution. In Robert A. Goldwin and William A. Schambra (eds.), *How Democratic is the Constitution?*. Washington, DC: American Enterprise Institute. (186, 187)

Subject Index